Beauty Enough

A Love Story in Letters

Rosemary Grebin Palms
with
Charles Palms

Printed by CreateSpace, an Amazon.com Company
Copyright © 2018, by Rosemary Grebin Palms
Cover design by Amy Palms, Copyright © 2018
ISBN-13: 978-1985020030
ISBN-10: 1985020033

For my beloved children and grandchildren

**and in memory of my
friend Gerald D. McCarty**

*I have crossed the streets of
nervous light
I have slipped through the fields
of wet grass
I have silently passed the
darkened houses
But nowhere, O Moon, rising full in the East,
Do I find beauty enough
For my lame soul.*

-- Gerald D. McCarty, circa 1968

**and in loving memory of
Charles Palms**

*I will be so happy when we can be
open. The strictures of tradition and
society bear heavy upon us, forcing
us to conceal something that is good
and beautiful and true – our love –
which will, like the sturdy and
majestic Brooklyn Bridge, twin
towers inseparably joined, survive
the storm.*

-- letter from Charlie to
Rosemary, May 12, 1970

Beauty Enough

Dearest Marion,
you will remember
a lot of this!
+ treasure your
friendship over
these 60! years.
Love,
Rosemary Graham Pacms

Contents

Preface

Dear Charlie,

I miss you. And I have an important question.

Much has happened in last thirteen-plus years. I've learned a lot: to pay bills on time, to prepare figures for income tax returns, to be independent, to be content living alone.

Meantime, I have found some of your writings – and I wish I had asked you this question before you were gone.

You left behind a family who loved you so much. We have photos that help us remember, and I have your poetic little love letters you wrote for me on special occasions. Now I have found letters that I had forgotten I had saved nearly 50 years ago: the ones you wrote the year after we fell in love, that year we lived apart while we made our decisions about our vowed religious lives and whether we would get married. And unbeknownst to me, you had saved my letters to you.

That year of separation was both difficult and exhilarating. Your letters were painfully honest as you shared your joys and fears, triumphs and struggles. So here is my big question: how much of your joys, fears, triumphs and struggles do you want me to share with your children – who loved you so dearly, who treasure their memories of the father they knew *after* these letters were written?

Probably they already know much of the gist of these letters, just by knowing and loving you for thirty-plus years. Won't they find this younger man, revealed in these letters, to be the same man they remember from their youth? I think they will love you all the more deeply – as I did as a young woman, when I first read these honest revelations.

I think of this memoir with our letters as part of our legacy – yours and mine – to our children and to their children. I wish I knew your answer to my big question. But I don't. I can't. So I will decide. I will proceed with this gift, this legacy. Because I love our children. They love you. I love you.

Rosemary
February 2018

Chapter 1 – A Minnesota Farm Girl

I was born in a farmhouse near Preston, Minnesota, the second child and first daughter of Francis Romen Grebin and Mary Eloise Gossman Grebin. There was no hospital nearby in 1940. I was named Rosemary Helen after my Grandma Rose Gresbrink Gossman, my mother, and my Grandma Helena Ibach Grebin. The Grebins originally emigrated in the mid-1800s from Alsace-Lorraine, so Grebin is a French name. But my other seven great-grandparents were of solid German stock. All were Catholic.

My father was a dairy farmer and milkman on his sister's small farm. He married my mother, a country-school teacher, in 1937, when he was thirty years old and she was twenty. In those days women schoolteachers did not continue to teach after they were married, so she became a fulltime farmer's wife and mother, eventually, of five children.

When I was three years old, my parents bought a 160-acre farm near Harmony, Minnesota. They moved in the autumn with their by now three children to a house with no running water and no electricity. My earliest memory of that farm was my father and his helpers digging ditches to put in water pipes from the well to the house. I also remember using the outhouse behind the house, pages from Sears and Roebuck catalogs serving as toilet paper. When spring  came, Daddy finished connecting running water to the house, including to a new bathroom. Not too long afterward, he installed a wind-charger and then we had electric light in the house. We had an icebox, but nothing that had to be plugged in. We had to wait at least ten years longer before Rural Electric (an FDR program) wired our valley, and we could then plug in appliances such as a clothes iron, a toaster, a refrigerator, and a radio.

My mother, at age 93 when I asked her about those early days, remembered that the farm had been in foreclosure, so my parents bought it from the bank. At the closing, after all the papers were signed, their money was so tight that the banker asked, "Now what are you going to live on?"

I asked her how she coped, back when she was still in her mid-twenties, mother of three little ones and pregnant with her fourth, taking on a mortgage and having to work so hard to make ends meet. Grandma Grebin once gave them $75, she remembered, to help buy groceries. She shrugged. "That's just the way it was," she said.

My father was the strong silent type. He was gentle, though strict, and a hard worker. He had to get up before dawn to milk the cows, but he always took a nap after the noon meal. He was creative and willing to try new farming techniques, like strip farming (for which he won a county conservation prize). I remember stories of his "Pinocchio" – a stickman robot installed on the tractor seat, with ropes tied to his "arms" so Daddy could manipulate the tractor controls while he loaded bales or ran the corn planter. After my older brother got big enough to help Daddy, Pinocchio was retired.

As a tomboy, I wished I could help Daddy more, but a girl's job was helping Mother. I did help with the garden as I grew older, while my sister, Kathy, did more cooking. By the time we were ages eleven and nine, the two of us always did the supper dishes together, and – since in those days there were no wrinkle-free fabrics – we girls were expected to iron our own clothes.

Mother was a reader and read aloud to us, to which I attribute my great love of reading. She would read "chapter books" to us from the few books we owned, and even Daddy would love to sit in and listen. She remembered reading us *Tom Sawyer* and *Huckleberry Finn*, and I remember fondly the *Bobbsey Twins* series, the Laura Ingalls Wilder books, and *Three Margarets*, an 1897 novel by Laura E. Richards.

When I reached the age of six, I joined my brother at a one-room schoolhouse about a mile from our farmhouse – or closer if we cut through our pasture and the woods. We would walk to school in all kinds of weather, unless a neighbor, when the snow was deep, came along with his team of horses and a sleigh (a novelty in the new age of tractors).

I took to school with joy, and soon pulled ahead of my two first-grade classmates. My teacher, Mrs. Hanson, borrowed textbooks for me from other country schools and let me proceed at my own rate. But this is how I remember why I skipped a grade: when the three of us first-graders started second grade there were only two sets of books, so the teacher promoted me to third grade.

A memorable event each summer was the day that five or six neighbors came to our farm to harvest our oats. The neighbors had developed a rotating system to help one another. One neighbor owned a big threshing machine, and the others would bring their grain wagons and tractors. When it was our turn, Mother would cook a huge noon meal, and in midmorning and midafternoon my sister and I would help her take cold drinks and cookies out to the field for the men.

In the winter, when the heavy farm work slacked off, the big social events with the nearest neighbors were card parties every Friday night. The adults would play whist, and the kids would have a great time playing hide-and-seek or tag or inventing our own games. When my siblings and I were old enough to take care of ourselves, Mother and Daddy started going to square dance parties every week. Daddy also was on a bowling team.

We grew up poor, but with lots of love and plenty to eat. Once the farm was established, we always had garden produce (Mother was canning all summer) and beef and chickens. Mother sewed clothes for my sister and me on her treadle machine, and taught us to sew for ourselves at an early age.

We children didn't have much spending money, though. I dimly remember our "war effort" – collecting aluminum foil from gum wrappers. Later Mother would pay my sister and me five cents a ball of rolled up strips of fabrics that we had sewn together, to be used for making rag rugs.

Sometimes when we visited Grandma Rose in her small town, we would be given a nickel to spend in the drug store. We could splurge it all on an ice cream cone, or we could buy penny candy in order to stretch out the pleasure.

A central part of our family life was our Roman Catholic parish. On Saturday nights we had certain rituals: the once-a-week bath when we were small, polishing our shoes over newspapers on the kitchen table so we would be at our Sunday best the next morning. The happiest day of our eight-year-old lives, we were told and we believed, was First Holy Communion Day. In those days of my childhood we fasted before the once-a-month Communion Sunday liturgy. Mother taped up the faucet handles so we would remember not to drink any water. On Fridays, of course, we ate no meat. I used to worry, if my mind wandered during Mass, whether I had satisfied my Sunday obligation under pain of mortal sin. At about age twelve we prepared diligently for the sacrament of Confirmation, memorizing large portions of the Baltimore Catechism because we knew the presiding visiting bishop would be quizzing us before the entire congregation.

Although many small towns had Catholic parish schools, Roman Catholics were a minority sect in this Norwegian-American corner of southeastern Minnesota. Our numbers were small, not enough to support a school. So for two weeks every summer, religious sisters came to our parish for "vacation school," a time for more doctrinal instruction for children attending public school. I was enamored of the nuns, fashioning veils out of bath towels in order to play at being one myself.

I felt my Catholic minority status in high school. I was a conscientious student – not difficult because I liked my subjects and liked my teachers. Having had a strict upbringing – Daddy wouldn't allow my sister and me to wear trousers to school, and Mother would warn us about fellows with roaming hands – I wasn't very confident around boys and didn't have many dates. In my senior year I went out with one Lutheran classmate a couple of times, and then his parents asked him to stop dating me because I was one of "those" Catholics. The summer before college, in 1957, I started double-dating with my sister, her boyfriend, and her boyfriend's perfectly well behaved friend Keith. We had a good time, but no sparks flew.

I wanted to go to a Catholic college, and chose the College of Saint Teresa, only fifty miles away. The school was owned and operated by the Rochester (Minnesota) Franciscan sisters, and I really liked what I saw. The young Franciscan candidates, called postulants, were studying at the college during their first year in the convent and lived in a separate house on campus. I found out that I could join them mid-freshman year, continue the same yearlong courses I was already taking, and simply move over to their house. I felt that God was calling me to this vocation, and I made the decision to join. How bewildered Keith was when I told him I was entering the convent. Why anyone would choose a celibate life was beyond his Lutheran understanding.

Parting from my parents and four siblings after the Christmas break was painful. The sisters had rules limiting visits from family to once a month, and my first visit home would not be until after I took final vows, five and a half years in the future. I wept for days before I departed for the convent Motherhouse in Rochester. My father and mother were proud of having a religious vocation in their devout family, but at the same time they made it clear that this was my decision. As I cried on the one-hour trip to Rochester, my mother said, "You know, we can still turn around and take you home." No, I insisted through my sobs, this was what I really wanted to do.

The instant they said goodbye at the convent door, I was happy. The regular hours, prayer, silence, and study suited me. Even wearing the same dowdy uniform as all thirty-four of my classmates was fine with me. With so many shared values and togetherness, friendships among the postulants

were easily made. We were kept very busy, with little time for loneliness. I "took the veil" – that is, became a novice – six months after entering. Along with the new habit I was given a new name, Sister Mary Francha. The trial period of the novitiate lasted two years, and then our class took three-year vows of poverty, chastity, and obedience. We called them "temporary" vows.

In a sense I had prepared for these vows throughout my young life. My religious superiors found me among the least unruly of the novices. I had been a fairly compliant, unquestioning child, and obedience in the religious life was not difficult for me. My understanding of chastity, at age eighteen, was also shaped largely, if inadequately, by my parents, and I was experiencing no regrets at leaving my rather infrequent and placid date scene behind. And I was used to living frugally, having grown up poor. Thus prepared by my childhood circumstances, I was a happy young religious woman.

However, I do recall a real sadness during those formative years. If a young woman decided that religious life was not for her, or if her superiors so decided for her, she was asked to keep silent about her coming departure, and then to slip away without saying goodbye to the rest of her classmates. Since we felt so close to one another, every parting was a sad one. In my class of 34 candidates, two novices left us before first vows.

Looking back, I think our superiors were trying to protect us from emotionally wrenching farewells, but also to prevent us from talking over the reasons for the departures, should others of us find similar reasons to depart. This stern practice was later discontinued, but the sadness lingered. Forty years after our novitiate, our class held a reunion, and one of those two former novices told us, "I came to say goodbye."

Convent life was a good fit for me for several years. My superiors assigned me various tasks that challenged me, and I felt affirmed in my successes. It was a women's world, and I grew in confidence and leadership skills without having to worry about fitting into or competing with the larger men's world outside our own circumscribed lives.

The first year as a "vowed sister" I taught a sixth-grade class, and I liked everything about that assignment – those children, my school principal, and my teaching colleagues. Then during the next two years I finished my bachelor's degree in my chosen major, preparing to do what I had always wanted to do: teach English in a high school.

My college graduation in 1963 coincided with the serious step of pronouncing final vows. Still content, still comfortable with my life as a religious sister, I made the commitment.

B.A. in hand, I was sent to a small village in western Minnesota, not unlike my hometown except that it was very Catholic. The sisters staffed the parish elementary school and the high school, with the help of only a couple of lay persons. I was basically the entire high-school English department, directing plays and coaching speech and debate. Twelve sisters lived in that convent. As the youngest, I was given additional jobs, such as driving sisters to doctors' appointments, training and scheduling the altar boys, and ironing their surplices. Busy but happy, I did what I was asked to do, and did it well. (The one exception was my assignment to teach Latin. I had never learned much Latin, and the second-year Latin students suffered the consequences.)

In the summer of 1965 I was sent to take two graduate courses at Notre Dame University in Indiana. One was a drama interpretation course and the other a writing seminar, both interesting but relatively stress-free, so I had time to take advantage of two film series on campus, sometimes going straight from one showing to another. I also hung out at hootenannies, a new experience for me, drinking in the excitement and some of the turmoil of the 1960s civil rights movement and war protests, singing the likes of "We Shall Overcome" and "Where Have All the Flowers Gone," not to mention "Cigarettes and Whiskey and Wild, Wild Women." I was trying to catch up on everything I had missed in those seven years since I had entered the convent.

There were long and earnest conversations with many other young sisters, brothers, seminarians and priests at Notre Dame that summer, about changes in the Church being discussed at the Second Vatican Council. Pope John XXIII had initiated the council, calling together all the bishops of the world to consider ways to modernize the Church. In his words, the pope expected "a little fresh air from it... We must shake off the imperial dust that has accumulated on the throne of St. Peter since Constantine." The bishops started meeting in 1962, and

now were in their fourth and final session. There were proposals
to use the vernacular in our liturgies, rather than the Latin we
had always known. There were questions about authority and
governance in the Church hierarchy, and about the principle of
subsidiarity in decision-making. Could an individual informed
conscience ever trump an official church law? What was the role
of the laity in the Church? And – I started asking for the first
time – where do religious sisters fit in this new picture? Should
we be setting ourselves apart by living in convents and wearing
these medieval habits? Or was it time to experience our
Christianity more closely with the rest of God's people?

At Notre Dame I basked in the new intellectual and
social currents and breathed deeply the fresh air from those
windows that Pope John XXIII had thrown open.

At the end of each school year in our Franciscan
congregation, every teaching sister would pack all her
belongings into one trunk and two suitcases. We would take our
two suitcases with us to our temporary summer assignments.
Toward the end of the summer we would receive our "mission"
assignments for the following year. If our assignments were to a
new location, it was a simple matter to ship our trunks to a new
address.

This summer of 1965 my letter of assignment brought
me a big surprise, one that would prove to be a major turning
point in my life. Instead of going back to the high school, I was
being sent to graduate school. (This was good news for the Latin
students: my replacement had majored in Latin.)

My superiors had applied to three universities for me.
The one that accepted me first, and therefore was chosen since it
was now late in the summer, was the University of Texas at
Austin. So in late August another Franciscan sister, Sister
Madonna, and I traveled to Austin. She was to study English
Education, and I was to study English language and literature.
Madonna was in her early thirties, a smart, vivacious, talented
woman who had already been a principal in one of the
elementary schools the sisters staffed. I was 25 years old, and,
although a good student, not exactly an original thinker. I had
never seriously challenged the authority of teachers or my
parents, and certainly not my religious superiors. Madonna had

always been a questioner, even as a high school student. She wondered whether our superiors had deliberately sent me to accompany her in order that I might rein her in a bit. As it turned out, I was the one who learned from her. Little by little I relaxed the reins on myself.

Chapter 3 – Nowhere Beauty Enough

Soon after I arrived in Texas I had gotten acquainted with a graduate student named Jerry, who was taking some of the same courses as I. He was from West Texas, in his late twenties. He worked part-time in the library, where he made sure that the people coming out of the stacks had properly checked out their books. Over the years I would see him often, since I was spending many hours in those stacks. We would chat a few minutes as I was leaving each day, comparing notes on our class assignments, professors, and fellow students.

I liked this friendly Texan, tall and a little skinny, with a dry sense of humor and a nice grin. Perhaps I seemed a bit exotic to his Protestant sensibilities: a young Catholic nun in full habit.

Full habit for me included black veil, starched white headband and collar, soft white cotton coif concealing every strand of hair on my head, long dark brown wool dress, matching brown wool panel falling from my shoulders down both front and back, black laced-up oxfords with sensible one-and-a-half inch heels, crucifix hanging from my neck, brown rope belt knotted three times to remind me of my three vows, and a rosary hanging from that belt.

Jerry and I exchanged pleasantries over the course of three years. And he watched with curiosity as the summer of 1968 brought permission for me – a change proceeding from the deliberations of the Second Vatican Council – to shed my medieval habit and to don, somewhat awkwardly, a modest modified habit: a small veil, a shorter skirt and shorter sleeves. It had been ten years since my hair, arms, and legs had been seen in public.

That summer of '68 Jerry was suffering from serious depression. I was drawn into the small circle of his friends when we all came together to support him through his illness.

One of those friends, Dolores, was a divorced mother of five young children, who had known Jerry from pre-graduate school days in West Texas. One evening he called her in distress, and she found herself sitting with him in his apartment as he contemplated suicide. He had a handgun.

As the hours wore on in this tense situation, her anxiety increasing as she worried about her five kids managing without her, Dolores recalled hearing that Saint Austin's Church, a Catholic parish on the border of the campus, always had a priest on duty to answer the phone, day or night. So she called.

The priest on duty that night was Father Charles Palms, who for the past two years had been assigned to the Catholic Student Center staff at the university. He immediately went over to Jerry's apartment to sit with him so that Dolores could go home to her children.

Father Palms was well liked by virtually everyone who knew him. He was gentle and soft-spoken. It was fun to be around him when he sang lively songs in his strong baritone, accompanying himself on his four-string guitar. The students and faculty who flocked to Sunday Mass at the Catholic Student Center appreciated his thoughtful Scripture-based homilies.

That evening in Jerry's apartment he engaged my distraught friend in conversation in his kindly manner, drawing on counseling skills learned in the seminary. Finally Jerry agreed to hand over the one bullet he had for his gun.

After that difficult night, Jerry's friends united in efforts to engage him in social situations, inviting him to picnics, summer concerts, whatever they were doing that they thought he would enjoy. Dolores organized many of these outings, and she invited my roommate Dora and me, as well as Father Palms and another graduate student friend of Jerry's, Carl. At one outdoor event, sitting on a blanket, I remember momentarily leaning against Jerry in an effort to express my fondness for him – however, feeling a bit flirtatious even as I instantly recognized the action's inappropriateness. "Flirtatious" and "nun," I thought, are two words that don't belong together.

A few days later Jerry voluntarily checked into a psychiatric hospital in town. In the course of a visit there from me, he asked me to take home and read several pages of French poetry he had copied in his own handwriting. Later, at home, I did my best to struggle through reading the poems in French. Suddenly I came across a couplet, also written in French, with my name in it: something about the desire to kiss Sister Francha on the lips.

I was horrified. It seemed that Jerry was playing a little game with me, testing me to see if I would read carefully through his French transcriptions. But beyond games, I saw an emotionally fragile man reaching out to a nun in a romantic way. I remembered my little flirtation and wondered if I had somehow encouraged him. What on earth should I do now?

I decided to consult someone who knew me and knew Jerry. Soon I was knocking on Father Palms' office door. He listened carefully to my dilemma, and said he could see the delicacy of the situation, dealing a disappointment like this to a psychiatric patient. Nevertheless, he advised, I had to explain to Jerry, gently but forthrightly, that although I was very fond of him, in fact I was not in a position as a nun to even consider anything more than a friendly relationship.

I knew Father Palms was right. So off I went to the hospital. Taking a deep breath and steadying my shaky nerves, I told Jerry exactly that, in as kind a way as I could.

Jerry just smiled and said, "I knew that." I relaxed; all seemed normal and friendly again between us. He was having a little fun with me, and now we could resume chatting in our usual comfortable way.

One afternoon, just a few days later, I was sitting in the apartment where I then lived, studying, when Jerry popped his head in at the door. Surprised, I told him to come in and asked him what he was doing here. He said, from the door, that he had a one-day pass to move out of his apartment, because it didn't make sense to be paying rent during his long hospital stay. Since his apartment was only a block from mine, he had taken a break, he said, to see if I was home.

"Let me help you pack," I offered.

"No," he said in a very definite tone.

"Why not?"

"If I tell you why not, you must promise not to tell anyone."

Puzzled now, I promised.

"The reason is that I have a gun. And I don't want you anywhere near it."

Although I was 28 years old, I was still in some ways the naïve, sheltered young woman who all my life had done what I was told to do – under the strict discipline of my devout parents, and then under my religious vow of holy obedience. I didn't even ask myself if this visit from Jerry was a cry for help, a plea for me to do something. I certainly didn't consider that Jerry might have been coming to see me one last time to say goodbye. All I could understand at that moment was that I had to keep my promise.

In a few minutes he returned to his packing, and I made a mighty effort to return to my studying.

Two hours later, I got a call from Carl. "Have you heard from Jerry?" he asked. "I've asked him to dinner, but he hasn't arrived, and he's not answering his phone."

With a heavy heart, but still honoring my promise, I said, "Carl, why don't you go over to his apartment to see how his packing is going?"

A few minutes later I heard the sirens.

Jerry had shot himself in the temple. He was unconscious but still alive when Carl arrived. He died at the hospital that night, on the operating table.

I don't remember a funeral.

I do remember the kindness of Jerry's psychiatrist, who gathered our little group together, along with Jerry's parents, who had traveled to Austin when Jerry died. The doctor knew it would be helpful for us to talk about Jerry's mental illness and to deal with our anguished questions and emotions. Jerry had attempted suicide several times over the years, the doctor told us; there seemed to be a chemical imbalance in his system that just couldn't be fixed. He had had a disastrous and very brief marriage. He had nurtured romantic interests in several other women, all of whom were already in committed relationships or otherwise unavailable. So, it seemed, I was part of a pattern.

When I confessed that Jerry had told me about the gun that fateful afternoon, the doctor said to me, "You did what you thought was the best choice. And even if he had not succeeded this time, eventually he would have. So you should not blame yourself for not reporting the gun. But if you ever find yourself in a situation like this again," and he smiled a fatherly smile, "don't honor any such promise." I felt as though I had received absolution.

Shortly thereafter I had a chance to read some of Jerry's poems. They included some foreboding passages. Father Palms for a long time carried one of them in his wallet, a tangible reminder of this young man's struggle and the deep impression he had made on those he had left behind. The poem was a little four-line question, asking the meaning of our lives, and finding no answers:

> *what do we know*
> *of life, time, the leavings of stars*
> *except the clippings of trash*
> *blown along a chain fence.*

A different poem stayed in my mind. The words detailed Jerry's search for whatever in his life could balance out the pain.

> *I have crossed the streets of nervous light*
> *I have slipped through the fields of wet grass*
> *I have silently passed the darkened houses*
> *But nowhere, O Moon, rising full in the East,*
> *Do I find beauty enough*
> *For my lame soul.*

Jerry's parents would have liked some of the poems to be published as a memorial to their son, and asked for our help. Dolores and I and another friend from Jerry's life before graduate school, the artist Marilyn Todd, explored the possibility of privately publishing a little book of his poems. Jerry's mother inked a series of black and white drawings that we thought could complement them, but the cost was beyond our means then, and the book project was shelved. Later I sent poems to a dozen periodicals, but there were no takers. Now, decades later, the poems are still in my closet.

Jerry died near the end of the summer of '68. That university summer session ended, and many of us left for vacation. I went to Minnesota, back to the convent, for two weeks, returning to Texas just in time for the fall semester and a new half-time job on staff at the Catholic Student Center, where Father Palms worked.

After I came back from my Minnesota break but before Father Palms returned from visiting his parents in Grosse Pointe, Michigan, letters came from Jerry's parents. They wished to thank Jerry's friends for their loyalty and to ask for help in obtaining the death certificate. Jerry's father also wrote to Father Palms, in part:

> *Jerry had never shot so much as a sparrow in all his life so it is most difficult to understand this tragedy. Dr. Wilson did give us some enlightenment that Science believes this sort of illness is organic and that some day they will find a proper treatment. Jerry was so intelligent and had such potential and was such a gentle person. We feel especially grateful in that you and Sister Francha were among his friends to give him help.*

I sent these letters on to Father Palms, and included a short note of my own. I reproduce it here to emphasize the close friendship that had developed among Jerry's friends, as well as the affection of other mutual friends. (Sister Belinda had been on staff at the Catholic Student Center the previous year, under the directorship of Father Walter Dalton, until the Bishop of Austin asked her to leave that position, presumably because of some of her unorthodox takes on religious subjects. She had lived that one year with Sister Madonna – now taking the new option of returning to using her baptismal name, Eileen – and me. Dora and Elizabeth, my summer apartment-mates, were among those who had gathered protectively around Jerry.) My note is dated August 20, 1968.

Dear Charlie,

    HELLO! We miss you!

    The big letter [referring to enclosures] *came yesterday in a packet for all of us. I hope this forwarding address finds you* [at his parents' home in Grosse Pointe, a suburb of Detroit].

    Sister Belinda came from Houston yesterday and left today. She really is hurt by the whole business of the bishop. She talked with Fathers Dalton and [former director] *O'Brien while here and says they are bewildered, too. It was hard to see her go. (Another blue day ☺.)*

    'Tis life, yes? A series of partings. 2 friends left last weekend, another today…. I look forward to your return at least.

    Reading a lot?

                          Love, Francha

Dora and Eliz. send their love…

Madonna (Eileen) returns in a few days….

Chapter 4 – Beauty Enough

College football reigns in Texas, and there are parties after every home game. After one of the new season's home games, I went to a gathering with some of my friends, and Charlie was there, too. He often was asked to bring his guitar and lead hootenannies at our mellow parties. When I was ready to leave that evening, he offered to walk me home.

Later he told a friend about that walk home. He had had a couple of Scotches, and he was feeling gallant, taking my hand as he helped me over some rain puddles. The festive air (we must have won that game), the balmy night, the couple of drinks, the shared intense drama of Jerry's last weeks, all combined to make something extraordinary happen.

As we got to my door, he reached for my face and kissed me on the mouth. Then he said, "I love you." He looked at me for a moment in wonderment, said "Good night," and turned and walked away.

I shut my door and leaned against it, my heart pounding in astonishment and consternation. I was taken totally by surprise. I had not seen this coming.

Over the next few days I tried to sort out my own feelings. My three years of graduate school had taught me to begin to question long-accepted attitudes and beliefs, especially on matters of faith. I had thrown myself into the civil rights movement and Vietnam War protests. The previous spring I had wondered aloud to my sister, Kathy, whether I should stay in the convent. Now I was finding myself receptive to exploring new possibilities in my life.

But, strangely, Charlie did not call. Not a sign of any new footing in our relationship. And now that I was on staff with him at the Catholic Student Center, I saw him often. Bewildered, I waited for a few days, and then decided to confront him. I marched into his office and closed the door. "What's going on?" I demanded.

He knew, of course, what I was talking about. But he was thinking realistically now. "I meant it," he said quietly, if a bit nervously. "I do love you. But here we are, a priest and a religious sister on the staff of a Catholic Student Center. We have both made vows of celibacy. So what are we to do? I love you, and I love what I'm doing."

It was an undeniable point. So I waited to see what would happen.

Before the week was out, he invited me to dinner, and then again, and then again, taking me to out-of-the-way restaurants in hopes that no one would recognize us. He offered to give me tennis lessons at 6 a.m. several mornings a week. He took me to movies and on scenic drives.

Our romance, surreptitious and therefore somehow even more romantic, was launched. Beauty enough.

Chapter 5 – A Michigan City Boy

Charles Louis Palms III came from a proud and successful Michigan family. His great-great-grandfather Palms made his money in lumber and linseed oil, and according to

legend married a Pottawatomie Indian princess. The reality seems to have been a bit simpler: she was a Pottawatomie or half-Pottawatomie girl adopted by an established Detroit family. She died giving birth to Charlie's great-grandfather, Francis F. Palms, and shortly thereafter his new stepmother (according to family legend) banished "that papoose" to relatives in New Orleans. He eventually came back to Michigan and further enhanced the family's business interests.

Charlie's paternal grandmother, Isabel DeMun, hailed from St. Louis. My favorite story about the DeMuns centered on a "Stradivarius" violin. According to this legend, certain ancestors, being French aristocrats, ended up on the wrong side of the French Revolution. They escaped by dressing up like minstrels and fiddling their way out of the country. They made their way to what is now the Dominican Republic, and eventually got to St. Louis. Fast forward to about 1980: Charlie's father, now in possession of the Strad, decided that he would like cash for his violin, and asked Charlie to peddle it around New York. One professional violinist said that it had a sweet but not aggressive enough sound for playing in an orchestra. She offered $3000. It was finally determined to be a fiddle, made in the 1700s in the Tyrolean Alps. (We interested our son in violin lessons for a while, but he really didn't enjoy it. Eventually we gave the violin to Charlie's nephew Mark, who plays folk and bluegrass music with it; so it is now officially a fiddle.)

Charlie's father, Charles Louis Palms, Junior, married Marion Dwyer, whose mother was a Fleitz. The Dwyers and

Fleitzes were well known families in Detroit. Marion's mother, widowed early, in 1928 built a beautiful house on Lake Saint

Clair in the Detroit suburb of Grosse Pointe Farms. Charlie remembered stories of "Granny" supervising the builders, climbing on ladders to check on their work. 78 Lakeshore Drive is still a celebrated house in Grosse Pointe.

In 1929, after the financial crash, Charlie's parents took their three small boys (Charlie, the oldest, was four) and moved in with Granny. There Charlie and his siblings were raised, with "the help" in the roles of nanny, gardener, chauffeur, cook and housecleaner. Marion professed to be rather helpless in a mothering role, although another son and a daughter were born a few years later. The boys remembered long weeks during school vacations at summer camp in New York State. Charlie, however, also fondly recalled the fun of playing tennis with his mother at the Country Club of Detroit (which is in Grosse Pointe). He also remembered that she took cooking classes in an effort to be more domestic. She must have been good-humored about this shortcoming, because her sons teased her, calling her "the chemist of the kitchen."

Charlie's father evidently had an easy relationship with his children. He was a warm man with an infectious laugh, who loved to sing and accompany himself at the piano (as Charlie did later). He, too, at one point tried his hand at learning a new skill: playing the cello. However, when his boys teased him by secretly recording his practice session and adding their voiceover, "Listen to those golden tones," he abruptly gave up the cello forever.

His warmth balanced his wife's formality, and Charlie remembered, on the whole, a happy childhood.

Charlie grew up loving the country club. He became a very good tennis and hockey player, and this country club was where he made and hung out with most of his friends. Later, when he left the Detroit area for good (the only one of the five siblings who did), he said he would miss the country club the most.

Even more formative than the privileged life style, however, was the deep-rooted Roman Catholic piety. The family daily recited the rosary together. The boys became altar boys. Priests were often guests in the house. Charlie's father regularly made retreats at a Jesuit retreat house. When Charlie, much later, visited his nearly comatose mother in a nursing home, she never responded to anything until he had the inspiration to say the rosary with her – and she would instantly pipe up with the answering half of the Hail Mary prayer: "Holy Mary, Mother of God, pray for us sinners now and at the hour of our death. Amen."

Charlie and his siblings mostly attended Catholic schools. After the parish elementary school, Charlie enrolled in the Jesuits' University of Detroit High School.

Graduating from high school in 1943, Charlie was immediately drafted into World War II. Because of less than perfect eyesight and "flat feet," he was relegated to the Seabees, and he spent most of his wartime in Trinidad – fretting that he was not able to be on the front lines of the war effort. "You're in more danger of being bombed in Detroit than I am in Trinidad," he wrote home to his family. He did have some fun with tennis and was a champion on the base. He was a talented boxer, but his heart wasn't in it: his mates called him Balmy Palms. And he picked up some calypso songs, with which he and his guitar later entertained his friends at parties.

After the war and his stint in the Navy, he attended his father's choice of college for him, the Jesuits' Georgetown University in Washington, D.C., where he earned his bachelor's degree in history in 1949. He enjoyed the Washington social scene, meeting Mimsie there, his first fiancée. And he played on the Georgetown hockey team. A teammate was Steve Smith, who later married Jean Kennedy. The Kennedy connection helped him out years later when he was looking for a job.

The next three years found Charlie at Harvard Law School. He often told me that his Jesuit education taught him to repeat everything he had been told, and he was very good at that. But at Harvard everything changed: retaining information was useless; he had to learn how to process the information and to reason to his own conclusions, and he struggled to pass his courses. He was now a C student, he confided.

He enjoyed Boston, however, enjoyed his roommates (Dick was a friend from Georgetown days, and Peter, his cousin, hailed from Grosse Pointe), and enjoyed socializing with, among others, cousins attending the women's Newton College of the Sacred Heart nearby. It was during law school that Mimsie called off their engagement. (After a few months she wanted to renew it, but this time Charlie, still feeling somewhat bruised, declined.)

After law school Charlie accepted a position with an established law firm in Detroit, where his Uncle Cleve was a principal. As the newest kid on the block he was assigned to minor cases, like repossessing refrigerators for banks, and found that, under those circumstances, he did not enjoy lawyering that much. He was searching for something else, a way to serve others in a meaningful way. He talked to the Jesuit priests about joining them. He also made a retreat with the Trappist monks at Gethsemani Abbey in Kentucky.

Meantime he got himself engaged to Jan, a Grosse Pointe native. Jan, however, soon observing his uncertainties, wisely told him that the engagement should be put on hold until he could make some decisions about his future choices. So he continued to explore, until he found the Paulist Fathers.

The Paulist mission, or purpose, was to preach to the people of the United States. The order's founder, Isaac Hecker, had been a convert to Catholicism, and no doubt that experience influenced the shaping of the Paulist mission. Charlie liked what he saw of the Paulist Fathers, and entered the order in 1954. The

Paulist central offices were in New York City, St. Paul's Church on 59th Street being the "Motherhouse" or "Mother church." The novitiate was in Oak Ridge, New Jersey. The seminary was St. Paul's College in Washington, D.C. For his Master of Divinity degree he wrote a thesis on the philosophy of one of his law professors, Lon Fuller.

Charlie was ordained a priest in 1960, at St. Paul's Church in New York City. His first priestly assignment was to go with two ordination classmates, Ron and Joe, to a Boston parish. The three young priests loved to tell stories of those halcyon days: preparing and teaching classes during the day, accepting dinner invitations and party invitations nearly every weekend, dragging themselves out of bed for early Mass the mornings after.

His next assignment was back in New York, working for Paulist Press as associate editor of The Catholic World magazine. He revered his editor, Father John (called Bas) Sheerin, and became very friendly with the head of the book publishing side of Paulist Press, Father Kevin Lynch. Charlie always stayed in contact with the art editor, Claude Ponsot. He fondly remembered meeting Dorothy Day and other Catholic luminaries during his stint with The Catholic World. His legal training and his clear writing served him well in this editorial job and in other career choices to come.

In 1966 Charlie was assigned to the Catholic Student Center, situated on the edge of the University of Texas campus in Austin – and that's where our paths first crossed.

Chapter 6 – Confluence: The Sixties, Charlie, and Me

For both Charlie and me, the university campus in Austin opened a whole other world. We had been unusually isolated from the turbulent sixties by living the religious life, doing what we had been bidden. For two persons who had come from such different class-influenced backgrounds and upbringings, the most formative factors were amazingly similar: our religious beliefs and our desire to live our Christian lives in service to others.

Charlie came to Texas a year after I did. I admired his conscientious approach to pastoring the students and faculty of UT. He was known as the priest who gave the homilies solidly based on the Scriptures. (A second priest, Ed Lundy, was known for his homilies containing perceptive insights into human behavior, with examples drawn from the movies.) Charlie had his light side as well. He came to parties with his guitar and could strum along with the antiwar songs of the moment, not to mention his large collection of favorites from popular and folk genres and some of those calypso tunes he had picked up during his wartime stint in Trinidad. He was an earnest man with a sense of fun.

Charlie, like me, grew from his experiences with both students and faculty at UT. One faculty couple told me recently that they had belonged to a Catholic couples group led by Charlie in which they discussed issues of church and society. Charlie helped them through a very difficult decision regarding family planning. Catholic Church teaching forbade all types of birth control except "rhythm" – a method combining abstinence and careful calendar watching that was not known for great successes in preventing conceptions. This couple had four children and a small income. They came to Charlie for advice after Pope Paul VI issued the unilateral *Humanae Vitae* encyclical in 1968 reiterating this church doctrine. The couple wanted to limit their children to four, but also wanted to remain faithful Catholics. Charlie reminded them of another important Church teaching, one spelled out in Vatican II documents – the doctrine of freedom of conscience. A well-informed conscience can make judgments about appropriate and acceptable behavior, he told them, and assured them that they had well-informed consciences. This couple gratefully accepted these words of advice. The number of their children remained at four.

Charlie helped this couple, but helped himself as well. There would be decisions in his own life soon in which the freedom of conscience doctrine would prove to be liberating. Especially, perhaps, concerning his relationship with me.

Charlie (like me) had arrived in Texas supporting President Johnson's stance on the war in Vietnam. But he (like me) was open to considering other well-reasoned points of view. A decisive turning point for him came in his work with students seeking conscientious objector status in this era of the draft. He was successful in helping several young men attain this status, and in the process had long conversations with them as they filled out the forms and prepared themselves for the application process. Eventually he was joining them in anti-war protest marches in Austin.

Civil rights causes were also a major concern for both him and me. He became an admirer of Martin Luther King, Jr. When King was assassinated in April of 1968, Charlie was deeply affected. Two months later, when Robert Kennedy, who was running as an anti-war candidate for President, was also assassinated, it was a second hard blow. (Charlie had met Bobby in the course of his friendship with Steve Smith, now husband of Robert Kennedy's sister Jean.) After Bobby's death, Charlie -- along with students and many friends, including me -- became a supporter of Eugene McCarthy for president.

By that summer of 1968, Charlie and I were separately but similarly primed for the Jerry McCarty chapter of our lives.

Chapter 7 – Love and Innocence

We were not all that young – Charlie was 43; I was 28. But in terms of experience, we were still in the age of innocence.

Jerry McCarty – his friendship, his infatuation with me, his illness and subsequent suicide – had represented a profound learning experience for me, including learning much about myself. But melodramatic as that episode of my life was, it was nothing compared to the heady first experience of requited love. Since he had been engaged twice in his twenties, Charlie had indeed experienced reciprocated love. Still, he seemed as inexperienced as I was. Yet we were both cautiously open to this new adventure.

How could this be?

I immediately realized that Charlie's kiss, though unexpected, was welcome, and I was intrigued by the possibility of exploring this relationship and seeing where it would lead. I had already started questioning whether I still belonged in the convent. My once certain faith had undergone some radical changes since that summer of '65 at Notre Dame. In Texas, in graduate school, I didn't ask a religious superior for everyday permissions. I didn't live a regularized day punctuated by praying with other sisters, eating with other sisters, socializing with the same sisters every day at a set time. I was in full charge of my own time. I started asking questions for myself pertaining to my chosen religious vocation – about the authority of the pope, about reasons for wearing a habit, about the purposes of the religious life, and most basically about doctrinal questions such as whether Jesus was God, and whether it mattered if Jesus was or wasn't God. I was moving toward a kind of cultural Catholic agnosticism. And, I wondered, if I didn't firmly believe in some of these fundamental Church teachings, what was I doing representing the Church as a woman in the religious life, vowed to poverty, chastity, and obedience? I had begun to feel that I was living a lie.

On my home visit in April of 1968, I had explained my quandary to my sister, Kathy. On the way to Minnesota from Texas I had stopped at her house in Illinois for a few days. She had met me at a nearby train station in the early morning hours.

At a quiet moment in her house when her three small children were otherwise occupied, she listened quietly and compassionately as I spilled out my doubts and my questions. When I finally finished, she expressed her concern and support, and then said, "But now I think I am having a miscarriage. I need to call Dick" (her husband).

I was astounded at her ability to listen to my long-range quandaries while she was dealing with such an urgent and emotionally-laden medical emergency. She was whisked off to the hospital, and I atoned for my self-absorption by tending to the three children until the next day, when she came home again, no longer pregnant.

The timing of this episode was important to me, I realized as I later reconstructed the sequence of events in my story. I was already entertaining the idea of leaving the convent before I entered into the romance of my life. There had been a vacuum, and nature abhors a vacuum.

I soon found out that Charlie had had similar questions and doubts. In the past year he had been invited to return to the Paulist seminary in D.C. in the role of spiritual director to the seminarians, and he had decided that he could not be a good match for this appointment until he had worked through his own personal questions.

As of September of 1968 I was a new member of the Catholic Student Center staff, a half-time position. I was to help out with various outreach programs and to be available to students who might want to stop by to talk. (The other half of my time was to be dedicated to writing my doctoral dissertation.)

Charlie and I saw each other daily at work, and at whatever other times we could find an hour here or there – in restaurants, seeing a movie, playing tennis. But it was not enough.

By Thanksgiving vacation he had hatched a bold idea: go to nearby Bastrop State Park with some of our trusted friends, including Madonna, Ed, Bill M, and a sister friend, Joan, for a couple of overnights in a rustic cabin. We had a wonderful time walking in the woods, making a home movie, picnicking, talking, drinking, laughing. Charlie and I grew closer, having been able to spend many hours together freely with friends. (And by the way, Madonna and Ed discovered a new love between them during these precious days.)

However, even as we grew closer, Charlie and I felt keenly the weight of difficult decisions to come. I recently found these notes among Charlie's papers, written in pencil with erasures and corrections as he strove to name precisely his ponderings.

Morning Prayer 12-5-68

> *God – where are you?*
> *I try to reach out to you but cannot touch*
> *I call to you but there is no answer*
> *I still believe you "are."*
>
> *The Evangelist describes you are "Love"*
> *Love is something real to me*
> *Clumsy as I am I struggle to give my love*
> *I know I have received it from my beloved*
> *Is this you?*
> *Are you contained in my love for Francha?*
>   *in her love for me?*
> *I believe you are*
> *Because my love is a gift that we did not create,*
>   *but suddenly discovered within*
> *ourselves*
>
> *Bless, preserve, and strengthen our love*
> *And help us to live it as your Son did – for*
> *others.*
>
>   *Amen*

The Christmas holidays brought our first separation. I was visiting my family in Harmony, and then making an eight-day prayer retreat at the Rochester Motherhouse. These letters I wrote to Charlie from Minnesota capture the emotions we were both experiencing. (Regrettably, I have not found Charlie's letters to me during these relatively brief separations before August 1969.)

ROCHESTER MN TO GROSSE POINTE MI

Dec. 27, 1968

Dear Charlie,

It is 9:30 a.m. after the evening I received your giant care package. I have lost my stamps; I overslept this a.m. through breakfast and Lauds (during which I was supposed to read a lesson over the microphone); and I just missed getting to the first conference. I couldn't make myself go in late because I already stand out in my green among the browns. Besides which, I have a headache, either from missing breakfast or from sore ears from wearing a veil [which I had stopped doing in Texas]. *That's that. Now I'll tell you why I'm happy.*

I'm happy because I love you and you love me. I told my sister about you and about the decision we have to make together, and she was wonderful. She said, "How can you stand the torment of being drawn in two directions?" I said it was simple: I am in love.

I talked to my mother and father a little about leaving the convent. The reaction was so definite I knew I couldn't tell them about you *yet. My reasons for leaving centered around disillusionment with the institutional church and changes in my own beliefs. Mother was good, though: she said I must do what I think best, regardless of whether it pleases or displeases my family. She knows I would rather please her than displease her. She knows I love her.*

It was good being home for Christmas. The entire family was present: Gary with three, Kathy with three, John with one and 8/9, and Michael, still a senior in high school. Dora [my apartment-mate and friend who drove with me from Texas] *is already part of the family. In fact, she went back to my home instead of spending the whole time with Sister Marya* [my convent classmate] *in Austin, Minn.*

I am lonesome for you! Your letter [unfortunately, not saved] *made me a little teary. You are so honest and beautiful! A year's separation from you is at the moment for me unthinkable! Yet I am still thinking in terms of returning to teach at CST* [the College of Saint Teresa] *in August. (On my own terms. Read on.) In fact, that is what I have been telling everyone. (I barely know anyone up here any more, so the conversation runs something*

*like this: "Let's see, you're Sister who? (Bad memories can hide
behind name changes.)* [After 1967 the sisters were given the
option to return to using their baptismal names.] *Oh, you're
studying in Texas. Where's your tan? Ha Ha. How is your work
going? When are you coming back? Oh, that's nice."*

*Up until last night I was depressed by playing this
superficial game with everyone and not being really honest with
more than one or two. It is the old dilemma: I want to marry you,
Charlie, more than anything else, I think; yet I feel like a traitor
to my own congregation when I start thinking realistically about
it. I feel like a rat leaving the sinking ship with all my friends
drowning along with the ship. Not just friends: they can leave
with me if they wish; but the dear faithful sisters who <u>can't</u> leave
(people the age and psychological makeup of Belinda, for
instance). The dilemma seemed to offer no way out: my
responsibility toward my sisters and my responsibility-love
toward you seemed mutually exclusive. There is no cognitive
dissonance between "I love you" and "I love what I'm doing"*
[Charlie's remark when we first talked about our love], *but there
is an actual dissonance in terms of existing structures.*

*But let <u>us together</u> forge new structures. The married
priesthood would answer part of your need; a married affiliation
organization with the Paulists would answer another part. Bill M
proposed that at our rectory party with George. Duke is saying
the same in his letter.* [Bill, George, and Duke were all Paulist
friends.] *Well, couldn't it work with Franciscan nuns, too? I no
longer feel committed to celibacy, but I still see the need for a
simple life ("poverty"), and I feel a strong commitment to our
<u>community</u> of sisters, to work <u>together</u> in the service of the
people of God (the church, not The Church). As long as I see
them doing good among the people of God, I want to support
them. As long as they want/need my help, I wish to give it to
them.*

*But they will have to take my support and help in the
way I can honestly offer it. I am open to other alternatives (I
can't think of any others right now, but there must be some), but
the present form of religious life would be artificial for me. (I
know I am not seeing things clearly right now, because any life
without you <u>openly</u> by my side is unthinkable!!)*

So -- *what would happen if I should return to CST (not necessarily: any work or place agreed upon by the congregation and me) as a lay affiliate of the OSFs? I would be either a single lay woman (Miss Grebin) or a married one (Mrs. Palms??). I would work for just enough to live on as our college board would (hopefully) begin to phase out of ownership of and corporate commitment to the College of Saint Teresa. In this way I would be contributing to the support of our retired members and the education of our new and active members. I would also have a hand in the direction our congregation is taking – in new forms of government and policy and community living.*

Well, what do you think? I'm going to try to write up a tentative draft of such a proposal. Eileen [Madonna had returned to using her baptismal name] *mentioned last night (when she brought me your welcome letter) that she was going to propose such a plan when the time is ripe, and when someone is willing to stick her neck out as a guinea pig, because she thinks there is a bond between friends she would not like to lose if (when?) she leaves the order. My reason for favoring the idea is rather a way to remain loyal and responsible to this group of women who educated me, and whom I respect, and whose work I respect and support. I am willing to be such a guinea pig. If you and I, Charlie, should decide against marriage, I still think I would rather be a lay affiliate of our Sisters of Saint Francis than remain vowed to celibacy. My vows would be promises to live a simple life ("poverty") in cooperation with the "apostolates" in the service of the people of God of the Sisters of Saint Francis ("obedience").*

Your homily [included in his letter] *was beautiful; and yes, the theme was a familiar one. I wish I could have heard you give it. I must learn more about this farm* [that is, the Catholic Worker Farm] *in New York, and I must meet your friend who wants to go there.*

Our plans for returning to Texas are (approximately) to pick up Joan ... in Davenport, Iowa, on Jan. 3, and drive back thru the slower but more scenic route of St. Louis, Springfield (Mo.), the Ozarks, Hot Springs (Ark.), Texarkana, and then Dallas and south. We will probably stop in Springfield overnight

*in order to do daytime scenic driving. We'll arrive, we hope, late
the 4ᵗʰ, and Dora will return to Laredo the 5ᵗʰ.*

I love you, Charlie!

Francha

Three days later I wrote again, still in retreat.

ROCHESTER TO AUSTIN

Dec. 30, 1968

Dear Charlie my love,

*I just got your letter of Dec. 26 and trust you will have
received mine before you left Michigan. After I read your letter
twice I sat down and re-copied a poem I wrote for you* [the poem
is lost] *as I was trying to sleep last night. You are with me
everywhere, Charlie. I catch myself saying goodby to this life, to
these people; and then I force myself to be less remote as I revise
and re-revise the proposal of a lay affiliate in my mind. If this
could be accepted, I would still be part of this group of dedicated
women. I feel so responsible for them (almost maternal: isn't
that ridiculous?)*

It has snowed every day since we hit Minnesota. (Dora
[from warm Laredo TX] *may never come back!) Like a hothouse
flower, I succumbed before the elements with a lovely chest cold.
Retreat's a good time to get sick, though, if I must at all. I can't
talk very well, and none of my closest friends are here, anyway.
The weather prevented at least one from getting here, and that
was disappointing. Another may still make it. With the rest, well,
there's nothing to talk about if I don't talk about you!*

*We have two retreat masters, and neither has impressed
me enough to value their opinion of a lay affiliate, for example. I
guess they strike me as so traditional I think I know already what
they will say. I may change my mind and go find out.*

*Joanie called me the other night. She's been snowed in
at her* [parents'] *farm and was getting antsy.*

*Be reassured, Charlie: I LOVE you. We'll soon know if
we should make the plunge. I pray as best I can.*

Love, Francha

Back in Austin our relationship grew, even as we contemplated a year's separation once summer came. In early March, 1969, I hand-delivered this poem to Charlie's office:

I love him because
>*he is lively*
>*talented*
>*fun to be with*

I love him because
>*he is older than I in wisdom — in some wisdom*
>*and younger in exploring his emotions — some*
>>*emotions*

I love him because
>*he is sunshine*
>*fresh air*
>*vigorous sports*

I love him most of all because
>*he is humble and honest and good*

and I love him
>*because he loves me in a way to which I can*
>>*respond*

I love him
>*in his zest for life as he strums his guitar*

I love him
>*as he admits his defeats*
>*confesses his battles with himself*

I love him
>*in his compassion for others*
>*that is evident in all he does*

I love him
>*because he loves me as I am*
>*with my own battles and defeats*
>*and victories*

I love him
>*for what he has done for me in accepting myself*
>*for helping me love myself*
>*for giving me self-confidence*

In these ways he has changed my life
>*permanently*

> *so that he will always be a part of me*
> *no matter what the future holds*
I love him
> *because I love him*

> > > *To Charlie because*
> > > *I love him.*
> > > *Francha 3-7-69*

By this time I had decided to teach at the College of Saint Teresa starting in September 1969. I returned to Minnesota over the Easter holidays, driving north with Nancy, a current roommate. Nancy was to visit her fiancé, Warren, in Minneapolis, and I wanted to get oriented for my new teaching job. In a way I hated to leave Austin at that moment, because the Students for a Democratic Society (SDS), planning to hold their National Council meeting in Austin, had been shut out of university buildings and all of the usual sites in Austin. In order to try to prevent violent confrontations between police (or even other Texas citizens) and SDS members, the university's religious student centers had jointly offered them shelter. The Jewish rabbi helped the other chaplains reach this risky decision, saying with a sense of humor, "Let's be Christian about this." The plenary sessions would take place in the Catholic Student Center, which offered the largest meeting space among the centers.

The first of my letters was enclosed in an Easter card saying, "You will show me the path of life, fullness of joys in your presence, the delights at your right hand forever. Psalm 15:11"

WINONA MN TO AUSTIN TX

> *3-30-69*

Dearest Charlie,
> *This card is the RIGHT one to send to you on Palms Sunday evening as I sit with you in mind in a lovely guest room in the Sisters' Residence Hall at the College of Saint Teresa. My welcome continues to be warm, and despite the zero° weather, my spirits are considerably better than at Christmas time. Part of it is knowing I shall be here, part of the picture, in a few short*

*months, and suddenly I want to know all I can about the way
things tick around here. I've had several good visits, asking so
many questions they don't get much of a chance to ask* me *any.*
☺ *Also hearing gossip and conjectures, like two of my
classmates are marrying priests in the next few months!! (With a
lowering of the voice as they tell me....) A wild but possible
conjecture is that one of my best friends may be the intended
bride of your good friend Bianchi in Atlanta!! If that turns out to
be the case, you and I may both be invited to the wedding. Isn't
that fun?* [This turned out not to be the case. Eugene Bianchi got
married, but not to anyone we knew.]

*Nancy and I had a good trip up. The roads and weather
were both generally kind to us. The car behaved beautifully. We
came by way of Macomb, Ill., to see my sister, Kathy – just in
time for lunch. I put on a skirt and pressed my veil and on we
headed for Winona. 20 hrs to Macomb and six more to Winona.
Nancy had three more to Minneapolis, where she probably
arrived about 12:30 a.m. Sun.*

*I eagerly await news of you, SDS, etc. The Sunday paper
here doesn't seem to be interested in us, which I take to be good
news. Keep the bishop happy.* [The bishop was very unhappy.]

Love, Francha

WINONA TO AUSTIN

April 3, 1969
Holy Thursday

Dearest Charlie,

*Happy Easter – probably a day late.... I have been busy
talking to people, relaxing, listening.... generally a very good
vacation. Nancy and Warren stopped for lunch Tuesday on the
way to Milwaukee, and I gave them a royal tour of CST* [the
College of Saint Teresa]. *I shall meet them in Rochester Monday
a.m. for our return trip, and that way they can see the
Motherhouse, too.*

*I am sewing for a sister while I'm here – it's nice to be
of service to them instead of always being on the receiving end. I
went to the "Chrism Mass" at the cathedral this morning to see
our new bishop of Winona, Watters, and I enjoyed all the*

*pageantry for a change of pace. Then choir practice and a lovely
liturgy of our own here in the p.m.*

    *I pored over your letter (I had to go to the bathroom to
read it privately – my classmate Marya came to see me ☺) and
news-clippings in the wee hours last night. I really am sorry to
have missed the excitement there. Glad of no big incidents. I
trust we all still have our jobs?? You write good letters; did you
know that? I could feel your weariness; I could sense the
excitement in the Center in the background as you typed away; I
know your love as you sat talking to me with distractions on
every side.*

    I'll see you Tuesday, dearest.

My love, F

For my birthday in May Charlie
presented me with my very own tennis
racquet, and whisked me away to San
Antonio, where we walked along the new
River Walk and saw the Barbra Streisand
movie *Funny Girl.* For his birthday in June I
gave him a framed color photo of myself,
taking advantage of a coupon from a
photography studio. (After all, I was living

under a vow of poverty, and was expected to account for my
expenditures to the Rochester Motherhouse.)

    The summer of 1969 brought an added intensity to our
relationship, fueled by the knowledge that we were on the verge
of making decisions about our futures, individually and together,
and that we would soon be separated. Charlie had decided to take
a leave of absence from the priesthood and was contemplating
the job market. He had decided to try to pass the bar exam in the
state of Illinois, where a possible job was in the offing.

    I had decided not to decide: that is, I had reasoned that I
could not make a decision about staying in or leaving the
religious life until I had returned to Minnesota and once again
was living a typical communal life. I had asked my superiors to
leave Texas ABD – all but dissertation – and return to Minnesota
in order to teach English courses at the sisters' college in

Winona. I would live in the large convent there with about fifty other sisters.

One of our last evenings together in Texas was the night of the first moonwalk, a long-anticipated space triumph. We chose to celebrate it together, alone, in a friend's house. Our mood was joyous, as the strain of always pretending – to be just friends – temporarily was lifted. The memory of that evening would sustain us in the difficult year ahead.

At the end of the summer session, together we drove north to my sister's house in Illinois. There Charlie first met a member of my family, and created a lasting impression on Kathy's children by singing them songs while he strummed his guitar. "The Second-Story Window" was their favorite, and Kathy kept Charlie's memory alive for the kids by continuing to sing that song to them at bedtime.

When I drove Charlie to the train station to point him in the direction of Chicago, it was goodbye time, maybe for a year. As we waited for the train, Charlie sang me the Fats Domino song, "Ain't Misbehavin'" ("...savin' my love for you...."), through his own tears. Parting from Charlie seemed like the hardest thing I had ever done.

I remember returning from the train station that day to Kathy's house and throwing myself into activities with the children, now ages 2, 5, and 6. We collected colorful paints and trooped down to the end of the driveway, where we painted flowers all over the mailbox and down its post.

The next day I headed north to my new teaching assignment.

Chapter 8 – A Year Apart

Charlie's train took him to Chicago, where he talked to a
Protestant coalition about working with the poor on the South
Side, perhaps as a legal aid lawyer. For that he would need to use
his law degree and pass the bar exam for the State of Illinois.
Even more crucial, he needed the approval of the Cardinal
Archbishop of Chicago in order to work in that archdiocese.

His next stop after Chicago was his parents' home in the
Detroit suburb of Grosse Pointe, where he studied intensely for
the bar exam. Our letter-writing began immediately. Note that
now I had returned to using my baptismal name.

GROSSE POINTE TO WINONA
Friday [August 8, 1969]

Dearest Rosemary,

It's noon. I've just put about four hours in on the law
books and am taking a break. Next to me is a can of Budweiser –
my reward for the long hours of study.

I called Chicago yesterday; there is still no further word
from the Chancery [the offices of the Catholic Archdiocese]. *But*
I did ask David of the Church Federation to make a further
check so that I can get in touch with our President [of the Paulist
Fathers], *John (Fitz) Fitzgerald. I plan to call New York this*
afternoon or evening. Jim [a brother Paulist] *called yesterday; he*
thought it would be wiser if we lived at Old St. Mary's rectory [a
Paulist parish in Chicago]. *It means losing some autonomy, but I*
am a member of the community and I can see the wisdom of
being with the community – a financial saving and other

members of the community can share in my
experience and less loneliness. However, if that
doesn't work out, I will get out on my own. I will
insist that I be free to fulfill my duties.

I love you and miss you. As painful as our tears
were, they made me feel so secure in my love, our
love. They flowed so easily in both of us. Our love to
me is like the mystery of the infinite. It's there and
whatever we may decide, it will never disappear.
The only things hanging in "my" room are a crucifix

and the banner you gave me: *"You just keep wondering."*
[Charlie had referred to this quotation from his devout "Granny"
in a homily a couple of years earlier.] *I woke up this morning
looking at that banner and felt a goodness deep within. I said a
few short morning prayers, wondering, hoping.*

> *It's now 4:15 p.m. I'm expecting brother George to pick
me up at 4:20 for tennis. Then I'll come home for supper and
study. (No word from Chicago yet.)*

> *I've only seen Brad* [a close friend from childhood] *so
far. Had dinner with him last night. He has been in great pain
from a combination of a torn shoulder muscle and shingles. But
now he's on the mend. He lives like a monk in a scantily
furnished apartment in Detroit. I promised to show him your
picture.*

> *George is here and I want to mail this. I love you,
Rosemary, and I love you so. I wonder what you are doing and
how you are feeling.*

> *Devotedly, Charlie*

Meanwhile, I had enjoyed a visit with my parents on
their Minnesota farm, and had now arrived in Winona.

WINONA TO GROSSE POINTE

August 8, 1969
CST

Dear Charlie,

> *People are so glad to see me that it helps a little! I was a
little physically sick when I drove in at about 2:30 p.m., but now
at 9:45 and moving in a little, I'm much better. I'm going down
in a minute to drink something cold (and soft ☺) in the kitchen.*

> *I told Mother right away that you had come to Macomb
and wasn't that lucky. She didn't bat an eye, but (we were on the
way to Grandma's) just said not to tell Grandma I had traveled
all that way with a priest. I had come waltzing home in my
cutoffs and Mom just laughed at that, too. (I couldn't believe it.)
In fact, she whisked me off to a farm auction immediately and
didn't even give me time to change. Even Grandma, who went
along, admitted she loved me anyway.*

You should have been with me at the auction! I had so much fun observing the local color – TECHNICOLOR! – and trying not to act superior. It wasn't hard, in cutoffs. To give you an idea of prices: Mom bought a sewing machine, pedal-type, that WORKS for $8.00. (!!) The proprietress was an old lady with gray hair, sloppily clad, with a perpetual drooping cigarette hanging from her lips. Farmers had come straight from the fields. Then a few well-dressed ladies from the city (population 5000) nearby, who take in every auction as a hobby. I can see that they are entertaining.

I was struck again with your resemblance in temperament to my father. Aren't you glad I have a healthy relationship with him? And with you? ☺ You're more nervous than he is, but you are both gentle. Like you, my father gets along with everyone. Never argues. Likes to sing.

I'm writing with a pen that goes with a stand that says ALLELU FRANCHA! on it. I have my little Mexican liquor bottles on the bookstand, so now I feel a little more secure. [These were farewell presents from Austin friends.]

How is the ILLINOIS LAW shaping up? I'd like to be listening to your problem cases again.

I need a navigator for my driving. I can't look at a map and drive both. Consequently I have taken the wrong roads twice since you left me.

I was home only 25 hours and I was already getting sassy. I think weekend home visits are the best idea yet. Sunday is the wedding anniversary of Daddy and Mother. I'll drive home Sunday p.m. and probably take the Bluebonnet to the Motherhouse Monday. [The little blue car, a Corvair, belonged to the Franciscans and had been made available for Eileen's and my use in Texas.]

Chapter ends tomorrow and no one here knows the results yet. ["Chapter" is the business meeting of the Congregation, with elected "capitular" representatives.]

Veils are still on.

First impressions after a 45-minute chat: the sisters here are living a dry life; all their interests are centered in their professional jobs or what other people are doing; no one talks about HERSELF, her own REAL THOUGHTS, REAL

FEELINGS. I can hear you say, "In 45 minutes you expect....?"
And you are absolutely right.

I'm going to bed now and will think about you till I sleep
– like I did last night. Greetings to your parents and I love YOU .
Francha/Rosemary

Permissions for Charlie to take the job in Chicago had
not been coming through from the Archdiocese, and the Paulist
Fathers were reluctant to stir up trouble with the Cardinal.

GROSSE POINTE TO WINONA

August 11 [1969]

Dearest Rosemary,

No word from you yet, but I assume you had a safe trip
home. How was the visit with your parents? I have been living in
peaceful co-existence. Study is the daily routine. No questions
about my personal life. The post-card was appreciated but no
further questions asked. Some rumors here have me already
married. This is embarrassing to Mother and Dad. I offered
Mass at our parish church on Sunday but refrained from
preaching. My social life is curtailed until after the bar exam.

I've spoken with Father Fitz. He does not want me to go
to Chicago unless I have the OK of the Cardinal. If the Cardinal
persists in his "no," Fitz does not want me to go under a leave of
absence as this would prejudice the existing community in
Chicago. This presents me with a very serious decision if the
Cardinal persists in his attitude. Fitz wanted me to return to
Texas, but I feel I have left the U of Texas. Walter [director of the
Catholic Student Center] *has hired Edmond B* [a Jesuit priest and
international student] *for next year since the Paulists couldn't*
supply a man. All of this fuss about next year makes it that much
harder to study for the bar.

I miss our early morning tennis games. I've only played
tennis once since coming home. I'll take a walk today to visit my
great Aunt Frances. I showed you pictures of her with her horse
and the cups she won.

I dream about us and think about you constantly. A blue
Volkswagon just went by the window. Remember the slow bug
that held us up for so long?

I look forward to hearing from you, sweetie. Meanwhile try out your tennis....

This carries all my love dear. I'll keep you informed on latest developments.

Devotedly, Charlie

(more)

I should have mentioned, dear, that I am in touch with Chicago (since John C is on vacation, I telephoned David M of the Church Federation). I have asked that an appointment be set up with the Cardinal and that I be present with John or one of the lawyers and David of the Church Foundation. I desire that this appointment be made as soon after the bar exam as possible. My hope is that the Cardinal changes position. My other alternatives are (1) to go with leave of absence, which Fitz opposes; (2) to go regardless; (3) to accept another assignment – none yet offered except Texas, which I refuse.

Love, Chas

The next letter followed a quick visit to my parents marking their wedding anniversary.

WINONA TO GROSSE POINTE

I enclosed with this letter a note to me from my sister, Kathy, who wrote that their "mailbox is cool!" And "We all love you. C is great."

Aug. 11, '69
3:00 p.m.

Dearest Charlie,

I started in wearing my contacts again today, and thought of you.

I put gas, oil, & water in the car today and thought of you.

My mother is vocal & upset by Bp. Shannon's actions. [James P. Shannon, a Minnesota bishop, had recently resigned after Pope Paul VI's prohibition of birth control in the encyclical "Humanae Vitae." He married shortly thereafter.] *My father agrees, but a little less vocally. "Christ never said it would be easy," and "Sex and marriage aren't all they are cracked up to be," are 2 central statements.*

I heard from Walter yesterday. A nice letter. He misses you – sent off your trunk, and hired Edmond to help at the CSC. I think that should work out very well, because the students like him & he'll keep everyone hopping.

I heard from Eileen, too. Ed left Mon. a.m., so she's a bit lonely, but he calls every night; says the meetings are profitable and he's getting more sleep ☺.

I miss you so very very much I'm tempted to beg you to come see me after your Aug. 21 test. I know that's playing with fire, but I would like you to see our beautiful campus. Excellent train connections between Winona & Chicago. I know I should not have suggested it, because the idea will torture both of us now.

I sure hope you write me – maybe I'll get a letter today. Otherwise I'll have to use your credit card! [I needed the card to make a long distance call.]

I'm going to Rochester tomorrow a.m. for Pat's [a close Texas student friend who joined the Franciscans] *ceremonies – making promises, not vows – in the a.m. St. Clare's Feast Day.*

7:00 p.m. LATER

Your first letter came. I guess it just takes a long time from Detroit. I miss you so very very much that tears still come very easily to my eyes just thinking about it.

So — you'd better NOT come to Winona!

I would say offhand, dear, that after 4 hours of law you need a Budweiser!

Note P.O. Box on address. 106. All faculty members get a private box. But the "postmistress" or mail-sorter is still a nun. But you can address the letter in a variety of ways and I'd still get it. Sister R. Grebin. Dr. Grebin ☺. [The happy face denoted a joke, since my status was "all but dissertation," no doctorate yet.] *Francha or Rosemary without the Grebin. Etc.*

I wonder if at Old St. Marys you will have the "out-of-the-wombness" that you are seeking....

I think [seminary professor] *Ben Hunt had a point about prayer. I'm praying more now, at any rate.*

I heard from Herschel [a Catholic Student Center friend], *too. He might be a little happier, but still is cynical. He's*

*sorry I'm gone, and you gone, too. (People seem to often
juxtapose our departures.!?)*

*Sweetie, it's 9:45 and I'm tired and I must get up at 6 so
I guess I'll close this & mail it.*

I love you.

Rosemary

WINONA TO GROSSE POINTE
August 12 [1969]

Dear Charlie,

*Six years ago today I made final vows. I went to the
ceremonies today and they were nice. The singing was beautiful.
I appreciate the lively music at the CSC, but I doubly appreciate
the lively on <u>key</u> music in the convent – at least on special
occasions!*

*News today: Joanie wrote that she has accepted a
position in the elementary ed. dept of Luther College, Decorah,
Iowa! That puts her within an hour and a half of Winona. She
wrote that she was impressed with the place, and Texas wouldn't
be the same anyway next year. I'm delighted that she is so close.
I may need a sympatico, you know!*

Aug 14

*Got my second letter from you (postmarked Aug. 12) –
telling of Fitz's not-so-understanding position and the
predicament that leaves you in. You may have to take a stand
sooner than you thought, dear. My feeling is that you have
committed yourself to the lawyers in Chicago now – and the
importance of following out <u>your own choice</u> is paramount, it
seems to me, at this stage in your life.*

*I have sent something every day or two, so you certainly
should be hearing regularly.*

*There are no books yet for my Early Am. Lit. class.
Takes 2 months and the order went in last week. Grrrr — what
shall I do??*

*Had "new faculty" pictures taken today – in sedate veil
and suit.*

*I will take the Corvair Bluebonnet to the Motherhouse
this afternoon and come back tonight by another car. I have*

become attached to it, I suppose because of the TLC we – you and I – gave it, and the memories that go with it.

Sister Bernetta says I act like I've always been here. I take it as a compliment. She is perhaps a bit myopic!

Our phone is anything but private, but if you need me, the Alverna line is 3755. Can't dial direct. That's the whole number – we're in the sticks! That would be the harder way to find me, I would imagine.

A better idea is for me to call you! I want to wish you luck personally before your tests, and so I'll call your house at about 10:30 Sunday night. Okay? You may not get this in time to plan to be there, but I'll take a chance and try.

So I won't send any more mail till I figure you'll be back in Grosse Pointe – about the 23rd? Good luck with the tests and with the Cardinal, and whatever else lies in your obstacle course to the fullness of life!

I love you, darling.

Rosemary

P.S. Sorry about those rumors. The rumors here about me range from (1) being married already, to (2) being on the sister formation team! ["Formation" was the preparation given to applicants on their way to becoming vowed sisters.] *What do you think of that?*

GROSSE POINTE TO WINONA

Aug 12 [1969]

Dearest Rosemary,

I'm not going to write you today because I just wrote to you yesterday. But I've been thinking about you all day. I remembered first of all at Mass, the feast of St Clare. I remembered it was something special at St Teresa's. Then your letter came which I read and reread.... I miss you dear and love you! (Now back to the books. Ugh!)

Aug 13

Dearest Rosemary my Francha,

There have been many interruptions today. I had to write Chicago re my appointment with the Cardinal. I hope to see him with John C and David M. Then the phone has been ringing. And my trunks came. Unconscionable! Eleven pieces costing $49.

But I can't continue studying unless I write you. I want so much to give you my thoughts and feelings. I'm not communicating with my parents. The gap is too great, I fear.

Your understanding and balance for my self-reproach is much needed. I don't know where to begin my remarks to you except to say something about prayer.

I believe in God. And I think I love God. But love is communication (I've learned this with you) and God does not communicate back, except thru persons and situations, and this can be very confusing and not conducive to growth in love. This is my prayer problem. But I guess I don't try hard enough. Maybe God is speaking and I refuse to listen.

I am overwhelmed by thoughts of my own selfishness. As I study for the bar, I isolate myself in one room of the house and spend hours with myself. I realize how much I have lived for myself throughout life. How much has my professed love for you been a love of self? (I hate even to ask the question.) At least I don't want it that way. I want to really love you and to love the poor and to love my parents.

I want to be a Catholic, but ... free to search and seek. My belief in the real presence, in Christ, in redemption is much different [now], *...but I need the Church in order to explore. I don't know how much I can act as the Church's official representative, believing as I do. At least I know I can't preach my beliefs. And how much is my shift in belief part of an honest search; how much is it a way of achieving my own selfish desires?*

Dear, these are my feelings. Don't try to respond to them. Just your listening is enough. And one other feeling that I save for now is my love for you which I realized in the joy of reading your letter and feel in the pang of your absence.

Devotedly, Charlie

GROSSE POINTE TO WINONA

Aug 14 p.m. [1969]

Dearest Rosemary,

My being at home this long has brought me into greater communication with Mother and Dad. Tonite I gave them, or rather witnessed to them on, two points: original sin and the sacraments. I said that I thought the biblical teaching on original sin was an existential statement on the human condition; and that sacraments, like a kiss or holding hands, was a sign of love that was already there (God's love) rather than a magical production of grace. They had no rebuttal. I felt they accepted me or at least were open to understanding. Then I waxed further on poverty, chastity and obedience. I said that these "vows" no longer meant as much to us – that they were a denial of the human person or dishonest. I said that poverty was unreal – that it would be much better to take the vow of generosity; I said that obedience was a denial of individuality and that Jesus had always appealed to me because he had affirmed his own identity; then I said I didn't know what to say about chastity – and they both laughed. I really felt I was reaching them. I didn't bring the subject of us up, but you were on my mind and in my heart. It's really a process of education. You and I have been thru it (this education) or are in it; and they are not on the same track so we can't blame them. You mentioned your folks' reaction to Bishop Shannon. I can still remember Mother and Dad (when I was in high school and college and would occasionally hint about a vocation) saying the same thing your folks say now -- "Sex and marriage aren't all they are cracked up to be." Well, neither is religious life! As Belinda said, "There's no such thing as religious life; there's just life." You and I can still choose life. We don't have to be what others want us to be. We have to be what we want! But I don't want to say we should be totally selfish. We are in a position to choose, you and I, a freedom situation that we have never been in before.

And for this reason I say, why not try to see each other when I come to Chicago? After all, Ed calls Eileen every night. I'm envious! I haven't been this much in contact. Life is too short. Why not a short visit! I'll call you at St Teresa. I don't know when the Cardinal will see me. Our get-together should be conditioned on that. But why not! Sweetie, life is too short! I've checked on the RR and there are three trains daily. We don't have to look at this as a momentous, decisive visit, but just as fun together. Let's really try! Remember the bar exam is from Aug

*19-thru-21. I'll call you in the evening of Tuesday, the first day
of the exam, as close to 7 p.m. as I can.*

*It's now Aug 15. I preached this morning at the 7 a.m.
Mass. I began by relating a new city ordinance against leaf-
burning to the Assumption as pertaining to the dignity of the
human body and God's love for it as symbolized in today's feast.
And leaf-burning causes smog and creates the risk of fires which
are harmful to our bodies. I then said that every successful
transplant and advance in medical science was a furtherance of
human dignity and was given meaning by this feast. And
alternately, every maiming and destruction of the body in
warfare, murder or riots was an offense against the body and
this feast. Vietnam; Londonderry, Ireland; Washtenaw County,
Mich. The Assumption is not just our awe at a miraculous event.
It must be related to life – to driving to work this morning; to
care and concern for the kids left at home. And the culmination
of the dignity of the body is in the Christian hope for the
continuance of human consciousness and the body beyond the
transition of death. "In the name of the Father...."*

*I had a dream the other night – really crazy. I was at a
large dinner party, a long rectangular table filled with guests. I
can only remember three people at that party now. I was sitting
opposite Pope Paul* [Paul VI, the current pope] *and, on my right,
at the end of the table was "You just keep wondering," my
grandmother. I recall that Pope Paul had a very small pug nose.
He was holding my hand (reaching across the table) and I recall
that his hand was very warm. My grandmother was speaking and
as she made points, she emphasized her remarks by tapping on
Paul's wrist with her middle finger. I can't recall what anyone
was saying except that Paul asked me if I were a priest. (The
thing I get out of this is that I must fight for myself and not let
beloved Gran argue for me.) She was a very protective person. I
can still remember that when I used to have headaches as a little
boy and she would rub my head with camphor, she would say
that she wished she could have the headache for me.*

*I wrote Kathy and Dick the other day. One thing you and
I should have done was sit down with them and talk about our
love. They accepted us without any explanation which was*

beautiful. Except for the first night, I guess a long discussion together was impossible because of Dick's studies.

This is a long missive. I guess I'm warming up for the bar exam. This intensive study has made me question about a future in law. As we saw in Oliver, *in many ways the law is an ass! One observation I make unhesitatingly is that it has changed less than the Church. There are so many antiquated rules! (Nixon's welfare reform is really exciting!)*

The other observation that I make unhesitatingly is that I love you, dear.... Let's pray, let's pray. The way that God can speak is thru Scripture. I'm making the effort to read more. Will call Tues.

All my love,
Charlie

Charlie and I discussed by phone, and even argued about, the advisability of him visiting me after his bar exam. Even though it was my idea in the first place, in the end I vetoed the plan.

CHICAGO TO WINONA

August 21 [1969]

Dearest,

I just wrote a couple of depressing pages to you and have torn them up. Instead, I went out for a walk and bought you a little anniversary present [Charlie and I celebrated the 21st of each month as our "anniversary," since Charlie's first declaration of his love was on September 21, 1968] *which you should receive in a day or so. And I feel like a million, darling, when I take myself out of the tailspin and think of you and your love for me, which strengthens me so!*

I'm going to stay here tomorrow. I'm going down to David's office and help him write a letter to the Cardinal and to Fitz. I hope to have lunch with John C. I was terribly depressed about not visiting you, but this is a decision we made together and I do think it fits with our plan and saves embarrassment to you.

I love you dearest. I wish you were with me. This is going to be a terribly difficult year for us. We've just gone thru a

crisis. I love you dearest. God bless you and happy anniversary.
I'll write soon.

All my love
Charlie

WINONA TO GROSSE POINTE

August 22, 1969

Dear Charlie,

This will have to be a fast note, but I want you to get
something in the mail as soon as possible after the tears over the
telephone. [The tears were over the decision not to see each other
after the bar exam.]

Don't you get low. You have difficult enough decisions
ahead of you without the added headache of wondering how I
am doing. I generally do quite well, you know. Last night after
supper I slammed tennis balls against the practice board
vigorously – if sloppily — for a full 20 minutes. (The board is too
small for me — about 12' x 16' – and I have a dickens of a time
hitting it!!!)

A couple of young sisters from Assisi Hall (house of
"formation") came over to chat soon after, and then a great
surprise: Pam [a Texas friend] *called me! It could not have been*
better timed. She loves, loves, loves, the [Lutheran] *deaconesses*
and the life in general, and LIFE, and next Wednesday will be off
to Baltimore to the inner city. (She probably could find you a
job!) She asked, cautiously, if I had heard from Chicago. I told
her a little of the Cardinal problems.

It's 1:30 p.m., and I must be over in the largest
residence hall in a few minutes to help register the incoming
freshmen. In cold objectivity, it's good to be available for
various errands today. I'm going on "bells" (phone and
doorbells) this evening from 7 to 9 in Alverna [the convent
building].

Oh yes, it looks like I'll be staying in Alverna. I got
corrected for sitting on the table in the kitchen last night. (I
didn't get off, either.)

The sun is shining. Let's keep it that way, dearest.

Love, Rosemary

WINONA TO GROSSE POINTE

I tucked in my next envelope for Charlie a little pressed fern sprig, and a letter from Kathy to me. She had written that a neighbor said to be sure to tell me how nice the mailbox looks, and she enclosed a diocesan newspaper story about two young Capuchin priests "testing the priest-worker movement in Milwaukee – living in an inner city apartment and working part-time." She added: "We sing Second Story Window at least once a day! Even Sarah [age 2] joins in."

"Choose life, only that and always, and at whatever risk. To let life leak out, to let it wear away by the mere passage of time, to withhold giving it and spreading it is to choose nothing.
–Sr. Helen Kelley
Dear Charlie,

Still August 22 – I really like the saying [see above] *– I feel sure you will too. Pat S sent it, and it looks like it was already a hand-me-down then!*

I have been thinking that one thing that has been bothering me about the sisters here is that far too many (all??) live on the FRINGES of others' lives. I cannot name one *sister who has deeply affected my life, except Pat S, and that was before she became a religious. YOU have deeply affected my life, and our relationship has everything to do with our personhoods, and only incidentally to do with our* roles. *The roles, it is true, brought us together: common interests, common friends, common service to others. And I don't know if I have deeply affected the lives of others, EXCEPT WHEN the role of sisterhood was incidental. I have made people happier for the moment, or supported them when they needed it, but have I helped them to BECOME???*

I think I'm trying to rationalize myself out of a job. ☺
Enough for tonight. I love you.

Rosemary

CHICAGO TO WINONA

Friday Aug 22 [1969]

Darling,

It turns out it was good for me to be here today. I sat with David M of the Church Federation all morning until we had hammered out a letter to Fitz. Then both of us had lunch with John C and clarified our respective positions further. Then after lunch I went back with David and reviewed a letter he composed to the Cardinal. We are trying to set up an appointment as soon as possible. If this doesn't work, then my appeal to the hierarchy is ended. David at lunch said that he would have to "think things through" if the Cardinal says "no." One thing that hadn't been clear to me before is that in accepting the Legal Services position I become a staff member of the Church Federation. The Chicago Volunteer Legal Services is a "Federation-related project." So I'm subject to the Protestant hierarchy too and would be under David! Thus David is afraid the Federation's relations with Catholics would be prejudiced by my coming in an unauthorized manner.

I just walked back from the Church Federation and am heading home tonight. On my way back I stopped at the art museum. I have enclosed a picture of it. And I also enclose something that touched me very deeply. I love Wyeth's paintings. I think this [postcard of a Wyeth painting] *will touch you too. Her sad expression says so much. I don't know why she's so pensive. Did she experience white prejudice for the first time? Did she have a fight with her boyfriend, or older sister? Does she think she spent too much money? Did all the people make her feel lonely?*

In a few minutes I'm going over to the Hilton to pick up my airline ticket. It costs $22 as opposed to $14.75 for the train.

I love you my love and I miss you. I love writing to you now. Knowing that you love me strengthened me today.

And I "meditated" distractingly for 15 minutes this morning!

Affectionately,
Charlie

P.S. What about the books? How is class preparation coming? How are the seniors? The freshmen?

GROSSE POINTE TO WINONA

Saturday, August 23, 1969

Dearest Francha my Rosemary

Somehow I don't think it's fair for me to write every day. I can just envision some snoopy person checking up on your mail. But I'm home now and it will take this longer to reach you so I'm going ahead.

I arrived last night around eleven. It's hard to live with the folks. I love them – and they do so much for me they make me feel like a little boy. They never ask me what I'm going through, or what it's like. They act more like loving parents who expect me to be a good little boy, to act out the patterns of life that they have always taught me. As they shower love on me, they seem confident that their son, in the end, will come through – the way they want him to. Only in this respect will I be glad to leave. It really is great to be home. To have this library to myself where I can read and write without interference (part of their thoughtfulness to me). Today I said I wanted to feel I was contributing something to the house, so I squeeze the orange juice and dump the garbage. They have the cooking and dishwashing down to such a system that I can't interfere.

I called Fitz this morning and advised him of my work in Chicago yesterday – that letters would be coming to him and that I needed community support. He advised that I write a personal letter to the Cardinal, giving my reasons for the Chicago assignment. I think Fitz is right. The Cardinal fears another Groppi. [James E. Groppi was a Milwaukee priest and controversial civil rights activist.] *I wish I were, but I know I'm not. I'm going to write this afternoon.*

Little Penny called long distance from Texas. She and Pan miss me. (I wonder if she weren't checking up to see if I were really here.) In some confused way Ed L and I are father figures for them.

I had a great letter of appreciation from Tom L whose marriage I worked out with Linda. Darling, I don't understand my effectiveness with people. But maybe if I did I wouldn't try as hard to give.

I called Toby. [Toby knew Charlie from his days stationed in New York City (1961-1965) who had become a

Catholic convert from Judaism.] *She had called while I was away taking the bar. She wanted to know all about the bar and about you and me. I said we had made a painful decision not to meet at this time. She wanted to know if she should invite you to the wedding* [in December] *and I said that you would love to be invited.*

I am enclosing two more little treasures from Chicago. I know you will enjoy the Utrillo. And Winslow Homer is another artist who moves me. All my love to you darling. I can't wait to hear from you.

Affectionately,
Charlie

WINONA TO GROSSE POINTE

August 23, '69

Dearest Charlie,

I too had a strange dream. Last night I dreamed I was home on the farm with my family. We were getting into the car (to go to church) (which could not hold us all) when suddenly 2 huge dogs, one striped like a zebra and one colored like a Hereford cow (red with a white face) bounded up to us and made us stand still. Then a bunch of men, with calm faces, surrounded us and pushed us together. Then without flinching, the man looking at me pulled out a pistol and shot me in the chest. I could feel no pain, just a smothering sensation as I lost consciousness, and I can remember knowing I had only moments to live, and I said to myself, "May God have mercy on me as He judges me. And I love Charlie." Then I woke up, to check if I was really shot, I guess, because the dream was so real that my chest felt smothered.

So I died with your name on my lips. I'm pretty proud of myself! I don't venture an interpretation of the dream. At least it wasn't my family that shot me. I don't know what happened to them. Maybe they were made to suffer because of me.

August 24. 9:40 p.m.

I manage to keep fairly busy but I have little to show for whatever I do. I haven't looked at my dissertation since my return.

*Today we had a lovely Sunday Mass with Freshmen and
Seniors present. Beautiful music, and I'm told it was just a
skeleton force. <u>WHEN</u> you come, you'll have to experience the
liturgy (music is best). Sister Lalonde, a great sister and a friend,
is in charge of the music.*

*I did a little work between 11 and 2:30, when my folks
unexpectedly arrived with Grandma and my nephew,* [4-year-
old] *Greg (who said not one word!). But I saw them only a few
minutes before a 3:00 freshman orientation discussion in which I
was to participate. Enough time for them to see me looking well,
but also for me to tell them it wasn't easy.*

And it ain't.

*I also got your beautiful and feeling letter sent on our
anniversary. I have sent 2 letters before this – I'm wondering if
you are in Mich. or Chicago??*

*Sister Bernetta yesterday agreed to teach one year at
Allen University, a black college of 700 students in Columbia,
South Carolina. She needs a break from here for a while — she
feels unappreciated here, and the students <u>don't</u> on the whole go
for her at the present time. I helped her move out of her office
this evening.*

*I heard from Pan today. She mentions a Heloise-Abelard
experience she had that was "hell," she said. It was in the
context of a joke <u>re</u> Walter, but it made me wonder if you
happened to be the Abelard.* [Very unlikely!] *It was nice of her
to write. Penny has written twice now, and Pat P once. Dora not
at all. Georgia* [secretary at the Catholic Student Center] *not at
all. (No news is bad news??)*

*I wrote to the McCartys suggesting I try to publish a few
of Jerry's poems singly to literary journals. A colleague and poet
here suggested that. Herschel wrote yesterday to offer to write to
some connection he has to see about a book publication. I
answered YES! Try!*

*I have been asked to participate actively in the Winona
Diocesan Sisters' Council. I am to think about it, but I will
probably plead dissertation.* [I chose not to participate.]

*Darling, I love you. At this point I really see no future
for me as a celibate Franciscan. As a lay affiliate, yes, but my
goals are so very different. But they are, by and large, a great*

*bunch of women. I am already thinking of writing up an
experimental proposal to submit formally, even for the second
semester. Maybe take a leave of absence (on the books) at
Christmas and finish out the year as an experimental affiliate.
This needs to be thought out, but you may have some initial
reactions for me?? Then if I left permanently in May, the sisters
would at least be prepared for it.* [See Appendices for my lay
affiliation proposal in its final form.]

    *The college is in dire financial stress at the moment.
This is a year of budget cuts and pounding the roads to find
donors. I guess it's good I'm here this year, at least, to save on
the salary of one English teacher!*

Goodnight, dear.

Francha

GROSSE POINTE TO WINONA

August 25 [1969]

Evening

Darling

    *I heard from you today twice! It makes the sun shine
inside me.*

    *I started my usual summer vacation schedule today. I got
up for early Mass. The Mass that I offer takes place in between
the 7 a.m. and 8:25 parish Masses. Dad preferred that Mass be
at our parish rather than at home. So Dad, who serves, takes the
first car with me and we arrive at about 7:25. Mother, who is
slower in the morning, takes a second car and arrives at 7:35.
(After Mass, Mother and Dad go home together and I usually
stay after for a little while and drive home by myself.) Breakfast
is usually ready when I arrive. (I'm spoiled.) After Mass I said to
Dad (who had served) that he was right on the ball. (I have him
do everything that the server-lector does.) He replied that
nothing gives him greater pleasure than serving Mass, especially
when I offer it! (While I was studying ten hours a day for the bar
exam I skipped daily Mass. I needed time desperately. Mother
and Dad asked no questions.)*

    *I tried to be more helpful this morning and did the
marketing. Then in the afternoon I was on the tennis court for
three hours playing with my college friends. Didn't do as well*

*today. Came limping in and spent a half hour in the hot tub.
Mother and Dad prepared a delicious lamb dinner. I invited
Brad over to share it with us and we just finished watching the
Detroit Lions whip the Boston Patriots. I'm really tired, but I
didn't want this day to go by without letting you know I love you
dear. And now I'm going to bed longing for you and I'll finish
this in the morning. I want to say something about two ways in
which you have helped me to <u>become</u> – in the growth of freedom,
and of love. Sweet dreams!*

August 26

   *Good morning Francha my Rosemary. It's a beautiful
day – 9:30 a.m. – sun shining. I don't know that I fully
understand what I am about to write. It is what I feel.*

   *There are three things that have happened to me
because of you. (1) When I am with you I feel at-one-with-myself
in a way that I don't feel with anyone else. When I'm separated
from you, I just don't feel this at-one-ness unless I concentrate
on your love for me. Although vacation is great for tennis, etc.,
living at home seems to fracture me, as much as I love the folks
and they love me. I drift into conformity patterns. Last night I
dreamt that someone was showing me a house for us to live in.
They said, "This is the perfect house in the perfect neighborhood
for you." I said, "No, no, no, no, no! I don't want to live here."
(Meaning Grosse Pointe.) (I also had another vivid dream. Bob,
my brother, told me I was being watched by the FBI. I woke up
very calmly trying to figure, why?)*

   *(2) With you I have felt great freedom. I have made risky
choices that I don't ordinarily make. Chicago is one such choice.
I can't explain it except to say that when I'm with you I feel
deliciously free. I don't feel that free at this moment. But with
you I have known a freedom that I have never known before.*

   *(3) Love. You have made me feel that I can love and be
loving. This is a joy. I feel it when I'm with you. Francha, my
Rosemary, you have helped me to <u>become</u>.*

   *I want to do something next year that will keep life from
leaking out and wearing away by the mere passing of time. It's
so much easier to let existence eke away. And I fear the
encounter with life. I need to anticipate it joyously, as you do, as
PL does. I picked up THE BLACK PANTHER newspaper while*

*in Chicago. It's full of hatred, but also self-assertion. I envy the
assertive quality. I have to fight the feeling that I am an "Uncle
Tom." When I confronted Father Cunningham* [the pastor of the
Paulist parish in Chicago] *about his insistence on clerical dress
(and when you continued to sit on the table) I feel so much
better. It's a very hard thing for me to do.*

*I miss you darling. This carries all my love. Why don't
we have a regular day to telephone one another? You can call
me on a specific day at a specific time and I'll be there.*

*Thanks for the fern. Keep up the tennis practice. You'll
soon be hitting the backboard. Pauline Betz became a champ by
hitting against a garage door.*

Affectionately,
Charlie

WINONA TO GROSSE POINTE

Enclosed: An aerial photo of the CST campus with
buildings labeled; and a news article, "Loneliness Causes
Change," with these sentences highlighted: In a study of rats,
isolated creatures have an increase in serotonin and "the animal
becomes significantly more tense and aggressive." And some
enzymes neutralize effects of serotonin, so "conceivably, an
'anti-loneliness' drug might some day result."

Aug. 26, '69 – Tuesday a.m.
Dearest,
*Both your Sat. and Sun. missives arrived today – our
erratic pony express! So I have enjoyed, luxuriated in, 4 letters
in 3 days!*

*I found your letter to His Eminence eminently worthy of
any eminence. How can he refuse? Allowing for a bit of bias on
my part, I'd say it is still a good letter.*

Tuesday p.m.
*The eve of the academic year. Tomorrow I teach my first
college class. The books have arrived!!! And all is ready.
Despite the fact that I shall be teaching (?) a 42-year-old nun
and ex-mission-mate, I'm not too scared – yet.*

I just finished writing for an appointment for a general physical at Mayo Clinic. (The Doctors Mayo established the policy of offering free care to the Franciscan Sisters.) It has been four years since I had a physical, and I would feel better just being looked over. A woman is supposed to have a checkup every 6 months, I'm told.

I hope no embarrassing questions come up.

Kathy writes that the McKays <u>won't</u> stop in Minnesota this trip – they are going to northern Wisconsin to visit friends. So the little kids won't have a chance to sing "Second-Storey Window" for their grampa and gramma ☺.

I really appreciate the art and post cards. Are you priming me for Chicago????

I love you –
Francha

(over)

My schedule: [I drew a chart showing two Freshman English classes and an Early American Literature class, each meeting 3 times a week spread over a five-day schedule. I added a note: *"3-5* [p.m., daily M-F] – *DISSERTATION (hopefully)"]*
Thanks for stamps!

WINONA TO GROSSE POINTE

August 28, 1969

Dearest C,

I received your fat and – always – touching letter of August 25-6. Know, dear, that you can still BECOME because our experience together IS. I don't think physical togetherness is always necessary, although, God knows, I miss you much and constantly.

Today I met my two freshman classes with much confidence. Yesterday I met one class of upperclassmen (majors and minors in English) with weak knees and thin vocal cords. For tomorrow I have two preparations to ready; then comes a long weekend, for we will not have school on Labor Day.

I also returned to my dissertation yesterday – the first time in almost a month. I worked about 3 hours on it and came home totally exhausted. I am motivated to get it finished; I hope the feeling lasts!

I'm on my way now to my office, where there is a good spirit of "we're in this together" among the colleagues of the English Department. My office and 3 others, separated only by bookshelves, are in corners of the room known as "English Department," of which the major features are a part-time student secretary, a typewriter, and a coffee pot.

7:15 p.m. same day

Home now, dear. Missing you so much I just wished to tell you so.

When will you see the Cardinal?

I like very much the idea of calling you regularly. Just say the word! I don't know what time or day to set – doesn't it depend upon what you will be doing – where you will be? But for a starter let's say a week from tonight, Sept. 4, Thurs., at 8:00 p.m. I'll call you at your house in G.P. If this is not satisfactory (your social life is getting heavier!), you call me at 8:00 p.m. on Sept. 3, Wed. As far as I know I can be home then. Okay? I'd rather call you, as you know. But who knows? The Cardinal may call you in or something.

Aug. 29

It's 7:20 a.m. and hot already! I'm having quite a time getting this finished, and now it's time for class. So I guess I'll just mail it and start another one soon. I love you, Charlie. You're the greatest, and don't you forget it!!

Love, Rosemary

GROSSE POINTE TO WINONA

Thursday August 28 [1969]

Dearest Francha my Rosemary,

Your dying with my name on your lips made your love for me seem so real. I read parts of your letter to Brad. Then we went out together to see If (you and Bonnie saw it together). After the movie we had a pizza and Brad dropped me off at a quarter to one. I went to bed hoping I'd have the same kind of dream. I wanted to die with you on my lips. – Well, I must have been too tired. I don't remember anything. I woke up for Mass at 6:15. Pretty early, despite the fact that I played 18 holes of golf yesterday with Dad and brothers George and Joe plus an hour and a half of tennis.

Your dreams seem more violent and decisive than mine. You are surrounded by men who "do you in." I am merely "tailed" by the FBI. In reading your letter I catch a decisiveness that I don't "feel" I have. But looking at my life this past year, I know I must have. I guess I feel like saying, "Hold on darling. Wait for me. Don't do anything without me."

It would probably help to clarify your own thinking and your own goals if you would begin writing up the experimental program now. I don't think I'd tell anyone, except perhaps Eileen. (I'd like to see it too.) Then the next decision would be, when to submit it. I'd give myself a few weeks of teaching before making that decision. Test your frustration threshold a little more.

I fear that being away from you has made me more cautious. Being at home has stopped my thinking. I miss the daily challenges and frustrations of Texas. Boy, I hope Chicago comes through. I can't wait to be confronted.

I had a long talk with Cleve [a cousin and very close friend] *Tuesday evening. He is thrilled about our love. He wants so to meet you. Cleve confessed, "I'm a bad Catholic. I only go to church a few times a year, but always when I'm with the folks on vacation." (He said that one week with his folks was all he could take.) I said that the depth of one's Catholicism or faith was not measured by church attendance. Then Cleve spoke beautifully about love and life. He said that this life is so short; that for us – himself, you, me, his wife – it had to be lived with and for others; that love was the most important thing in it. And then he said something remarkable. I asked him about having children at my age. He smiled. He said, "Having a child is God!" He explained that love is God and the child is the visible expression of that love and that it's the closest thing to God that we know. Cleve and I grew up together practically from babyhood. I felt so much closer to Cleve that night than I ever have before. Cleve is in the cautious banking business but his advice to us is to <u>act</u>. I think he suspects that we are too cautious. (He knows me.)*

Darling I love you. I'm going out now to visit brother Joe's plant. Then I am going to do something for the folks. Mother and Dad have admired a beautiful little tree that grows next to our parish church. It has a white blossom that makes me feel it's a cousin of the magnolia and the lily. I am going to plant one of these in our yard. I called up a plant nursery this morning and have located my quest. It's called a Rose of Sharon bush. I've picked one or two to plant for you in the morning. It will be a symbolic way of our being present to the folks. Then I'll tell them the story of the little tree on our first visit.

No word from Chicago yet. I am waiting optimistically. The only thing I'm wary of is the point you raise about living too much in the womb. Well, the first thing is the job. I'll begin living in community, but I'm almost positive that my duties and schedule will make community life a mere pretense. And that's part of the whole problem.

I want your name on my lips and you in my arms – always –

Charlie

WINONA TO GROSSE POINTE

August 29 '69

Dear Charlie,

It may seem to you that you write longer letters than I, but that's because you write with a [thick-nibbed] *pen like this!*

I just got your anniversary present (finally!), and I am touched. It's from a song in "The Sound of Music," isn't it? At any rate, I agree with the message: "Love isn't love until you give it away."

Have I told you lately that I love you? [Glued picture of girl holding lollipop and looking furious: "Without yooou my lollipop tastes flat!"]

Aug. 31

Hi dear,

Two + days later. Labor Day weekend is a nice time for unwinding. Sister Lalonde's best friend left today for Boston and graduate school, so I have been thinking about others for a change and spending hours with her. Sooner or later I'm going to tell her about us, *but it will make her sad, although she'll understand if I time it right.*

A really nice happening today: Joanie called from Decorah and then came over. We had a good visit. She even *talked about herself some! She wants to share herself but feels the risk in doing so. She has applied for an indult – a dispensation. I told her I hoped she fell passionately in love this year, and she laughed. She's glad she has made her decision about religious life before involvement with a man. I agree it helps one to stay objective. ☺ I guess it was especially good to see her because I could talk about <u>YOU</u> freely. I rattled on and on, dear. You see, I love you.*

I worked on my dissertation maybe 5 hours yesterday. Last night Lalonde, her friend Briana, and 5 of us went to the lake with wine, bread, cheese, & sausage. It was just what we all needed – Lalonde & Briana because they were aching inside, I because we had just had a sub-committee meeting on the government-to-be in our big house. On the whole I like the big things that emerged; but the little bitsy petty stuff you have to plow through. GOD! Some want specific NORMS for the house – signing out to exact destination when off campus, no baths after 10 p.m., etc. etc. I said – again and again — the norm should be courtesy, the common good, and THAT'S IT! I should have added trust of one another.

I'm off to have a snack with Lalonde, then to bed. Sweet dreams —

I wonder where you are – will be....

Love, Francha

GROSSE POINTE TO WINONA

Last day of August [1969]

My darling,

It's before Mass, 6:45 Sunday morning. You've been on my mind so much these last couple of days. When I woke up this morning I thought first of you. I wanted to begin this letter before Mass. You will be very specially with me during Mass, and I'll mail this sometime this morning after Mass.

' *Walter telephoned yesterday. He wanted to know about me. I still have nothing to report. It was thoughtful of him to call. He appreciated your letter.*

The color photo of St Teresa's compact campus helps me to imagine where you are, any given moment. Right now you may very well be on your way from Alverna to the Chapel.

The schedule of classes looks sensible. No more than two classes on any given day. Are you teaching three different classes or are those two sections of frosh English? I hope you schedule yourself a day off.

I wore my green Texas tie last evening. Many compliments. I went to dinner at Pete and Ellen's. They had two other couples. I missed you. Part of the reason for the dinner was to celebrate a tennis victory. Each year we have an "ecumenical match." Pete and I (the Catholics) play Jack and his brother-in-law, Bill (the Protestants). [Pete's labels were the "Romans" v. the "Barbarians."] *We lost the first set 10-8, but then crushed them 6-1, 6-3. We won last year too, but lost the year before. There are lots of laughs, accusations about cheating, etc.*

I paid a brief visit to the University of Detroit's (Jesuit) legal aid clinic. It's modeled like U.T.'s. I'm going back this Thursday for a more extensive study. I asked about the priest who had founded the clinic and was told that he is now married!

Dad and I have had one confrontation on priests who leave. He feels that a priest who leaves isn't facing life and that the trouble is rooted in seminary education which shields young men from life. I said that maybe the man who leaves is facing life – emerging from the womb! And then we got on commitment. I argued that the reason for stability in marriages (children) was very different from the reason for stability in religious life – that you couldn't really make a proper comparison or analogy between the marriage vow and the priestly vow (a squeak in the cosmos, in Belinda's delightful way of putting it). We were getting louder and louder and Mother kept trying to change the subject, telling me I'd be late for dinner. So I left for Pete and Ellen's when the telephone rang. I'm sure we'll get on the subject again.

In a few minutes I am going to pick up Marie, Brad and Carol's daughter, my godchild. She's about 11, and totally deaf since birth. She's a great little athlete, very competitive. We are going to play tennis. I'll be thinking of you so much!

I really miss you dear. I know you must be very, very busy. I feel in a kind of limbo. I need to get my teeth into something. I'm reading – still plowing through Rollo May's

Man's Search for Himself and yesterday I finished Updike's
Couples which is beautifully written, but the meaninglessness of
their lives, the self-centered erotica, the non-involvement of the
couples with the problems of society and even the development of
their own children is DEPRESSING. It's a brilliant indictment of
contemporary suburban station-wagon jet-set life.

 My love and my life are wrapped up in you dear. The
sun is shining.

Devotedly
Charlie

WINONA TO GROSSE POINTE

Sept. 2, 1969

Darling,

 It's 10:15 p.m. and it has been a good day. Before I
jump in bed I want to tell you I love you.

 I love you.

 The mail was good to me today; despite the Labor
Weekend I got your Aug. 31 letter. Thanks for the extras –
leaves, stamps, card — as well as the letter. Did you know you
write good letters?

 One of our English teachers was called home to a dying
mother. I offered to take her freshmen. (I feel so much happier
when I try to be generous. Not the purest of motives for my
charity – to make *me* feel happier!)

 We had our first faculty meeting tonight. Must be 60%
lay. Good spirit. Sense of humor. A sister at the end of the
meeting said, "Now aren't you glad you're here?" She said it so
enthusiastically that I immediately agreed!

 We have a large number of new teachers, especially
sisters. Also new president and new organization of
administration with lots of brand new posts created. New dean of
studies (now called V.P. of Academic Affairs) and new registrar.
We are in the middle of a curriculum change; we are also in
financial straits. I guess that all makes for togetherness – either
that or we fall completely apart.

 I played a little tennis on this beautiful day, but my
opponent was terrible ☺ and the backboard was being used by
someone else. No one gives me the workouts you do.

Still no word from Dora.... I finally wrote a letter c/o her brother in Austin, since I didn't have her address. I'll soon be worried enough to call.

Honey, sleep well.

Much love, Rosemary

GROSSE POINTE TO WINONA

September 2, 1969

My dearest

I just drove in with two Rose of Sharon trees for our yard. Dad and Mother decided they wanted two instead of one.

I got a letter from Fitz saying that the Cardinal was still adamant, and that he, Fitz, would like to discuss with me another assignment. My next move is to call Chicago tomorrow to see if they will still have me despite the Cardinal's stand. I feel very low at the moment – as if I were a pawn in the hands of the Cardinal, John C and Fitz. I wish I could erupt in indignation, and yet I'm not that sure of myself. It's the desire to be free and to be challenged and to be doing something meaningful rather than that particular job. I'm afraid the Protestants will not accept me if the Cardinal doesn't. I may go to New York next week and talk things over.

I'm going to go out and play tennis in a few minutes and play as hard as I can. Then tonight I go to brother George's and his wife's for dinner with Mother and Dad.

I don't want to go back to Texas. I feel I have to grow some before I can face the students again.

I love you dear and wish I could talk things out with you.

I feel as if I'm bungling through this Chicago appointment. I want to be able to "lay it on the line."

You are in my heart darling
My love always
Charlie

WINONA TO GROSSE POINTE

Sept. 3 1969

Darling,

It is 10 minutes after your call and you are of course so much in my thoughts that I'll push the red pencil your way for a minute, instead of toward freshman themes.

I feel your helplessness in the face of hierarchical insensitivity, even stupidity. The "leaders" of our church lead us right out of the church. Ach!

I guess you hit the nail on the head when you said you had put all your eggs in one basket. Who would have thought so many wrinkles would appear in the lining of that basket? Maybe a less trusting man than you would not be caught in such a position. It's really depressing to feel that one has to be a slick fella to make his way in the world.

I'm getting more and more depressed.

Did you happen to watch Cronkite's news tonight? The heartrending account of the Pikes in the desert? [Former Episcopal Bishop James Pike and his wife, Diane, got lost in the Judean wilderness, where he died.] *I remember being so very impressed with him when he came to UT. I remember George L staying to listen to him even longer than I did.*

Do you remember me telling you about my friend Marion in Atlanta who married an ex-Glenmary? They are expecting a baby now, and she has been the breadwinner all summer because – I hate to depress you! – he found that being an ex-priest was no asset in job-hunting. I hope by now something satisfactory has come up.

Well, just be assertive, Charlie. That is, providing you don't lose your Christlike gentleness.

I wish I were with you and we could face this thing together. I mean really together. Somehow it wouldn't be so hard for either of us.

I feel bad that the mail is so erratic. I have been spacing my little missives, hoping to enter your life every couple of days. So the ones you got today must have come after a drought of 5 days?? And I made a special trip back to my room and over to the mailbox Mon. a.m. to prevent disasters like that....

*I led office tonight. Theme of love. My voice cracked
continually as I thought of you and read 1 John 4:7-11 to the
sisters.*

> "Beloved, let us love one another, because love is of
> God; everyone who loves is begotten by God and knows
> God. Whoever is without love does not know God, for
> God is love. In this way the love of God was revealed to
> us: God sent his only Son into the world so that we
> might have life through him. In this is love: not that we
> have loved God, but that he loved us and sent his Son as
> expiation for our sins. Beloved, if God so loved us, we
> also must love one another."

I suppose I sounded scared. Well, just let them think that!
*Would you like to follow us in our office themes? I'll
send an extra program just in case the answer is yes. The sisters
take turns composing the office for the day. Usually the
Invitatory, Oration, and Blessing are from a special book of
which there are no extra copies, but you may be interested in
following the Scriptural readings and themes as they correspond
to the Mass for the day.*
Simply must get to those themes!

I love you ---- Francha

WINONA TO GROSSE POINTE

Enclosed: Part of a CST brochure with item titled
"History and Location: Wenonah and Winona."

Sept. 4, '69

Hi dear,
*Since we talked 26 hours ago, and since my first
thoughts written you 25 hours ago, I have had new ones re your
eggs in one basket.*
*You really should be persistent! Sit on the chancery
steps if they won't let you in the waiting room! (Maybe not quite
that strong, but you know the direction of my thoughts.) I got
your letter of Sept. 2 today (record time and not air mail!?) in*

*which you speak of your need to assert yourself and act freely.
Darling, do it!*

*By a 1000-1 chance, I ran across a Mark Twain bit of
cracker-barrel wisdom in one of the books I'm using in Early
Am. Lit. I couldn't believe it when I read it tonight:*

> "Behold, the fool saith, 'Put not all thine eggs in the one
> basket' – which is but a manner of saying, 'Scatter your
> money and your attention'; but the wise man saith, 'Put
> all your eggs in the one basket and – WATCH THAT
> BASKET.'"
>
> --Pudd'nhead Wilson's Calendar

Honest to God, that's a direct quote. 'Nuff said.

*Sister Lalonde came in to chat last night and in the
course of the conversation scolded me for saying so often that I
may be leaving. She said, "If you say that often enough, that's
just what you'll do." I said I was doing my best to give it a fair
trial, and she said I certainly was not. She even said she hasn't
been able to let herself get close to me for fear I will leave and
she will have to go through that all too familiar anguish of
separation. I acknowledged that I was dimly aware of having my
own shields up – for the same reason, and with everyone here.*

*I really must try to give of mySELF – and not just a
friendly smile. Otherwise – she's right – I'm not really being fair
and the whole year will be in vain.*

So ---------------- to work!

*I hope this letter reaches you before you depart for NY
or wherever. Bon courage!*

My love, R

GROSSE POINTE TO WINONA

Thursday nite [September 4, 1969]
Almost 10 p.m.

Darling,

*It was so wonderful just to hear the sound of your voice.
It made me a little high. I was conscious of laughing more than
the conversation called for. I wish I could have understood you
better. I had dinner with my great-aunt Frances – who is in her*

80's. I made her laugh a few times and enjoyed the evening. I'm home now and it's so quiet. I'm tempted to call you, but realize this could be very awkward for you, so I'll just be very thankful that we were so close yesterday.

I had lunch today with a priest friend and a professor from the University of Detroit Law School. I told them my sad story and after lunch was introduced to the Dean of U of D Law. Our chat was informal, but there is a <u>possibility</u> of two offers emerging. One, to teach jurisprudence at U of D. (This I would refuse, because I want to plunge into the problems of the community before I try teaching law again. I felt I was speaking too much from the ivory tower in class.) [Charlie had taught a "law and ethics" course in the UT Austin Law School.] *The other offer was to do research and legal work in housing in Detroit – working for a change in law. I'm not too clear on what this offer involves, but again, I can say I don't want to be a legal researcher either. Pure research also is too far removed from the real problems. At least, I'm heartened to find that I am attractive to lawyers and law deans.*

I haven't had the final word from Chicago, but I am pessimistic. Apparently, if the Cardinal doesn't love me, neither do the Protestants.

I've been gaining weight even though I play tennis daily. I've been playing harder and with more effectiveness and abandon than I have in years. My game is at a peak.

Francha I really miss you. And I love you my Rosemary. We have been apart for a month now. We can exist and survive and live physically apart from each other. At this moment I can simply say – I DON'T WANT TO. I'm willing to take the risk of sharing life. But I do think we need to decide this together and that we must give it more time. Darling, I just wanted you to know how I feel.

I'm happy to see that you are plunging back into the dissertation. I envy you. I feel as if I were in a kind of limbo.

Sweetie I'm really tired. I'm going to get this in the mail now. I'm enclosing a clipping which tells it pretty much as it is. [The clipping was a report on why priests leave the priesthood.]

I'll be in touch darling. I miss you and love you.

Affectionately, Charlie

WINONA TO GROSSE POINTE

Sept 5 '69
CST

Hi!

    I feel invigorated, and that's unusual for me lately at 11:00 at night. That's because we had our first local meeting concerning [convent] *government for the year. I said one (good ☺) thing at the meeting and that did it: they took up my suggestion (mostly) and put me on the committee to follow it up. The job was to pull together all ideas about gov't and set them clearly on an opinionnaire, so that the committee can see in which direction to plan specifics. I was soon recorder at the follow-up committee meeting, & then later I was re-writing it into opinionnaire form, and now it is run off and distributed to each member of the local community. I had an expert secretary at my disposal, one of the other committee members. I'll keep you posted on developments. (My stomach can't take my excitement and perturbation at the stubbornness and obtuseness of others!!!) Well, I guess they can't all see it my way....G'night.*

Sept. 7

    I got your letter of Thursday night today, Sunday, and thank you, darling, for loving me so much!

    What of a job in Detroit???? Would you live at home???????

    You are attractive to more than lawyers and law deans....

    In fact, the only one who doesn't like you is the C-A-R-D-I-N-A-L, and he, I say bitterly, seems to think he's God. Others seem to think he is, too.

    Don't you DARE get fat! I'm glad you're playing tennis so well, dear, but don't work up an uncontrollable appetite!

    I thought the report on why priests leave was valuable. Thank you for sending it.

    I just re-read the Sept. 5 part of this letter and have to smile a little. Tonight our committee met to interpret and tabulate the opinionnaire, and I was tired and said about 1/5 as much; and we waded through misunderstandings and semantics and .... I sort of got disinvolved. I begged out of doing a major part of the general meeting next Wednesday by saying I had been

gone 4 years and didn't seem to have a common understanding
of basic terms. E.g., "directress" as opposed to "co-ordinator."
    Well! My bell just rang (9:45 p.m.!) and since you were
so immediately on my mind, I decided it was you and tore out of
my room. It was still a nice surprise: Barb calling from Houston.
She had tried to call earlier today and couldn't find me, and it's
too bad, because Ron and Angela were there too, as well as Nick
who talked to me just now, too.
    They just wanted to know how I was doing, and Ron's
message was that if I would come to Georgia's wedding, he
would sing. (? wedding ?)
    So the weekend is gone: I shopped, and "committeed,"
and visited with Pat S and Kathleen (Sister Marya) who came to
see me, and that, my dear, took care of the weekend, and I'm not
ready for tomorrow so I had better get ready. It's 10 o'clock,
and I was tired at 6. Good night, my love.

                                                                        R

P.S.   I pray for you daily, and sometimes even aloud, disguised
in such petitions as: "For those who must make decisions in
their search for truth," or "That our church leaders may be
receptive to the Holy Spirit, we pray to the Lord." Tonight we
prayed the beautiful blessing of St. Francis and you were in my
heart: "May the Lord bless thee and keep thee; may He show
thee His face and have pity on thee. May He turn His face
towards thee and grant thee His PEACE."

                                                                       XXX

GROSSE POINTE TO WINONA
Saturday Sept 6 [1969]

Dearest,
    Well Francha, the Chicago opportunity has now sealed
shut. When I spoke with you Wednesday evening, there was one
more chance: I could still offer to come despite the nay from the
Chicago Chancery. When I called David M yesterday, he said
that the Greater Church Federation of Chicago could not risk its
ecumenical future with the Archdiocese by defying the Cardinal.
He said that he had also spoken with some Catholic priests and
they felt that the way to fight the Cardinal was from within his
jurisdiction, not outside of it. When I called John C, he was

*terribly disappointed, but his group of lawyers depends upon the
Church Federation for office space and secretarial help and if
the Federation could not accept me, neither could Chicago
Volunteer Legal Services. A very sad state of affairs. My letter to
the Cardinal has never been acknowledged which I consider an
indignity. Nor has any reason for refusal ever been given to me.
The Cardinal is trying to protect a system that has no future.*

*My hopes were stimulated by an offer that opened up
through a contact at the University of Detroit. The Wayne
County Neighborhood Legal Services is an Office of Equal
Opportunity funded service. They have approached U of D and
want the Law School to handle the housing phase of the service.
This means they will recommend two staff attorneys to work on
urban renewal, zoning, rehabilitation, community development.
The salary is $9,000 to $12,000 per year. At first I was very
interested in this. It would involve intense legal activity and
community involvement. I had dinner with Brad last night and he
was sour on the offer. He had two reasons. He felt that I would
make many enemies within the Detroit establishment,
embarrassing Mother and Dad. And further, he continued, that if
we got married in a year the story would make the front page of
the paper, further embarrassing Mother and Dad. Brad
acknowledges the importance of the work, but he feels I should
do it somewhere else because of the uncertainties about the
future. I tend to think he's right at this moment. But I am not
completely decided.*

*I would like to get your reaction. I'm going to New York
on Tuesday for a Paulist pow-wow. I will also consult our
President and Council on my future assignment. I felt it would be
a good idea to catch the spirit of the community and to sound out
our administration once again. Why don't we plan to get on the
phone again? I expect to have dinner with Toby and Dan on
Friday evening September 12. Call me at 8 p.m. your time at
Toby's apartment.*

*Walter called me this morning. I gave him the Chicago
story and we both felt I could not return to Austin at this time.
Georgia tells me that one of the Austin priests is the source of
gossip about us. He gets a few drinks and hints about our special
relationship, says he thinks it's "wonderful"! I want to get the*

facts straight before I write, but I feel I must do something for your protection and mine.

Francha my Rosemary, I love you! Your letters give me a tremendous boost. I wish I were more solid about what I want to do. I just feel I would love to plot my life with you. Whatever I do now is not a solid plunge. But it might become a lifetime interest. This is also a reason for finding something outside of Detroit where I fear the older generation would not understand. When I go to New York, I think I will level even more honestly than I did in June.

In my last letter I commented on our separateness. Later I realized that dependence upon one another depends upon life together, children together, decisions which together we have yet to decide about. Can we promise ourselves to each other, can we risk our futures, can we give to each other and others with all the responsibilities we now have? Isn't this what we must face together?

I love you Francha, my Rosemary, and this carries all my love on a hot Saturday morning in September. I look forward to hearing from you in New York.

Devotedly,
Charlie

DETROIT TO WINONA

Monday Sept 8, 1969

My dearest,

Its 11:10 p.m. I'm down at Brad's bachelor apartment. I catch an 8:35 a.m. plane for NYC tomorrow morning, and Brad offered to take me to the airport. Brad is in bed. It's very quiet. I LOVE YOU.

Today there was a real nip of fall in the air. As I watched the kids walking to and from school, felt the chill of the September breeze and crunched the dead leaves underfoot, I felt my childhood. It was a kind of lonely feeling.

And I have felt lonely often lately. I miss you. And I know I have to make decisions. Even the prospect of making a decision makes me feel lonely. The greatest cross for me is to be assertive. Christ was both gentle and assertive. The gentleness seems to fit easily into my nature. Assertiveness is hard for me. Yet it is just

*as essential to the character of Jesus. It is why he faced his
death. He would not take back who he really believed himself to
be. For me to go to New York is, once again, to be assertive.*

*I love you because you want to bring out all of me, the
potential assertiveness especially. I really would sit on the
Chicago Chancery steps if (1) I thought it would do any good;
and if (2) the Greater Church Federation were in a position to
back me up. The lag in our (you-me) communication makes it
difficult to contemporize our thoughts and lives, but I'm sure that
after my Saturday letter you can better understand why this sit-in
wouldn't work.*

*Meanwhile, another possibility burst in on me, almost
out of the blue. A lawyer I knew during my practice in Detroit is
Romney's undersecretary in HUD. A Jesuit priest who travels
the country for this young attorney, also a friend, gave me a ring
because he had heard of my plight, and now urges me to visit
Washington, which I may very well do. And then Mother urged
me to call on Steve Smith, my old college buddy who married
Jean Kennedy. I hesitate, I don't know why. Really, there are a
great many opportunities… if you have a law degree. I hope to
have good news when we talk on Friday.*

*Bishop Pike's tragic death touched me. There is
beautiful symbolism in his burial in the Holy Land. This is where
he belongs. He was gently assertive. I was driving downtown as I
heard the news reports of his burial. Life is so short. How do I
spend it? I do not want to be a product of what others expect of
me. I do want to be responsible, but I have never felt so strongly,
as on this trip home, that I cannot simply live out others'
expectations. There is no reason why either of us has to be a
WENONAH.* [According to legend, the Dakota Sioux woman
Wenonah leaped off a precipice to her death rather than marry a
suitor she did not love.] *I will pray for the courage to live, not to
die. As Hammerskjold put it, my death must be a gift to life, not a
taking away. As your card put it, life must not simply ebb away,
leak out. Bishop Pike died affirming life. So must we.*

*I read 1 John 4:7-11 this morning before Mass and my
heart cracked. Thanks for the office readings. Sleep well my
darling. There's someone who loves you dearly – me –*

Charlie

SCARSDALE NY TO WINONA

Sept 11, 1969

Francha my Rosemary dearest,

    It's a beautiful morning in Scarsdale New York [at that time the Paulist Fathers' headquarters]. *I got up early and offered Mass in a greenhouse extension of this old house. I could see the sky and the lawn and trees. The pear trees were heavy with their yellow fruit. As I recited the* <u>Gloria</u> *amidst all this nature, a beautiful cock pheasant strolled across the lawn, about a hundred yards from me. It was early and quiet. The sun was reflected in the diamond dew. I could see my breath. I offered a Mass for peace. You were in my heart.*

    As I got up this morning I thought of your beauty and the mornings at Govalle [site of our Austin tennis lessons].

    Now I've finished breakfast and in a few minutes I have my meeting with Fitz. I'm anxious darling.

    I just spent an hour with Fitz. There are still some questions about Chicago. I am free to seek out employment in accordance with my desires. My temporary base of operations will be Detroit. We can talk about this Friday evening.

    Now I'm on my way into New York City to visit the Press [the Paulist Press, where Charlie was employed 1961-1965], *to see cousin Jody,* [friends] *Lily, Toby, Harry and Anne B – all I can possibly squeeze in – also to continue job investigations.*

    The community is being very good to me. I am free. I am also in conflict as you are; conflict of loves and loyalties. We have three types of relationships to the community: (1) the traditional pastor-curate relationship; (2) the team (without a superior, but one man as coordinator); (3) the man whose primary community is outside of a Paulist house. This would be someone like the Paulist who is chaplain at the state Hospital or Father Justin M who does cancer research – or myself. It would also include, it seems to me, the married Paulist of the future – though no one has suggested this.

    Time for me to move, darling. I want to get this in the mail to you. I look forward to hearing your voice tomorrow nite. I love you.

Affectionately and devotedly
Charlie

NEW YORK CITY TO WINONA

Sunday September 14 [1969]

Dearest,

 *It was just great hearing from you on Friday evening.
And I look forward to Tuesday. I trust you so my darling, and I
know you trust me. I was tense before you called; I had had my
fill of wine. But talking with you brought me to a new high. I
guess I was nervous about meeting Dan. Toby had led me to
believe that Dan would help me in my gropings. Actually
darling, it seemed to me that I was the one in control. Dan
seemed much younger, much less mature. And though I am
aware of my own immaturity, I felt the greater maturity that
evening.*

 *I returned yesterday evening for a Mass in their
apartment. The liturgy was very moving, composed by Toby and
Dan, celebrating three forms of newness: (1) the Jewish new
year; (2) the new opportunities in the lives of all present; and (3)
the new relationship between Toby and Dan. I read the
communion prayer.*

 *Today I didn't go to Mass, but did go to church at St.
Paul's. The neighboring Congregational Church is being torn
down and for six months that congregation has celebrated its
Sunday liturgy at St. Paul's at 11:00 a.m. I participated in that
liturgy. There was no communion, but Paulist Frank R gave the
homily. The beauty of the singing and the meaning of our
sharing our old church with the Protestant congregation brought
tears to my eyes during the service. I reflected more than once
how much you would have loved to have been next to me in the
pew. Part of my love for you is knowing what you love.*

 *This afternoon I am to meet a N.Y. poverty lawyer.
Tomorrow I'm going to call PR of "Bearings" and play tennis
with my black priest friend, Harry. I'll keep in touch my darling.
I love you.*

Devotedly,
Charlie

NEW YORK CITY TO WINONA
Wed. Sept. 17 [1969]

Dearest,

You are fantastic! That little trip [a suggestion for us to meet during Thanksgiving or Christmas vacation] *you sprang on the telephone last night was ingenious. I hope we can do some or all of it!*

I get so excited when I speak with you on the phone that I can't remember all of what we say. I know I'll try to reach you again on Saturday or Sunday from Warren and Nancy's – unless I have to make a trip to Washington, D.C.

I told you that I refused a $12,000 offer from Detroit. They called me long distance with the hope I'd accept. But for all the reasons we reviewed together, Detroit is not the place.

I am also afraid New York is out too. Though the Office of Equal Opportunity attorney I spoke with yesterday was encouraging and wanted me to submit my résumé – and the poor are really poor in this city – it's (1) terribly expensive to live here (Joe and I had dinner and two drinks at a Chinese restaurant near his apartment and it cost $19 +); (2) New York is like Chicago in that it wants its priests dressed in the collar and not in secular positions; (3) the bar exam is one of the roughest in the country; (4) I would probably have to live in this rectory which is terribly impersonal – like a hotel (tho some of my closest priest friends live here).

Most of the cases that the OEO attorney (I met with yesterday) handles are (1) domestic problems, e.g., divorce, child custody, cruelty to children; (2) problems with government agencies, e.g., social security, unemployment compensation; (3) problems involving debts to department stores, etc. My attorney advisor said that one of the most important aspects of the work was interest in the people – that this is the most important quality a priest-lawyer could bring to the neighborhood. I told him I was not in love with the law but would want to use it as a tool to help in a poor neighborhood.

I am in love with you darling, and I will be in touch very soon. Will try to see Patricia R at Bearings today.

All my love always
Charlie

NEW YORK CITY TO WINONA

Friday [Sept 19, 1969]

Dearest,

I'm up in Harlem with my friend Harry. We just played two sets of tennis, had Tom Collins, and now Harry's in the shower. I'm thinking of you, as I do so often my dear. I love you!

So much has been happening, so little has been happening. I visited Bearings yesterday. Had a good talk with Patricia R. She gave me a few leads which really haven't fructified. One of the great difficulties is, I'm afraid I don't want to be in New York, so I'm very vague when I interview with people here. The greatest favor I can do for Patricia R is to get her some money. I opined that the Paulists really couldn't help. We have too many in-debt foundations. Patricia remembered my connection with the Kennedys and requested that I feel out the Kennedy Foundation, which I promised to do. I am having dinner with Steve Smith Monday night. Patricia was encouraging to me. When I explained that vocation was more a response to self than to a "voice" or rather statement "Come follow me!" outside self – she smiled and said that I would do well in the secular. Patricia also said that many priests were leaving for the wrong reason – they are dissatisfied, but don't know what they really want!

I've really been mixing business with pleasure. I've had dinner with George L and his lovely gal Diane. I know where it's at, but George L is still vacillating and not sure of himself.

Joe and I had a good evening. Joe knows where he is going, but there is no gal in his life at the moment. He had a difficult experience last spring.

I've also spent two evenings with George H who is depressed. He's a perfect example of a guy who doesn't know his own real worth.

John (Bas) Sheerin, my old boss at the Paulist Press, and I had two long bull sessions. Bas is so much like my own Dad in his dedication and religious faith, that I had great difficulty communicating at the gut level. I told him I was going through a kind of clerical menopause. I also insisted that commitment these days is more to the self, one's potential, than to a person. Bas sees the clerical vows as fealty to a person

*which must be lived up to, despite all obstacles. Bishop
Shannon's marriage is incomprehensible to him.*

   *Darling, it's now Saturday afternoon. Harry and I had
dinner in the Bronx at the apartment of his secretary. After
dinner they decided to have a party and two couples were invited
over. I didn't get home until 5:30 a.m.! It was a fantastic eight
hours filled with music, drinking and conversation. Harry's
secretary is an ex-Handmaid of Mary and very bitter about the
Church. She shouted many times during the course of the late
evening and early morning: "All the white bishops care about is
the dollar bill, and brother, your picture is not on that bill."
Another friend, Bill, was a black power activist. He drank the
most and did the most talking. He conversed endlessly on
"power in the people" and when he wanted to pay the highest
kind of compliment to a person, he would say, "He's together,
man." Malcolm X is a "together" person of the highest type in
Bill's eyes.*

   *Tonight I'm going to visit Nancy and Warren and we
will be calling you. I look forward to hearing your voice. I'm
feeling anxious and not all "together" because I'm not very
productive. I have no job, but I do have the freedom to search
and seek. Yet I haven't really experienced hardship. I'm still
within the womb of the rectory and felt the indignity yesterday of
asking the folks to send a little money.*

   *Last evening, one of the girls read my hand. She said I
had tremendous feeling and awareness but that something was
blocking me. She also said I was the most affectionate person in
the room (I was the only white). My affections have been blocked
too, my darling. I love you and miss you. It will be great
speaking with you tonight.*

Devotedly
Charlie

NEW YORK CITY TO WINONA

Sept 20, 1969
My second letter today

Dearest,

When I joined Nancy and Warren upstairs after our conversation, I realized I had forgotten to wish you a happy anniversary. I excused myself and went back to the phone booth, but the circuits were busy and I couldn't get through. I would have tried again, but I felt I was being impolite to my hosts, and thought also that for your sake, one long distance call in an evening was enough.

So here I am back at 59th Street, ready to put the light out and thinking of you. It was one year ago today that I told you: "I love you and I love what I'm doing." The Texas-California game was on TV this afternoon. I thought of you. Seeing Nancy and Warren was made complete by speaking with you. One year later – I repeat: "I love you." My love for you is stronger and deeper. I can't say at the moment that "I love what I'm doing."

You mention "touch." When I hear your voice, you touch me within. I tingle. And I long to touch you. I want to be with you.

Bas wants me to keep up my relationship with the Catholic World. *He wants to see my paper on homosexuality. He is also willing to consider some of Jerry's poetry for publication. Do you want me to submit a few poems?*

I haven't got anything special for our anniversary. I decided not to wire you. But darling, I give you my love, my feelings, my efforts, my religious idealism, my humor, my music, myself. And when you tell me you love me, I feel strong and happy. It's four minutes to midnight. I am going to sleep smiling.

Devotedly,
Charlie

P.S. Have you seen "Midnight Cowboy"? See it and then we'll see it together.

The next letter, dated September 9 and September 20, was mailed to Grosse Pointe when I thought, incorrectly, that Charlie was returning from New York.

WINONA TO GROSSE POINTE

September 9, 1969

Dear Charlie,

Even though I know I can't mail this to a specific address yet, I want you to know I am with you in spirit. I have a spirit that spreads around a lot, I guess.

Some ironic coincidences have occurred that I don't want to forget to tell you:

1) *The bishop's hat among my cactus plants shriveled up on me for lack of care. Why that one and not the other three???????*

2) *Jeane Dixon reads your horoscope for today as warning that travel connections will be difficult! Hope you got to NY okay.*

3) *My horoscope warns that I must stick to decisions and not do things by the wavering of the moment. This is coincidental because I read Karl Rahner's long article on priestly celibacy, which I think is well-written and fair. I would like you to stop right now and read it, but if you can't, I'll sketchily summarize and say that he is in favor of continuing the church's stand on it; that promised vows have special merit above a single life that is unpromised; that just because priests <u>do</u> not often find love among the people of God as celibates does not mean it is impossible to find it, rather that priests should concentrate on meeting this lack within the bounds of celibacy, not by changing their minds about commitment; <u>but</u> that it is impossible to talk about celibacy as an abstract good, that it must be considered in the context of each individual's life.*

Putting Rahner's article together with the clipping you sent me on why priests leave — because they are frustrated in their goals, not because of celibacy per se — I started putting these two articles and everything else in my mind together and came up with this contention:

WHEN YOU SAID 'I LOVE YOU' TO ME, AND I SAID 'I LOVE YOU' TO YOU, IT WAS THEN THAT I MADE MY DECISION, OR AT LEAST IT WAS WHEN I DELIBERATELY TOOK ON THE RESPONSIBILITY OF A DEEP RELATIONSHIP WITH YOU THAT EXTENDED BEYOND OUR ORIGINAL UNDERSTANDING THAT IT WOULD BE 'WITHIN THE CONTEXT OF OUR PRESENT COMMITMENTS.'

When that moment was is hard to pinpoint. But what makes me think that I can play god with you any more than the cardinal has a right to? Another contributing circumstance was a letter from Dora. She warned me not to play puppets with you or my family. Am I pulling the strings? Am I keeping you dangling? I decided in church yesterday to write to my parents immediately and tell them all.... Which gets me back to my horoscope in this horribly rambly letter! I decided to put it off till I could talk to you Friday about it. So I didn't write the letter home ....

But, darling, I don't have a right to keep you dangling. I made a decision that is just as binding as my final vows in 1963. I decided to be responsible to you in a love relationship. If I had the right to take on that responsibility – I don't yet know. But the fact remains that I did and that changes everything.

My thinking, as you can readily see, is muddled. I only know that you came into my life when an old way of life was waning for me, and that may well have been providential.

~~*Dear, I changed my mind and am going to send this to Toby's address. Hopefully you will get a chance to read it before I call Friday night. I will also send it immediately rather than go home and get the article. No, I see it's already too late to catch the last mail pickup here, so I may as well wait and include Rahner.*~~

Oh heck, I'll tell you about it Friday.

Sept. 20

Remember when I told you about this? Well, I have calmed down a bit and still have told no one here about the complexity of my commitments. I love you, dear, and I always will. What expression that commitment must take is what we together must still work out. But whatever happens, I love you.

I'm sending this on now dear, and eagerly await hearing
from you – Thursday, Sept. 24, hopefully.
    Greetings, if it's prudent – to your father and mother.
                                    My love, Rosemary

      The following is written on a card, which reads: "I Love
You!" And inside: "My analyst said that once I said it I'd feel
better." It was mailed to Grosse Pointe when I thought Charlie
would have returned there, when in reality he was pursuing a
new job lead (described in his letter of September 22 below).
      Enclosed in the card is a chart titled CHRISTMAS
VACATION – A MODEST PROPOSAL, followed by a kind of
map starting with Winona, December 19, turning in grades, then
on to New York to attend Toby's wedding on December 20, see
Warren and Nancy, visit Pam in Baltimore, and maybe a Father
Clarke about lay affiliation. (Clarke had published an article
about lay affiliation.) On to Atlanta to visit Marion and maybe
Eugene Bianchi, also about lay affiliation, and the McCartys
about Jerry's poems. Then to Austin about dissertation business
and to see friends, and maybe go to Mexico. Next, on January 11
see Marilyn Todd in Frederick, Oklahoma, about the poems.
Return to Winona on January 12. (The Atlanta, Mexico, and
Oklahoma pieces did not happen. A visit to Dolores in Midland,
Texas, was added.)

WINONA TO GROSSE POINTE

                                    September 21, 1969

Happy anniversary, Darling –
    My love, always—

                               Francha, your Rosemary

NEW YORK CITY TO WINONA

                                   September 21 [1969]
                                        11:40 p.m.

Darling – happy anniversary once again.
    I've written you three times in these precious hours. And
it is because I love you and am thinking of you.
    I'm on a terrific high right now because I spent the
whole day, practically, with Steve and Jean Smith. I got up at

*6:30, went to 7 a.m. Mass, grabbed some breakfast and caught
the 9:15 train to Pawling, New York. It was a superb day.
Brilliant blue sky without a cloud. I arrived a little after eleven.
They live in an old beautifully appointed farm house with their
three kids, three maids, and the kids all had guests for the
weekend. Steve and Jean were alone. We had a number of long
talks interspersed by touch football (with the kids), swimming
and tennis. (Jean and I defeated Steve and an afternoon guest.) I
am a physical wreck at the moment. I ache all over. I had the
feeling I wasn't really doing anything except having a good time
until this evening over supper. We drove back to NYC at 6:30,
went to the apartment, had a drink and then went out to a
restaurant. It was there that Jean made the suggestion that I
become a Kennedy Fellow for a year. I don't quite know what
this means yet, except that I am to meet with Steve at his office
tomorrow to make further arrangements. Apparently, if I have
something I want to do, they will finance me in what I'm
interested in. Without really knowing what's involved, I'm
elated. I remember that you said one day when you left* [i.e.,
temporarily put aside] *your thesis, "I guess I'm more interested
in people." Well I've been touched by the reaction of two people
and I'm hopeful. They want me to stay at least another week and
to come back to Pawling again next weekend. Steve says there
are all kinds of people in N.Y. that I should talk to. I have
nothing specific in Detroit and perhaps I should take advantage
of my opportunities here.*

*Darling you were in my heart so much today. I picked
three leaves for you before we left. I don't know how to show my
love for you except by these leaves, these words and these
feelings I share with you.*

*We can also keep planning our first meeting. Will it be
Christmas or Thanksgiving? Both??? It's easier for you to plan
now because you know your schedule. I feel badly that I'm so up
in the air. Nancy and Warren are aching to see you. I feel much
warmer toward NYC after today, but I can't base my life on the
Smiths and Kennedys.*

*Dearest I love you, love you, love you. And now its
12:05. I go to sleep again, smiling, but missing you.*

Devotedly, Charlie

NEW YORK CITY TO WINONA

Monday morning [Sept 22, 1969]

Dearest

I thought you might find the enclosed interesting and perhaps useful. The author calls for a theology of meaning. What he perhaps doesn't realize is that the Church is in a crisis of meaning.

I've been telephoning and can't get anyone either in N.Y. or Washington so I've decided to do my own laundry and a little reading... and a line to you, my love.

I brought our travelers cheques with me and had to dip into our fund for $20. This seemed to me better than using the folks' gift. I can replenish our fund when I return to Detroit. There is still plenty in it for our travel plans.

The grit and grime of New York gets in your hair and under your fingernails.

But darling, you're the only one who's under my skin – and in my heart.

My love always
Charlie

NEW YORK CITY TO WINONA

Wednesday Sept 24 [1969]

Dearest Francha, my Rosemary,

Yesterday was fantastic. It all began Monday evening. I had dinner with Steve and Jean Smith and they invited John and Ann Doar. John heads up perhaps the most successful and imaginative poverty program in the U.S., in one of the blackest and poorest of ghettos – Bedford-Stuyvesant, Brooklyn. I was invited to visit the next day (yesterday) and arrived at 10 a.m. sharp after a long subway ride.

First I was given a tour of the area – 653 blocks, stretching over nine miles, with 450,000 people. (It's the second largest black community in the country. Chicago's South Side is #1.) Bed-Stuy infant mortality rate is nearly twice the national average, seven out of every ten high school students are dropouts, about twice as much unemployment as the U.S. rate....
Robert F. Kennedy wanted to do something about it and did – hence the Bedford-Stuyvesant Restoration and Development

program which John Doar and Frank Thomas head. John Doar was a brilliant attorney with the civil rights division of the Department of Justice. Frank Thomas was a deputy police commissioner, black, and a lifelong resident of B-S. Programs include job training, educational improvement, housing building and restoration, attraction of business, weekly television, etc.

Another program that John Doar wants to run is a school for poverty lawyers. There is money available, about $400,000 annually, to train 250 lawyers to be poverty-law specialists. For the last three years, the program has been run primarily by the University of Pennsylvania. This past summer there was a kind of revolution. The 45 (out of 250) black lawyers met separately and demanded that there be more black law students included in the program, that the courses be more relevant, that the financial assistance be re-adjusted. Pennsylvania Law School has thrown up its hands. Bedford-Stuyvesant wants in. John Doar feels that the lawyers will be better trained if they learn and live in a poverty area and that the community will benefit from the economic gain of having lawyers living in (rent income). John wants a full time administrator and he urged me to apply (without promising I would be accepted). I would be a kind of Dean of a poverty law school having responsibility for curriculum, selection of faculty and students, housing, etc. It's an extremely complex assignment. John and Frank would front for the school and I would follow up and arrange behind the scenes. John felt that I would learn the poverty scene by living and working in Bed-Stuy.

I came home last evening overwhelmed. I woke up this morning fearing the acceptance of responsibility, doubting my capabilities, wondering if I would fail, reproaching myself for my lack of courage. Darling, I don't know my limits and it's taking all the guts I have to test them. I prayed silently for a half hour this morning and felt "together" enough to face the day.

And it was a simple day. I bought a ticket for my train ride to Washington tomorrow. I visited the Paraclete Book Center where I purchased books for the Smiths. I had lunch with Diane (GL's dearest friend) and brought Toby to the airport. Toby is delighted about the prospect of your coming to the wedding. She is still on crutches and I had to get a wheelchair at the airport.

Tonight – the Smiths again for Steve's 42nd birthday. Tomorrow I go to Washington to talk with a man at the Kennedy Foundation and to look into opportunities at OEO. I called Pam up and will have dinner with her and we plan to call you. We are both excited about this.

Telling you my day has helped me. I feel "together" as I write to you and think of you. I wish we weren't so far apart.

How are you my darling? How do you feel?

I love you, Francha my Rosemary.

> *Devotedly,*
> *Charlie*

NEW YORK CITY TO WINONA
Friday [September 26, 1969]

Dearest

After we hung up, I took Pam out to dinner and then I caught the 11:01 p.m. train for NYC, arriving at 2:46 a.m. I was exhausted and slept most of the way, even tho the chairs were the non-reclining type. Knowing my propensity for falling asleep, this should not surprise either of us.

It was exhilarating seeing Pam. She seems very happy, is challenged by her work and is pulling for us. I have never been so open with her about my love for you.

Sweetheart, it's so difficult for us over the phone. I still get carried away talking with you and jump from subject to subject so fast – and we try to cover so much – that I can't remember enough when we hang up.

I gather you are lonely and doing your best to live out your commitment for the year. I admire you so. Pam and I agreed you're the most honest and gutsy person we know. My thought at the moment is that we must keep to our year-of-trial agreement; but this does not mean we must wall ourselves off. At this writing I think it imperative that we meet as soon as possible. We need to talk and express our love and see where we are. I'm more and more inclined to accept Bed-Stuy. It will be the kind of challenge which is best for me – hence best for us. I will live right down there in the problem and succeed or fail on

my own ingenuity and creativity. Darling I love you and will
continue to keep in touch.

Devotedly
Charlie

[Written around all four margins of the page:] *Off for the*
weekend. The leaf [enclosed] *is from Ethel Kennedy's, picked*
while waiting for the door to be answered. (I also visited the
National Gallery and will be sending other lovely paintings.)

We were now trying to devise a plan to see each other
soon, rather than wait until Christmas vacation.

NEW YORK CITY TO WINONA

Monday [September 29, 1969]

Rosemary my darling, I love you
    This morning I paced the floor and thought and thought
for two hours – and prayed – and then I called John Doar at
Bed-Stuy. I simply said: "I am prepared to make a formal
application for the job." He thanked me and reported that there
is to be a meeting tomorrow. He asked me to telephone him late
tomorrow afternoon and he would let me know about going
ahead. I feel relieved, but there remains the uncertainty. I will
know so much more on Thursday when I call you.
    Darling, I thought of you so much last weekend at the
Smiths – when I looked at the beauty of the fall colors, while
playing tennis, when sipping a daiquiri.... You are a soft golden
colt .... And I thought of you when going to bed. (I slept without
pajamas.)
    Dearest, as you think about our meeting point, try to
choose a location near a good sized airport. Our time will be
short and the distance is great. Also a place where we can be
alone and be free with each other. We don't have *to choose*
Joanie or Mary B [another Texas friend who lived in the Twin
Cities]. *We could choose any city and be by ourselves. But I do*
think it would be fun to see either of them. My impression is that
Joanie's [in small Decorah, IA] *might be inaccessible or rather*
too inconvenient.

This day has been one of deep self-searching. I am struggling to grow my dear, and just the effort to make the job application gave me the experience of liberation.

I rejoice in your love and your trust. I hope my love and my trust strengthen you.

Love always,
Charlie

WINONA TO GROSSE POINTE

Sept 30 '69

Darling,

I have only a few minutes and I don't really know when you will get this anyway – but you are often on my mind and always in my heart.

I hate to see you go from Detroit to Brooklyn and then back to Minnesota and then again to Brooklyn. Maybe you can come here before you return to N.Y. It really doesn't have to be a weekend you are here, does it? The airfare you save could maybe help pay for renting a car here.

My calendar of events:

Oct 3-5 – going to Owatonna to visit Pat S & another friend. But this could be postponed if necessary.

Oct 7 – clinic appointment in Rochester in afternoon. Possibly a follow-up appointment the next day, or the next.

Oct 9 – 8:00 p.m. a meeting I must superintend at CST.

Oct 10-12 – Barb will visit me – coming to Rochester Airport.

I'm thinking maybe you could fly into Rochester, rent a car, meet me around clinic appointments. Oct. 7 I teach till 11:20 a.m. The appointment is at 1:00 p.m. Wednesday. In the only class that day I have scheduled a test, which I could ask someone to monitor.

I have a feeling that the weekend of Oct. 3-5 is better for you. So be it. I have no heavy commitments here until Oct. 7. Come if you wish.

Or if you prefer to leave it at the weekend of Oct 17-19, that's fine, dear. I just want to see you!!

Because I love you.

Rosemary

NEW YORK CITY TO WINONA

Wednesday [10/1/1969]

My dearest,

I called John Doar of Bed-Stuy last evening and he cannot give me a final answer. I'm still cliff-hanging – wondering like the Murillo postcard I enclose. Apparently the people who fund and direct the legal education program are not convinced that Bed-Stuy is the place for the poverty-law-education program. I have to check back Monday.

I'm leaving for Detroit this afternoon. I'll call you from there tomorrow evening. At least I've gone thru the process of commitment. I thought and thought, paced the floor, called you, finally said I was ready to make my application, my commitment. Once again I'm frustrated. But I do feel good about having been able to make a decision.

The last lines of this letter are for you. I love you dear. I can't wait to read what you have written me. [My last several letters would be awaiting him in Grosse Pointe.] *I want to see you, touch you terribly. (Writing is so inadequate.) I can't wait to see you, be with you! Darling I wouldn't be in a position to choose life as I am in these moments if it weren't for you. I LOVE YOU FRANCHA MY ROSEMARY.*

CHAS

Back in Grosse Pointe, Charlie decided he would move soon into a large old house in the historic Boston-Edison district of Detroit, perhaps for more privacy or more independence.

GROSSE POINTE TO WINONA

Oct. 3, 1969

Dearest Francha my Rosemary,

I feel more like this Toulouse-Lautrec [a postcard enclosed] *today, after having spoken with you last night and finally checked up on my Michigan Bar Status. To practice in Michigan all I have to do is send $25 to Lansing (capital) with an affidavit that I have not practiced law since 1954. It was quite a blow to have flunked the Illinois Bar. I dreamt that evening (after having opened the letter of "regret") that the letter stated that "this is a bad day in your life" and I kept insisting in my* *dream that it wasn't a bad day. I argued that I was happy to have taken the Bar Exam – that I was in a better position having taken it, etc.*

Mother and Dad asked me before we went to bed last night if I would like to offer Mass at home in the morning. I said I would be delighted and we celebrated the feast of St. Therese at 8:30 a.m., just the three of us. It was touching. Mother read the Epistle and Dad the Gospel. We chatted informally during the liturgy. I said that the Mass had always been at the center of our lives and that offering Mass at 64 Moran was symbolic of that fact. They thanked God that I was with them to bring Christ to our house. I added that I felt that the Spirit of Christ was always with us and that the Mass was a sign of His presence. Darling, I hope and pray that some day you will be in our living room with us; and that I can visit your home with you, so that we can celebrate our love, our parents' love, and the mystery of the Divine – which is so uncomplicated for us!

My darling, this carries all my love. I can't wait to see you and to be with you. Thanks for your prayers. You were in my heart and on my lips during Mass this morning because I love you.

Charlie

WINONA TO GROSSE POINTE

Oct. 3, 1969

Darling,

I have a few minutes before I must do a couple of errands before going to Owatonna for the weekend.

It occurred to me that I may not be in Winona Tuesday when you call at 8. I may stay overnight in Rochester, as that is the day of my 1ˢᵗ clinic appointment. And I don't know where I would stay – most likely at the Motherhouse. Will you try again Wednesday night at 8, if I'm not here Tuesday?

Today Mrs. McCarty called me. She & Mr., in the process of moving to Mississippi, got caught in Hurricane Camille. She therefore did not have an abode and did not get my letter of mid-August until now. So now I can say I am authorized to ask you to submit some poems to Catholic World *as you*

offered to do. Please let me know which you select, and I'll
submit others to various literary journals.
I will see you soon in person!! None too soon, darling.
Let us not lose each other. Or let memory distort or romanticize!
I love YOU better than memory of you!
I must go. Thanks for leaves, cards, & YOU.

Rosemary

Charlie has now moved to downtown Detroit.

DETROIT TO WINONA

Sunday [10/5/1969]

Dearest Rosemary,
Tomorrow I call New York and will get the word on
Bedford Stuyvesant. Tuesday I'll be speaking with you again,
darling. We will know more about our future.
This morning I offered Mass at 64 Moran at Mother and
Dad's. At the Prayer of the Faithful I prayed for all who are
"dear to us." During the silent times of the Mass I was tempted
to pray aloud for "Rosemary." Rather, I prayed silently (once
again) that some day soon we can share the Mass with both sets
of parents. Darling, I am hopeful!!!
It's now midnight. I went out for dinner with a young
Paulist and a black student at Wayne State. Lots of good
conversation and plenty of Italian food. I'm full and tired and
anxious about tomorrow, but secure in my love of you.
Darling, I'm going to mail this and then I'm gonna hit
the hay. Tomorrow another step. At this moment I want it to be
Bed-Stuy. I want the challenge.
It's very quiet. I'm in a big room in this creaky old
house. I miss your touch. I love you dear. I want you to be happy
and fulfilled.
God bless you, sweetie, and good night.

Love,
Charlie

A meeting in Minnesota was finally agreed upon.

Charlie flew to Rochester to meet me around my Mayo Clinic appointments – our first meeting since our tearful parting in early August. We spent some delightful hours together. By rental car I showed Charlie the Rochester Franciscan

Motherhouse grounds, including a close look at the apple orchard. We drove to Winona, standing on an outlook above the city situated in the beautiful Mississippi River Valley, and we visited the College of St. Teresa campus. And I took him on country roads past the farm of my childhood and the country school I had once attended.

I had arrived at my decision to leave the convent and was ready to embark on the process that would lead to marrying Charlie. During the evening we had together I told this to him. But at hearing my decision, Charlie experienced a panic attack, finding that he was not ready for a full assent. In this letter, written on the motel letterhead, he tried to explain his emotions.

ROCHESTER MN TO WINONA

Thursday 9:30 a.m. [10/9/1969]

Dearest Francha, my Rosemary,

I woke up early and took the car back. Do you realize that we drove 247 miles yesterday, darling!

I feel so alone in this room. I had difficulty swallowing my breakfast at our restaurant. The same waitress waited on me but she didn't recognize me without you.

I telephoned Brad. He was so cheerful and will meet me when I return to Detroit this afternoon. He is my community at this moment in my life. You are my love.

So many things that we said and did keep racing through my consciousness. There is terrible dissonance. Self doubt is gnawing at me. But there is an underlying self-assurance that comes through. Darling, I am worth the risk. Please be patient for a little while. I am moving toward new depths as a person.

You are helping me to face myself at deep levels that have been armour plated. The protective covering is stripped away and I don't know how [to deal with], and therefore fear, the degree of personal involvement and responsibility that are called for. I have demonstrated that I can reach out romantically to you. You pierced the veil of the romantic and entered that holy of holies of personal commitment and responsibility and it was dark and wet. Remember the perspiration! I am now entering that long-sealed holy of holies with a light. I want the light and air to get at it. You have helped me open it. You can help me carry the light, but I must bear the light in my two arms. The same two arms which can so lovingly hold you.

My hope and faith are grounded in my humanity, revealed in Jesus. We die and we rise. This is the hope that God gives us in Jesus.

You forgot to give me the photos last night and I forgot the cash. I enclose some now for reprints and stamps.

I love you Francha, my Rosemary. It's not age, or children or community, even priesthood that holds me now. It's the deeper part of me. You have called me to respond at the deepest level of my being and I have shown naiveté, confusion and fear. I know I love you and I know the response is possible. This response is at the core of my Christianity. Without it I cannot live; I will only exist. And Christianity is LIFE.

As I reread this letter the dissonance is dissipated. When I began it, I did not know that I could express myself to you, but I have, and I see it all so much more clearly and my love for you is stronger.

I fell in love with you again over these two days.
Give me time my love. I gave you time.

Your devoted Charlie

DETROIT TO WINONA
Friday afternoon [10/10/1969]

Darling,

It's a dreary, dreary day. There is a slight drizzle. Automobiles drive by under my window, the sound of the water and the tires is louder than the engines. I'm alone and lonely. I love you. I need you. I need your reassuring touch, and glance, and smile, and warmth.

And how are you? When I think of how you must feel, I get more depressed. I can't let myself tailspin this way, so I reach out. First I reach out to you. Here is what's happened.

Brad met me at the airport and we had dinner together. I slept at his apartment last night. I couldn't face this lonely house. We had a good time, joining another friend later.

This morning I called New York. The Bedford-Stuyvesant prospect is still open. John Doar said that the legal education prospect looked closed, but asked me if I would be interested in working for him. I replied: "I am interested." I am to call him back on Monday. Then I'll telephone you on Monday or Tuesday evening around 8 p.m. It will be so much better for me to have a job and a challenge and to be on my own.

Then I had a frantic message from Toby. She wants me to write a letter to the Patterson Chancery office (where Dan's case is pending) saying that it will be a scandal if they don't get permission to be married in the Church of St Paul the Apostle. I will do that as soon as I seal this letter.

I called long distance to Fort Sill, Oklahoma, because Tom H (of Austin) wrote a note pleading for my support in his appeal for a discharge from the Army. The letter was dated Sept 17 and I didn't get it until today, so I decided to try calling him. Tom was out on "detail" so I will call again later.

The Paulist appointments were mailed and reached me today. I am listed as in Detroit on "special assignment." You and I know what my special assignment is. It's summed up in Rollo May's <u>Man's Search for Himself</u>. To me this book is a contemporary companion of the New Testament. It's what Christianity is all about. Jesus died for what he believed and found himself to be.

I believe in death and resurrection. I believe in you. I believe in myself. I believe <u>I am worth the risk</u>, as I wrote you yesterday. I am living thru a crisis in self-confidence, and I thank you for your patience and understanding which are beautiful manifestations of your love, which I treasure and <u>need.</u>

Darling, I give you my love, always,

Charlie

WINONA TO GROSSE POINTE

Friday night
Oct. 10 '69

Dear Charlie,

I haven't had a <u>minute</u> to write you, dear. Right now I am sitting at my mother's kitchen table, waiting for her to get dressed to go with me to Rochester to meet Barb at the airport. I came home with [brother] Mike and his Winona State friends – following exactly the same route you and I followed 2 days before. I brought <u>selected</u> pictures with me to show the folks, including a few of the Ozark shots and the one with you and Kathy's three. She (mother) looked thoughtfully at it – the latter – but didn't ask me just how much you mean to me. I was almost hoping she would. I was prepared to say, "I love him," but I guess it's just as well I didn't. Just now she asked about ex-nun Marion and I told her she had married a priest, and mother looked <u>terribly</u> crest-fallen. "Now what did she do that for?" she said.

I have been trying vainly to get caught up with school. I barely can scrape enough material together to face one class at a time.

Later – 10:00 p.m.

We are in the Rochester Airport waiting for Barb's plane – delayed at least 2 hours by bad weather over Chicago. I'm sitting in the john (biffy) writing this so my folks don't ask me what I'm doing! I'll mail it in a minute and get back to them.

But I really wanted to send you at least a line of appreciation – for YOU, dear Charlie. I loved your wine, daiquiris, cheese & rye bread, the long drives, the visit with Joanie. But I was strangely and beautifully moved mostly with our long night together that you explain so well in your letter. I am WITH you – in Christ's Paschal Mystery – and we'll see this through together.

Know that I love you!

Rosemary

DETROIT TO WINONA

Sunday [10/12/1969]

Dearest Francha, my Rosemary,

You are on my mind every moment it seems. I think of you as I go to sleep and as I rise.

If you don't read any other chapter in Rollo May's book, read SEVEN: "COURAGE, THE VIRTUE OF MATURITY." It hit me where I am. I wish I could read it with you. I am taking the steps that lead to maturity, but I am slow. When we said "Good night," you pointed out that I was moving, i.e., the car was. And I called back, "Not fast enough."

Darling, I love you. I am moving toward you, faster, faster.

Devotedly,
Charlie

P.S. How was Barb!

WINONA TO GROSSE POINTE

In this letter I enclosed a "school photo" and my first "purple letter," a weekly "dittoed" newsletter mostly written by me to the sisters away – those studying, on special assignment, or on leave.

Oct. 13 ''69
Monday night

Dear Charlie,

Enclosed is something I'm not so sure you want – a veiled me.

Don't worry about me, dear, although I appreciate your concern. Your doubts help me to realize that our marriage will be a long time away yet – if, indeed, we do marry. And, strange to say – (PHONE CALL FROM YOU HERE!) I feel more at ease now that I don't have the enormous pressure about making up my mind so fast. (Now I have explained that to you on the phone....)

Barb's plane was 3 hrs. late Friday night. My folks met her with me, and it was a long wait. My mother talks freely – at least more freely – with me about her feelings now. This is a new experience for me. I think part of the reason is that I am more free with telling her my doubts; but also I may be a little more sensitive to her as person rather than mother-role. I just wish I could tell her all. I hate so much to hurt her or make her think she has failed with me.

Barb liked her a lot. Barb is so zestful, full of life, and <u>cares</u> for people (made my grandma feel great!) that everyone liked her, too. Saturday the family picnicked with her. I drove her to Winona Sat. night, where we saw a CST play. Sunday it was cold & rainy. Again her flights didn't work out right, and she spent almost all last night at O'Hare Airport.

Our English coffee-and-cookies gathering last Thursday went all right. Friday night Barb & I talked till 2:30 a.m., so naturally I couldn't stay awake during the play Sat. night, which, by the way, was well done & interesting – Jean Anouilh's THE CAVERN. But I got caught up by sleeping late Sunday. I'm back into the routine now – finally going to prayers again!!!

Take care of yourself in Brooklyn, dear. NY scares me mightily. I REALLY CARE SO MUCH FOR YOU, that you find yourself – then give yourself.

Go in peace – with my love. Happy fasting!

Rosemary

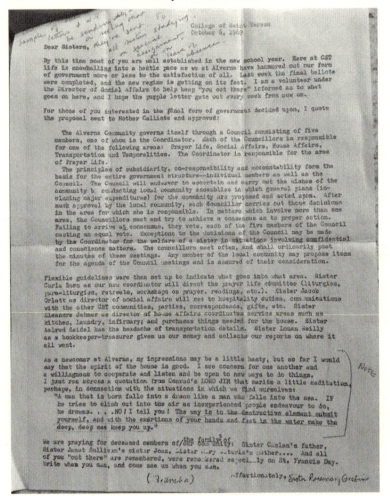

Charlie received a firm offer to work at Bedford-
Stuyvesant D & S Corporation, which he accepted.

DETROIT TO WINONA

Tuesday [10/14/1969]

Dearest Rosemary, my Francha,
    *The combination of the Bedford-Stuyvesant offer and
your letter made yesterday a great day in my life. Both signified*

*"acceptance." Frankly, your expression of love meant the most
to me. It made the job mean something!*

*I plan to fly down to New York Thursday evening. I will
spend the first few days with Duke* [a close Paulist friend]. *Then I
will try to get a place on my own. I think it will have to be
furnished. I have no chairs, no towels, no blankets, etc. I think I
will just bring two suitcases with me. Just a few books.*

*In getting my airline reservation for N.Y. last evening,
the clerk reminded me that holiday plane reservations should be
made early, so I suggest you get on that phone and make your
reservation for NYC now. You can always make a change and
you don't have to pay now. (This means that we will not be with
our folks at Christmas, doesn't it? It means we will spend
Christmas together, doesn't it? Let's go to midnight Mass
together in N.Y.!)*

*This morning I submitted five of Jerry's poems to <u>The
Catholic World</u>. I am enclosing a separate sheet indicating the
ones I chose for publication. We probably won't know the
answer for a few weeks. I submitted the author's name as G.D.
McCarty. Is that OK?*

*Francha, my Rosemary I love you. We will see this
through together in the Spirit of Christ's Paschal Mystery. The
constancy of your love – through that long night and the next day
and now – is simply EXCITING to me. That's all I can say for
now except you have me, my love, always.*

Charlie

P.S. Will call Fri or Sat p.m.

DETROIT TO WINONA

Thursday [10/16/1969]

Dearest Rosemary, my Francha,

*I'm packing up for New York and plan to travel light –
two suitcases and a briefcase.*

*I'm light of heart too. Your love and the job give me that
feeling of being "together." I have what every man needs: his
love and his work. I realize these are the first steps in a new life,
but I am hopeful. Your love means so much to me.*

I go in the spirit of Christ the healer, so beautifully etched in the card enclosed. I hope to etch the likeness of Christ by my life.

Brad will drive me to the airport this evening. I'll be staying with Duke tonight and report to Bed-Stuy tomorrow. I'll be calling you, my love, tomorrow or Saturday.

Know that I love you my darling, more now than ever.

Devotedly,
Charlie

The letters now began to flow between Winona and New York City's East Village. I addressed my letters for the first time to Charles Palms, not "Reverend" or "Father," in care of Duke.

WINONA TO NEW YORK CITY

CST
10/17/69

Dearest,

Thanks for taking care of the poems. About the name: I think the McCartys prefer Gerald D. McCarty to G.D. McCarty. Their note of authorization to me reads:

October 7, 1969

TO WHOM IT MAY CONCERN:
This is to authorize SISTER ROSEMARY GREBIN to represent a group in the effort to get Publisher's Bids on publishing poems by Gerald D. McCarty, deceased.

Signed by Parents of
Gerald D. McCarty (signed)

(You are the legal man. Do you think this is sufficient authorization? I do.) I don't think you need to change G.D. to Gerald for the <u>C. World</u>. Do you? I hope they do publish one or two.

10/18/69

<u>*Tempus fugit!*</u>

I have such a funny feeling – that I am so concerned with meeting each day's demands that life is passing me by. I have the *feeling that you and I – together – shall have to wait a long long time before we are really happy together. I guess I am in a sad mood that you sort of detected on the phone last night, and which I can't quite figure out. Pat S was here today, and I was trying to explain our current status. It's an over-all pervasive but not intrusive sadness – not dramatic, not hysterical, not even teary. I just can't figure it out. But I feel that I have to <u>do</u> something to shake it off.*

I love you.

I believe you love me. I believe you when you say to me so simply, so beautifully: "You are the <u>one</u>." I never doubt you, dear.

I believe <u>in</u> you. I know you can do the job well.

And I fear for you, darling. I fear and I want to protect you. And I know that's the <u>last</u> thing you need right now. This is one time when you must go it alone.

But you are never alone as long as I love you. I love you.

I love you.   Francha
10/19/69

Darling, it's Sunday now, and this letter still sits on my desk. I'll mail it in the morning, and hope it will arrive at Duke's before you move out.

Joanie called this afternoon and invited me to Decorah next weekend. It is their mid-term. I readily accepted the invitation, telling myself that my head really doesn't have holes in it; rather, it is important to <u>Joanie</u> that I go. (I really did hate to leave her right after the phone call that night with you.)

This weekend, at CST (for a change!), was a welcome chance to start getting caught up. But it was only a start. Today, for example, when I was planning on correcting bunches of term papers, I got involved with a <u>dear</u> but psychologically messed up sister who can't make community work. She is a good friend of Eileen's, so I urged her to call Eileen collect tonight. I hope she does. She really was LOW today.

Tomorrow is Monday, and then Tuesday your big day and new job. My thoughts (prayers?) are with you.

Yesterday's letter was a sad one. Today I feel more cheery, less melancholy. I slept a lot this weekend, which probably helped some, too.

My parents will be leaving for Florida – today, I guess!
– driving my aunt Julia and my widowed aunt to their winter
abode. They will stop by at Kathy's going and coming back. It
will be a quick trip back, but they plan to go through the scenic
spots like the Great Smokies on the way down. Mom got
Marion's address in Atlanta, so they may stop to see her, but
now that they know she married a priest, they may change those
plans! At any rate, they should be back in 2 weeks – in time to
help the boys [my brothers] *pick corn.*

May your next days be exhilarating, challenging ones –
take care, and don't let yourself get discouraged.

Love, R

NEW YORK CITY TO WINONA

Saturday night
Oct. 18 [1969] *10:30 p.m.*

Dearest Francha my Rosemary,

I could almost write a book to you tonight, I'm so full of
thoughts and experiences. I've been reading about Bed-Stuy for
the past three hours. My mind is full of facts about the
developing and deteriorating of Brooklyn (which statistics I will
soon forget) and I'd rather talk about developing Palms.

Duke and I got up early this morning and walked around
the East Village, which is one of the most fascinating areas of
New York. This is where the "Bowery" is. There are poor sick
men, black and white, dirty, two- or three-days growth of beard,
slovenly clad – about every 100 feet. They are terribly sick, dear.
Their lips are wet. Their eyes are half-closed. They invariably
ask for a few cents, which I can't refuse. Dorothy Day takes care
of them (she's just a few blocks away) and there is a Sacred
Heart Home for Homeless Men down the street. There are places
for them to go, but the sight of them wrenches your heart. Duke
commented: "So many are so young." One man walked up to me
on crutches yesterday. I'd say he was about 50. His eyes were
blackened and he had a broken nose. When I gave him a little
change, I said, "You've been in a fight." He replied: "Aw, that's
nothing. I've been in plenty of those." He wanted money for
transportation so that he could get "dried out." Really, both he

and I knew he was bumming enough to have another drink. We certainly need a realistic program for alcoholics.

But there is much more to my temporary neighborhood. There are hippies galore, with long hair and wild clothes. The shops around 4th Street sell beads and colorful hippie attire. So many of the kids look to be high school age. Duke is in the ideal neighborhood for his work of reconciling these homeless kids with their parents.

Then there are the various nationalities in little pockets close by. The Puerto-Ricans, the Italians, the Chinese, the Ukrainians, the Jews. I don't know how many others. I even saw a couple of Anglo types today in Buddhist garb. They take the Eastern religions very seriously.

After a good breakfast at a special restaurant where Duke always goes on Saturday mornings (one of his luxuries), we bought the NYTimes and came back to our apartment, climbed those six long flights (the smell of pot hits you on the second floor landing), and unlocked two of the three locks on the door (the third one is a dummy). I started looking at the want ads for an apartment and Duke got interested. He pulled out a city map. He got so interested that he decided to come with me apartment hunting in Brooklyn.

But before we got on the subway, he took me to visit the apartment of the "Little Brothers of the Gospel." These are two young men from France who have come to New York to live and communicate the Gospel. The brother who is an artist was out, but his companion, Joe, was most gracious. He gave us espresso coffee, and I could hardly carry on a conversation I was so taken with the paintings and artifacts and little chapel they had. Duke occasionally offers Mass for them. Joe goes down to the employment agency each day and gets a different job – hard labor. I could feel the work he does in the strength of his grip and roughness of skin in his handshake. But he is a fellow who reads all of the latest theology. I felt he had great depth. I hope to offer Mass there, too.

Then we were off to Brooklyn via subway. John Doar suggested that I live on the edge of Bed-Stuy. He feels that Bed-Stuy is dependent on the white communities that surround it and likes to place his staff around Bed-Stuy and in it. He gave me

*three possible locations and Duke and I visited the one location
that was open for possibility according to today's paper. It was
immediately attractive to me because it was near a big park, the
Brooklyn Public Library, the Brooklyn Museum and the subway
(only five minutes – four stops – from my office)* [temporarily
located in the old Granada Hotel near Flatbush and Lafayette
Avenues]. *The building was attractive from the outside, red
brick, windows with white trimming, a sort of colonial effect. It
turns out that it was built in 1940. We saw some of the rooms.
They were pretty dirty. The elevator in the building was poor so
we walked up to the sixth floor. There were the usual signs of
shabby N.Y. life – the empty wine bottles, stomped out cigarettes,
etc. I looked at a 1 ½ room apartment on the* 6th *– large
bedroom, two windows, bathroom and kitchenette. Rental $84
now, $97 in May. The previous occupant had not completely
moved out and I was kind of revolted by the mess. I told the
landlord I'd think about it. He showed me another three-room
apartment for $145 per month. (Duke pays $120 here in the East
Village for 1 ½ rooms.) I felt, what would I do with three rooms
all by myself?*

*Duke and I left and walked to the park. We sat down on
a bench and talked about this first stop on our tour. The location
was perfect. It was an integrated apartment building in an
integrated neighborhood right on the edge of my job territory.
And with the park, museum, botanical gardens, library, and
subway so close…. I got up and said, "Duke, I'm going to take
it!" (Even tho it was the first one.) So I returned to the crusty
landlord, made an application, and discussed particulars. I will
have to sign a two-year lease, but I can break the lease if I forfeit
a $97 security payment. (I could also sublet, of course.) I felt it
would be worth the risk. I won't know until Monday or Tuesday
and we can discuss it Wednesday when I call.*

*Dear, I could go on, but I must bring this to a close. I am
excited. I thought of you so much today. I wish you had been
with me. It's not a place I could ask you to live in, but it is my
little room where I will find myself, so that I can* then *give myself
– as you so beautifully put it in your letter. I want to give myself
to you. You are the one who sees into me most clearly; you are*

the one who has seen the best and the worst, and I can trust in your love. It has been a rock of support for me.

Darling I have charmed John Doar; I charmed the landlord, Mr. P, today. Duke was amazed how I "defused" him, as Duke put it. The landlord started out very hostile and ended telling me all his troubles about rent control, etc. I'm getting into black power, and I realize that I have "Palms power" that I don't fully understand or know how to use. I laughed long with Duke about this. He insisted, "If you give people the impression of this kind of power, you must have it!"

Darling, though I miss you terribly, I'm so glad I'm here. I'm planting my tree in Brooklyn, and I can feel it begin to grow. Life is new and <u>wonder-ful</u>.

I love you my darling. Travel to any airport in the NY area (including Newark) and I'll meet you with open arms.

Your devoted
Charlie

P.S. Mailed at midnight Sat Oct 18. How long did it take dear?

NEW YORK CITY TO WINONA

Oct 20 [199]

Dearest Rosemary, my Francha,

My anniversary present to you is myself, my life. I report for my first day of work tomorrow! I'm really excited!

Darling, if it weren't for you, your love, your confidence in me, your hope in me, I wouldn't be here. I wouldn't be on this voyage of discovery. I am discovering myself so that I can give myself. And you are the one I want to give myself to. In giving unreservedly to you, I will be able to give to others. I have much to give.

I know I have given much in the past. But you call forth a gift on a new dimension. Do I make myself clear?

Today I washed clothes. I used one of those complicated washaterias for the first time. I was so confused that a Puerto Rican lady in broken English asked me, "Where is your wife?" I said I had none. She laughed. She helped me – too much, she even put bleach in the colored clothes wash.

This afternoon I wanted to walk around Bed-Stuy. I walked less than a mile and ran into a Lutheran Pastor who was

once a great confrere. We were on the radio together in 1964.
He invited me to have coffee. I talked mostly about you. We spent
two hours and my walk will have to wait.

I realize, darling, I have to do something about the leave
of absence. In effect, I am on "one" and you are right, it's not
something you are given, it's something you must request. I feel I
must make my request, though it pains me. I must separate
myself. Though I don't see why ministry or marriage should
separate one. Hence, the rationale of affiliation. We Paulists
have no concept of this yet.

My dear, I love you. You'll receive this after we talk on
Wed and after our anniversary.

My love always,
Charlie

WINONA TO NEW YORK CITY

10/21/69

Dearest,

I received your long, long letter (mailed at midnight,
10/18) this a.m. Three days, then. Really only 2 ½!

And thank you for the long, long letter. The Palms
personality is transforming New York! And do you know whom I
like immensely already? Duke!

I am glad you found an apartment so readily, Palms
personality! The convenience is so important; your safety is
important (3 locks on your door, too?). I hope that
psychologically you can take the environment. Well, there is
always the museum nearby for a change in scenery. But images
of the New York of <u>Midnight Cowboy</u> *come crowding into my*
imagination....

10/24/69

It's now Friday at 3:30 p.m. You are, I see, much the
better letter-writer of the two of us. It's becoming more and more
evident.

But somehow I remain really and truly busy – living, I
guess, although it seems to me that my life has slowed down
considerably. It's a paradox. An enigma. And I'm a conundrum!

This week our mid-semester grades were due, and I
made the deadline, if barely. But I did call Joan to plead no time

to take off this weekend in Decorah. Instead, I invited her to stop off <u>one day</u> here on the way to Mpls. to see Mary B. So she will arrive in an hour or two, and I've got jillions of things – like getting <u>this</u> letter mailed – to do before Mass at 4:30. This is UN Day, and there's a special liturgy planned; the international students are planning something this evening, too, which I hope to interest Joan in, so we can go together.

I <u>must</u> get some winter clothes put together, too. It's already colder than Texas at Xmas, and I just haven't a winter wardrobe suitable to Minnesota.

And then there is the job of Jerry's poems which I must get at.

And then... the Double [my dissertation subject] *is* haunting me!

I did dash off a short letter to Eileen early this morning, trying to say in a few words the state of our relationship – yours and mine – at the moment. As I expected, she doesn't write to me, but would rather telephone. (I did get one letter, and it was worth getting – last August....)

Barb and Nick wrote a darling epistle to me. I am really terribly fond of them both. Nick says to send him a picture like I sent Barb (the veiled smug-mug shot) and he'll trade 1¼ books of green stamps for it. The idiot. Barb is frantically hoping for a married priesthood [Nick was debating whether to enter the seminary], but can't really picture herself as the wife of a priest. Oh, the complexities of life.

Pam wrote a "Good Grief" letter, saying she wants to join the nunnery and to please talk her out of it. Now how do I answer that???

I laughed at the picture in my mind of you in a Laundromat. I was touched by your words of love, dear, and by your growing belief in yourself.

Take care, dearest. I love you.

Francha

NEW YORK CITY TO WINONA
Thursday [10/23/1969]

Darling,

*Today I finished my third day at work. It's now 6 p.m.
I'm tired. I've been reading background stuff most of the day.
Attended one meeting and made some pertinent suggestions. I
felt pretty good at that point. The need to <u>act</u> is gnawing at me. I
could sit on my tail at this desk forever, assimilating and
analyzing the problems. I have to get out and act. I have to ask
people to give me things, to do things for me, to accept things
from me. Palms power has to be put to use. It is an effort for me
to assert myself.*

*This thought came to me today. My job is to revitalize
the city and life in the city. I am to devise ways of bringing
people with needs and people with resources together. I guess I
am a kind of renewer or reformer; maybe a broker, to put people
in touch with people. I am strategizing for the people of Bed-Stuy
with a purpose and a determination that I never used within the
Church structure. I was for, and am for, change in the Church;
but never strategized for change. I guess I was satisfied with
changing the climate of opinion through preaching and
conversation.*

*You know it's funny, darling. I feel at home in my new
job. (I'm confused and in awe of my responsibilities, but I feel at
home with the people I work with.) I'm surprised that I don't
miss the ecclesiastical role. I have the same dedication I've
always had. I feel the same need to pray (and difficulty in doing
it). I feel I am working for the good of my brother, as before. I
feel the responsibilities much more. I don't feel as secure about
being able to produce. But I feel at ease at my desk and in the
office and on the streets.*

*There was a little coffee party this morning for a gal
who is getting married and another who is leaving town. There I
got a better picture of the staff and secretaries. There are about
25 people. The staff is mostly male and white. The secretaries
are mostly Black and Puerto Rican. I am a member of the Bed-
Stuy Development and Service Corporation. There is a brother
corporation called Bed-Stuy Restoration. It is headed by a Black
man and its staff and secretaries are all Black. Though we share*

*offices in the same building (an old hotel—every office has a
bathroom! BIFFY!), there is a sense of separation, of
independence, of pride, of going-it-alone in the brother
corporation. Both corporations have the same goal, revitalizing
Bed-Stuy.*

*Dearest Francha, my Rosemary. I've read your lines of
the 18th again and again. "I love you. I believe you love
me....You are never alone as long as I love you. I love you, I love
you." So beautiful. So strengthening.*

Last night [on the phone] *I said something in response to
you, that our love was a union of great hearts. There is an
inscription over the Brooklyn Public Library that begins,
"HERE ARE ENSHRINED THE LONGING OF GREAT
HEARTS...." We will stand hand in hand before that library in a
few weeks! You are the one, darling. My heart is yours. And
when I give to you I will give to others. When I act for you I will
act for others. And my giving and acting will, in the St. Francis
paradox, be a receiving. It's an easy prayer, love.*

Devotedly,
Charlie

P.S. I'll call again next Wednesday, OK?
P.S. – next page

*You know dear, I write as if I'm the only one going
"through it." It must be so difficult for you, trying to live
something that you find deep down, not what you want; yet,
loving the sisters. I don't feel I am much help for you. I want to
be. I will begin by sharing it with you; by trying to understand.
You are such a tremendously loyal person, the anguish must be
all that more piercing. But you also are courageous and
decisive, dear.*

*Help me to share, to understand, to grow in my love of
you, darling.*

Chas

NEW YORK CITY TO WINONA

Saturday [10/25/1969]

My dearest,

*I've spent all day at a conference on the new NY school
legislation which decentralizes (like the Church) school*

*decisions and policy from a monolithic central hierarchy to the
local community board of education. I went because we have to
use this for the advantage of Bed-Stuy. The legislation is a can of
worms, full of ambiguities. It was passed by the N.Y. legislature
with reluctance, and apparently with evil design, i.e., it is so
complicated and involved, that hopefully (for the powers that be)
it won't work. But we have to make it work! Well, anyway, I'm
exhausted from all the verbiage. And confused.*

But not confused about you. I love you dear!

*I'm also excited, because after sitting on my tail for
three days, I finally brought forth a memo with a concrete
proposal. You have no idea how the chance conversation with
my Lutheran pastor friend made my day, and made his idea
about a high school seem like the inspiration of the Holy Spirit.
He is the friend I met when I strayed into Bed-Stuy that day last
week when I was attempting to walk around it.*

*You know darling, I don't know how to keep a budget.
I've been living beyond my means. Friends of Duke come down,
or people in the office, accept my hospitality, and I find myself
financially depleted. I realize that I must learn that I can be
loved without spending money. I must also learn not to accept
every invitation. These are funny things to have to learn at my
age.*

*I hope you got my last letter, a long one, the first one
written without a return address. And so with this.*

*Now I'm going out to do my laundry again. Sheets and
everything. I love you Francha, my Rosemary. I'll be calling
Wednesday. No Brooklyn apartment yet.*

So long Great Heart
Charlie

WINONA TO NEW YORK CITY

Oct. 26, 1969

Dear Charlie,

*Do you mind when I write to you when I'm blue? My
words at such times are blind and searching, without definite
direction, trying to spell out to myself as well as you just why I
feel the way I do.*

It may be that I'm a slow reactor. Maybe your uncertainty about the future is finally seeping into my consciousness. Maybe I'm afraid that the new Charlie of a year from now, say, will not still love the girl the old Charlie loved. Maybe Francha fell in love with a guy that won't be the same guy she did love.

More maybes. A convergence of ideas, all co-incidentally converging, raise new doubts. (1) We studied Emerson's "American Scholar" and "Self-Reliance" last week. "Trust yourself," he said over and over again. Don't be bound by the past. Etc. Then the criticism points out the idealism and fallacies in such extreme individuality. Emerson's ideas, to which I <u>resonate</u>, are harpooned, short-lived (in their full idealism). (2) Reading for Vespers Friday: Christ's words: "I am the vine, you the branches. My Father is the vinedresser, and you bear the fruit. Sometimes the vinedresser <u>prunes</u> the branches, so that they may bear more fruit." (The need for suffering, discipline, renunciation.) (3) In Freshman English we are reading <u>Antigone</u> by Sophocles. Antigone defies the king to bury her brother so that he may be at peace in the afterworld. She therefore must also die. She renounces her happiness, her very life, for the sake of her faith in a divine order. This is nobility. In this play, written in the fifth century B.C., a philosophy of renunciation and self-denial is admired and condoned. I asked the students to compare it to the traditional doctrine of Christian suffering, redemptive suffering. (4) Tonight I watched the TV special on "Peanuts" – mainly on Linus in the sincere pumpkin patch, enduring the taunts of his sister and playmates, missing the tricks-and-treats and Hallowe'en parties, for the sake of his faith in the Great Pumpkin, which, year after year, <u>never comes</u>. Linus blames his own judgment about choosing the wrong pumpkin patch, or blames the pumpkin patch, but <u>he never loses his faith</u> in the Great Pumpkin.

What the <u>HELL</u> am I saying? Out of this hodge-podge, what the hell.... I think, Charlie, at this moment, that I am crying out of a vacuum. I have lost my faith in the Great Pumpkin (which in my allegory is the reality, not the beautiful idea, of the religious life) (Great Pumpkin ≠ -- does not equal – God). I still think the idea is great, and my heart goes out to the Linuses of

*the world who brave the mockery of the multitudes for the sake
of their faith. The "fools for Christ." Linus is admirable. In his
own way he is even noble, for he acts on his convictions.
Antigone is admirable for the same reasons. I am attracted to the
nobility of such behavior, of such a life (as religious life). But I
don't believe in it. At the moment I don't believe in it. I don't
know if it's a dark night of the soul, after which there will be a
brighter dawn, or whether it's a new phase, linear, not cyclical,
in my life.*

*In the meantime, as I hang in indecision, my life seems
to be going in slow motion. I seem to be trying to run through
quicksand and am getting sucked under. I am panicking and I
just want to GET OUT.*

*But where to? Into your arms? No. (Not yet. We are at
arm's length now, so to speak.) Will you act the spiritual
director, Charlie, and tell me what you believe is the value of
redemptive suffering? Of self-denial?*

*Darling, I'd better stop. I'm really getting tangled up! I
love you – I really do.*

Francha

NEW YORK CITY TO WINONA

Enclosed is a New York Times article, "Thousands Hear
Ousted French Abbot's Final Sermon," by John L. Hess –
10/27/1969. The Abbot had converted a Brittany Cistercian
monastery into a "community open to everyone, demanding no
vows." Charlie had written in the top margin, *"Let's join this
community dear!"*

Monday [10/27/1969]

Dearest,

*When I came home this evening there were three good
things. (1) Your letter. (2) Duke had supper simmering. (3) I had
a good experience to tell him. Let me say a little about each of
these.*

*First, your letter. I have been most open with you. You
have seen me at my most gallant moments; my most gruesome.
And you love me. I believe you. Hearing from you is a*

*reaffirmation of my being. My being and becoming are primarily
my responsibility (in mystery = God), but darling I can't do it
apart from my relationship to you. The fact that you have not
rejected me in my weakness is a strength to me. Yet I almost feel
guilty because I am appealing to the feminine instinct to bend
down to the weak; to hold the unsteady arms of the toddler. But I
must say, I am becoming more aware of my own power. How do
I continue to attract a John Doar, a Steve Smith, a gruff
landlord, a black economist..... I don't know how to relate the
reality of myself to the real world. My family and the Church-
role-situation shielded me from this. I'm glad I am where I am at
this moment. But darling, I go through the day experiencing all
sorts of contrary emotions that teeter from "Palms power" to
tottering feelings of inadequacy. Maybe this is what life is.*

*Francha, my Rosemary, when I say <u>you are the one</u>, I
mean it. There is no one I would rather face the mystery of life
with than you. You speak of yourself as a conundrum. Can you
join yourself to an enigma? Let's spend hours and hours on this
at Christmas. Darling, I love you and don't want to lose you!*

*The second good thing today was Duke's simmering
supper. I realized yesterday, that the reason I couldn't hang on
to money was that we were eating out too much. Duke's stove
had <u>dust</u> on it! Tonight both of us brought home the "bacon."
Duke was more provident. He had corn and potatoes and
hamburger. I got a good recipe from one of the gals at the office
and bought a package of Lipton's noodle soup, plus a small can
of chicken. We had Duke's choice and it was delicious. Mine
comes later.*

*And third. Each day I've had some kind of a funny
experience. Duke enjoys them. Today, I lost my sense of
direction on the way home. I decided to get my bearings by
going into a little grocery store (for Lipton's soup). Who did I
meet there but Sallye Wright, one of the girls in NOW THE
REVOLUTION on tour. She was also in my Bible class. The
whole cast is living in a theater a few blocks from here. They
open early in November. They have changed the name to
STOMP. Isn't that a fantastic coincidence!*

*Dearest, I spent the whole day at a meeting on poverty
law. There is so much to learn and to do.*

You are my love; the one I love; my dearest. Keep
helping me to live out my love, darling – you're beautiful.

Your
Chas

WINONA TO NEW YORK CITY

October 30, 1969

Hi dear,

I felt that our conversation last night was a good one.
Usually telephone conversations leave me empty or unsatisfied
or lonesome. This time I felt lonesome (of course) but satisfied. I
really miss you, and it seems like a long time till Christmas.

I'm curious about your talk with Georgia [in Austin],
and if anything were settled, like a decision about a date for the
wedding.... Naturally I would like to be there, but my
convenience is not the most important thing to be considered.

I feel slightly guilty about not getting letters to you more
often. I hope you accept my bad habits in correspondence along
with all the other shortcomings you manage to overlook. You are
so appreciative of my letters when they do come that I read
between the lines and regret that I write so little. Compared to
you, that is. I have never written to anyone as often as I write to
you. Of course.

The last three days have been "conference days" with
my freshmen. I tell them the grade I gave them on their mid-
semester reports, and talk about their progress or lack of it in
writing. I also tie name and face together for the few I don't
know for sure yet. If they don't speak up much in class I have a
dickens of a time remembering who they are. They really are
nice girls. No complaints in that line.

I feel less adequate with the upperclassmen. I need more
confidence in myself. (You are not the only one.) I had another
sister in as guest lecturer yesterday, on the influence of Poe on
the French Symbolist Poets, and she awed them and me with her
background knowledge. I come out badly in contrast. But I am
studying the problem and learning some techniques to apply in
the next course, Later American Literature. Would you believe
we have to have our book orders in by tomorrow? I run all the
time and never catch up!

My friend Sister Lalonde, who has had a back fusion and is now hospitalized for problems in the neck region, is in worse shape even than we thought. It seems that her spine is deteriorating. *Can you imagine? She's only 31. And a real saint. I really mean it. No one has suffered more than she has, and she remains cheerful through it all. Always worrying about others, not herself. Worrying about me, for example.... Her father is dying of cancer.*

Must run. Will get this in the 2:00 p.m. mail.

Much love, Francha/R

NEW YORK CITY TO WINONA

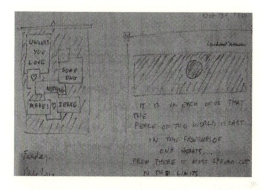 On the top of this letter Charlie sketched two banners: "Unless you love someone, nothing makes sense" – an e.e. cummings line from a poem; and "It is in each of us that the peace of the world is cast… in the frontiers of our hearts;… from there it must spread out to the limits of the universe." – Cardinal Suenens

[10/31/69]
Friday.

My love,

These are the sayings that hang above my bed. Duke's choice. I've adopted them as my own because they express me – my love for you and another way of looking at "Palms power."

Dearest, your last letter moved me deeply. Your "maybes" told me what you must be going through. I can (and now it's hours later – I got up at 6:30 this morning to write to you but didn't get very far. I'm sitting in my office. It's twenty minutes to eight. I can hear the laughter and excitement of the

*kids on Halloween fifteen floors below my window. I'm hungry,
more for you than for food, so I'll finish this before heading back
to the Village.)*

*It's quiet up here. I just reread your letter again. What
an evening to be thinking about the Great Pumpkin! Did Martin
Luther King believe in the Great Pumpkin? Did Robert
Kennedy? I think they did. I think all of us have to have a Great
Pumpkin. But I agree with you sweetie, it's not the religious life.
The religious life shields me from having the courage of my
convictions; it protects me from the cross of self-affirmation.
Self-denial or mortification is so much easier than self-
affirmation, than the effort to live what one believes. I think that
we must live what we really believe and that means we may be
rejected and disliked. The religious life doesn't make sense for
me. Besides, as Oliver B [his psychotherapist in Austin] used to
delight in saying, "You do what you damn well please, anyway."
I've been trying to have my cake and eat it for so long, darling,
that I feel kind of split, not together, dishonest. I know I'm being
too harsh on myself in that statement, but I think I have my finger
on the problem. And I think this whole problem is involved in our
love for each other. We have to make choices and live them out.
You were moving "together" in an honest forthright manner; I
was threatened by choice. I didn't want to face a decision. It was
more comfortable, have cake and eat it, to just float through,
romantically, like a flower child. No sir, Charlie. Please bear
with me as I try to zero in. Our love makes us responsible for one
another. I balked at the responsibility. But not entirely, darling.
I'm writing this from Brooklyn, N.Y. I love you from Brooklyn,
N.Y. I am living out the consequences of one decision, a decision
that I consider a crucial stepping stone in our relationship. I
know what it is to make a decision. And I am preparing to make
others. I have to carry this same spirit into my work, because I
can have the cake and eat it here too – no one hound-dogs me.
But the day of reckoning will come. I have become so aware of
my lack of self-discipline and my constant self-indulgence.
Sweet, I don't want to lose my humanity. I realize I'm fully
human. But part of that humanity is giving of self. That's the
business I'm about right now. That's what Jesus did. And
religious life has no relationship to it for me, right now. I love*

my Paulist brethren, but my love for them cannot imprison me within a structure that has the effect of emasculating me. (Would I hurt them if I said this to them?)

Darling, I've got to get off that subject, but writing this has helped me to think things out. I think I'm moving in the right direction. I feel good.

I called Georgia and we had a good talk. I was enthusiastic about her marriage to Ron. She said, "Glad to hear someone who approves." I guess she's not getting much support. But I believe in Georgia, and that's what I told her. I said I would come and that now you and I could be in Texas together. They need to set a date, and because much depends upon when Ron's folks can be there, it looks like the date should be between December 21 and 27. I suggest after Christmas. So when I call on Wednesday, let's pick a date and then I'll call Georgia.

Rosemary, my Francha, I love you. I feel stronger about it now than ever. Things are clearer for me. You look better and better to me. Isn't it funny how your "maybes" brought out my affirmations.

Happy hallowe'en,
Chas

NEW YORK CITY TO WINONA
Halloween – later letter [1969]

Darling,

You're constantly in my thoughts. I mailed that Goblin letter two hours ago and I have some more to talk to you about.

First, my rejection of religious life is not a rejection of the <u>priesthood</u>. I feel very much a priest. I am presently ministering outside church structure! But as dear Belinda said, "There is no such thing as religious life; there is just life." I am more convinced now of this than ever. I reject "religious life" as structure, not the reality of the priesthood as <u>life</u>.

Second, check NCR [The National Catholic Reporter], October 29, p. 5. "Former Peace Corps members say it should be abolished." Some of the reasons are: It "supports status quo." It gives legitimacy to the local power structure with which

*it works. It provides an illusion of progress. It diverts local
energies from challenging the underlying injustices…. Do you
realize, dearest, that this is what I am doing! Here I am, trying to
improve health and education within the present system. Here is
our corporation working hard to create black capitalism by
inviting Blacks to set up businesses in Bed-Stuy. Aren't we really
substituting a White form of status quo for a Black form? I can
foresee that I may have to leave my job already! How do we get
at those crucial underlying causes of all the trouble? Darling,
don't fret. I won't leave yet. Maybe I should risk working from
within. As I wrote in a previous letter, I realize I didn't make the
"sacrifice" to work at revolutionizing the Church from within.
But I didn't realize that until I planted the tree in Brooklyn.*

*Got a great Halloween card from U of Texas CSC
friends. It really gave me a boost. I love you my darling. Good
night and God bless you. Don't you believe in the Great
Pumpkin?*

Charlie

NEW YORK CITY TO WINONA

Charlie sent this quotation sometime in Fall 1969; it was wrapped around flowers or a vine "Picked on Park Ave."

"Natural flowers are better (than artificial) because they are dying and therefore infinitely more pathetic. Those that do not die are merely lent to the feast day; those that die are given to it. Because they are, they become identified with the passing day and with mortal man. We can see ourselves in them. They tell us our own story in terms of beauty. This bunch of flowers cannot be used twice or pass from hand to hand. It is an image of absolute fidelity, of a marriage or a friendship." – Pierre Charles

WINONA TO NEW YORK CITY

October 31, 1969

Dear Charlie,

Happy Hallowe'en! Two little boys just came into the office trick-and-treating for UNICEF.

Which reminds me. I have only 20 minutes left of this p.m. before Mass and supper, and the day students have invited the faculty to a Halloween party, so I had better get down there. To be continued....

November 2!

Such a busy life! I just got back from a weekend in Rochester, for a series of talks on community by canon lawyer Kevin O'Rourke. I am happy to report that they were good talks, and spaced leisurely enough to allow for discussion of the ideas, rag-chewing, and caucusing for capitulars and president of our Franciscan congregation. It was good talking especially to classmates, one of which I had not seen for 2½ years. Half of the class was there (8 out of 15). And I almost gave a pitch for lay affiliation during the open forum. Almost. I am terribly disappointed in myself; I had the ideas all written out and everything, and then my courage failed and my rationalization powers worked full speed ahead. Darling, I need someone (you!) to pat me on the back and reassure me just as much as you do. One little push and I would have done it. My rationalization was that I would have had to twist the direction of the questions a little in order to relate it to the topics Father had talked about.

I'm still waiting to hear how your conversation went with Georgia.

Shall I capsulize the O'Rourke talks for you? My notes aren't here, but briefly his three topics were: (1) the need for primary groups or "we" supportive community, and the importance of not letting the secondary group or task-oriented group supplant the primary group; (2) prayer – "we have an irrepressible desire to confront God, to pray"; and (3) the function of law is to guide to freedom. Written, external laws are necessary because we are imperfect, but their function is only to lead us to the practice of Christ's law, which is written in our hearts: to obey out of love, out of freedom, out of the desire to serve, not out of fear or coercion.

I'll get this in the mail, dear. Remember that if you call Wednesday, to call about 9:05 p.m., and then I will have the doors locked and will be "off bells." (Can you afford to call so often?)

Love, Rosemary

NEW YORK CITY TO WINONA

Sunday
November 2 [1969]

Francha my Rosemary,

I'm cooking my supper. Lipton's soup and I added half a can (small) of chicken for flavor. I just sipped a little. It's delicious! Now I'm eating it and it's really good. I just burned my mouth.

Well, that's that. One thing I have had trouble with is laundry. My shirts don't get clean. My cousin Jody recommended something you soak the clothes in overnight before washing them. Jody and I went to Mass together and had a good talk over lunch.

Toby I've seen only once. I've been invited for dinner next Saturday with some close friends of hers. She is wrapped up with Dan and concerned about the details of her forthcoming marriage (no official Vatican dispensation papers yet).

Today has been dreary, raining all day. I've spent most of it reading background material for my job. The school system of N.Y. is too centralized, just like the Church.

George L called a little while ago. He's lonely. I promised him I will go out hiking with him next Saturday. Diane and he are having trouble making their decision.

Duke just came in and the television is blaring. I'm trying to finish this in our kitchen – the scene of my supper triumph.

Monday

Dearest, it's now early Monday morning. I couldn't get enough quiet to finish writing you last night. Now it's very still. I went to sleep thinking about you; I wake up with you in my heart and thoughts. What we went through in Rochester I now believe was a good experience, though painful. It seems to me it could have had two effects. It could have been a prelude to withdrawal,

or a stepping stone to decision. I can say very honestly, darling,
that I am moving closer to you very day. I could make the
decision at this moment, but I want to do it with you. I guess I'm
thinking, is Christmas too long a time to wait? Ed and Eileen
suggested we get together over Thanksgiving in Decorah with
Joanie. I don't know if this is very sensible timewise or
moneywise for us. It's tempting. We'll just have to see. They said
that Bill M might come all the way from California. Let's keep it
in the realm of possibility anyway.

Today (Monday) is Black Solidarity Day. Black people
are staying home. Tomorrow is election day. I can't vote, but I
would, for Lindsay. If John Lindsay doesn't get elected there will
be a bloody revolution in New York. He has fought for rent
control, for community control of schools, for minority rights.
The middle-class Jews, Catholics and Protestants (those of
narrow vision) despise him because of his attention to the
"privileged minorities." But I have enough confidence in the
common sense of New Yorkers to believe he will be re-elected.

God bless you darling. I love you. I look forward to
crossing voices with you on Wednesday.

Devotedly,
Charlie

WINONA TO NEW YORK CITY

. Enclosures include a version of Psalm 40, starting "I
waited for my Lord with a poor and empty heart." I wrote in the
margin: *"I find this really quite expressive of my own efforts at*
prayer, and the positive outlook I long for but don't yet have."

[November 4, 1969]

Charlie dear,

I got, today, your postscript Halloween letter, but have
not *received the "goblin" one you say you mailed earlier! My*
curiosity is worked up!

Further investigations into plane fares [for a Christmas
trip] *reveal that excursion rates (over 7 days, less than 30) make*
quite a difference. Rochester/NY round trip is $102. Chicago –
NY round trip is $80.00 (circa). That really isn't as much as I

had expected. So, my dear, if you can afford it, I will be happy to accept $100.00 in whatever way you deem most prudent. If money order, why not just make it out to Rosemary Grebin? What do I do, just take it to a bank and identify myself?

Tonight, at my initiation (!), the college community [of Franciscan sisters] *is doing some open politicking as we talk about "The Making of a President: 1970" – what are the qualifications and who fits those qualifications of a major superior?? There are some of us who believe that caucus-ing can be inspired by the Holy Spirit if it is done honestly, in the spirit of good will, and in charity. This means it can be done openly, even should be done openly. Therefore we dared to make an open invitation, and I'm still shaking at my own audacity. (Maybe I'm trying to make up for my failure in courage at the O'Rourke lectures?) And I really fear the ill feelings that may come out of the evening. If only I had that saving sense of humor when I have to stand in front of a tense situation!*

But the "if onlys" don't build a new world....

Thought for the day: (If the shoes fits....) "Absence is to love what wind is to fire. It extinguishes the small and enkindles the great."

I love you.
Rosemary
Later

P.S. The meeting went all right. Sometimes I manufacture fears.
☺

WINONA TO NEW YORK CITY
November 7, 1969

Darling,

You would be shocked at me tonight. It's Friday, and I need to let off steam, you know, scream or play tennis or something, and so – after I read a few pages in Rollo May about the meaninglessness in people's lives these days — I jogged over to the office without my coat, found a half-smoked cigarette and a match, lit up, took off my veil (after pulling the shades!) and here I am, feeling much better. I have an appointment in an hour to go play pool – relax, it's a table over in our nursing home a few blocks away! I'll put my veil back on.

The cigarette didn't last long and tasted awful. Viceroy. Strong. Served me right....

And tomorrow night I'm going to discuss curriculum changes in our department with other English teachers here, in one of the men's (single!) apartments, over beer. They hesitated long and hard over inviting me; I finally got a shy invitation and offer of a ride today, and I've had intimations of a "beer-bust brain-storming" for over a week. Part of the reason I feel stifled here is that everyone expects me to be stifled. It's maddening. And silly to talk of these things – cigarettes, beer — as symbols of emancipation or something. I really can't explain exactly why I feel stifled, except to say it's in the very atmosphere. (So I don't say to anyone I'm stifled.)

I'm rambling, but somehow I feel you're following me.

And now I heated up the dregs in the coffee pot to get rid of the cigarette taste – aaugh! And, incidentally, the smell....

Tuesday afternoon and Wednesday morning I finally got back to the task of Jerry's poems. I went through the magazine racks and selected journals I thought might possibly be interested in publishing one or two, and then picked out three different poems for each of six of them. That means, counting your three to the CATHOLIC WORLD, there are now 21 of the 54 poems currently being reviewed by editors. Let's hope all that work was not in vain. In the covering letter I briefly explained the situation and asked them for suggestions by way of criticism or possibilities for publication even if they did not want to publish any themselves. Now I wait again. Did you hear anything from the WORLD yet?

Thomas Clark, who writes such a promising article on new forms of religious life in the current SISTERS TODAY, is speaking to 1700 sisters in St. Paul Sunday. I decided not to go, and maybe get back to the business of dissertation this weekend, or at least get preparations for class out of the way so that I can start at the d. next week again. I wrote to my major professor today, asking for an appointment sometime between Jan. 5 and 9. That will be an incentive to get some more on paper. [Our Christmas vacation plans now definitely included a visit to Texas, for Georgia's wedding.]

I really need deadlines. That is becoming more and more obvious.

I thought you might enjoy a taste of the high-quality underground newspaper that comes out weekly here. See enclosed [with topics like the Vietnam War and the "death of God"]. *The first two entries are by professors here, in social science and in theology. The title, Esgaroth (in case you are as ignorant as I was), comes from Tolkien's Hobbit world of LORD OF THE RINGS.*

Thanks for all your clippings – always very interesting. I especially enjoyed Ethel Kennedy's trip through Bed-Stuy. Did you see that The National Catholic Reporter features Austin's crusade to save the trees – current issue?

I am really getting excited about Christmas vacation. You won't be taking off days while I am there, will you? I can manage to amuse myself during the days, maybe even go to a big library and browse, or arty places, or visit the Funks. I know how important your work is, and there is Sunday, Christmas Day, and evenings. Can I cook for you???

I wrote an enthusiastic letter to Georgia.

Darling, enough of this banter. Maybe I will feel more meditative next time. My brain is tired now.

My love,
Rosemary

NEW YORK CITY TO WINONA
Saturday November 8 [1969]

Dearest Francha my Rosemary,

I have just returned from an enjoyable afternoon with George L. He picked me up at Duke's at 1:30 p.m. and we headed for Brooklyn. I brought my first load of stuff to my new apartment. When we got there I couldn't get into my room because the Super had the key and the Super was not in evidence. So George and I traveled to his apartment which is about five miles away (also in Brooklyn) and there he made me a sandwich and we had a beer and talked. George is going through something which is something like what I've been through. I think I was helpful to him. I urged him to be as honest as he could with Diane and to keep in communication. In time, I told him, the path would be clear. Darling, I am sure I am right. Meanwhile, I telephoned my landlord and said that I would not pay the rent for today since my apartment was locked. He quickly made arrangements for me to get into my digs, and I brought a suitcase full of books and things to 195 Underhill Road, Apt. 6E, Brooklyn. [Charlie did not have his address exactly right, which caused confusion and some mail returned to Winona for a couple of weeks.] *I don't know the postal zone yet, but you can write me there beginning now. I won't have a phone for a while because the telephone men are on strike. We can keep our same plan about the telephone Wednesday nite. The gas and electricity start in 6E on Monday. Honey, I'm on the move!*

When I asked how you were feeling the other evening you replied, "So, so." I know you must be going through a great deal and I want to bear it with you. I'm sure the pressures of teaching and of participation in community life must keep you thinking about what you are going through – what we are going through. I just feel so proud of you when you tell me about your initiation of open politicking (the Lindsay syndrome?) and when I read your newsletter and when you describe your efforts to open up the lives of your students. No doubt about it dearie, you are the one. I can't wait to see you.

Here is the transportation schedule. In due time I'll send you the tickets. Problem: to take advantage of the "excursion" fare, if you leave on a Friday, you have to leave the airport before noon. Since Chicago is where the excursion rate begins for you, it means getting up at the crack of dawn. I know this is inconvenient, and I will be ready for your suggestions when we talk on Wednesday. Also, it means we have to leave NYC before noon.

December 19 – leave Rochester 7;55 am; arrive Chicago 9:04 am --Northwest #414. Leave Chicago 11:00 am; arrive NY LaGuardia 1:47 --American #312
December 26 – leave NYC Kennedy 9:15 am; arrive Dallas 11:57 am -- Braniff #1. Leave Dallas 1:50 pm; arrive Austin 2:34 pm -- Braniff #131
January 10 – Austin to Chicago to Rochester open

I'll be with you on the flight to Austin on the 26th,
returning to NYC on December 28 at 4:05 pm (from Austin). I
hope Ed and Eileen will be in Austin. Put the pressure on them.
This will take the pressure off us for Thanksgiving. I don't think
we can afford both. Incidentally, while you are in NYC, you
should certainly be able to see Pam. She's in Baltimore, only
three hours away by train.

One bit of sad news. Bas, editor of the <u>Catholic World</u>,
returned Jerry's poems. He wrote: "I have read these poems, put
them aside, and then re-read them, but I still do not react to them
in any enthusiastic fashion. They are tragically melancholy, ...
not my dish of tea." We see so much more than the printed line.
I'll try another publisher.

And now I'm off darling, to Toby's who has also invited
her friend Millie. And Dan will be there. Tomorrow I go to Mass
with cousin Jody. We are going to a jazz Mass in Harlem. My
Aunt Frances is in town and I have dinner with her tomorrow
evening at the St. Regis Hotel.

[Here Charlie quotes the e.e. cummings poem "Out of
the mountain/ of her soul."]

> *I LOVE YOU   LOVE YOU*
> *THANKS FOR ALL THE PRAYERS   LOVE YOU   Chas*

NEW YORK CITY TO WINONA
Sunday [11/9/1969]

Dearest,

I'm writing you again, following up on the long letter of
yesterday, because I just want to. You are in my thoughts
constantly.

Last evening was very pleasant. Dan was there. So was
Millie's husband Peter whom I had never met before. Millie and
Peter were a few days away from their 25th wedding anniversary,
so they were toasted as well as Toby and Dan. I reminded Toby
about sending you an invitation, and she was indignant that I
would even think of saying anything about this. I'm still glad I
reminded her. Toby cooked a delicious chicken dinner. During
the evening there was much conversation about what made for a
successful marriage. Peter (who is Puerto Rican) remarked
much to Millie's embarrassment (Millie is Jewish) that fighting

in marriage was good because it was so nice to make up afterwards. Millie and Peter have college-age children. They felt that the college generation has a sense of honesty, but not a sufficient sense of follow-through and responsible commitment.

I'm enclosing the NY Times clipping on Stomp *(*Now the Revolution*) which opens here on Thursday. I hope it's running when you come to NY. There is going to be so much for us to see I won't know where to begin. This morning I saw Eddie B. Remember, he is the Black composer whose recording (*Mass for Every Season*) I played for you one evening. Eddie advised me to go to the Black plays in town to get the feeling of the Black mood. Tuesday Jody and I will go to* No Place to Be Somebody.

That gets me into this morning. I met Jody at her apartment and we taxied to Harlem for Mass. Mass was offered in the auditorium of one of Harlem's public schools. It was a very moving experience to watch Eddie again and feel the joy and reverence of his music. Both Father Kevin K and Eddie remembered me and treated me like the returning prodigal. I felt great. And as an added bonus, Eddie teaches in the NY Public School system and is presently assigned to one of the most important areas of the system, an area in my territory, Ocean-Hill Brownsville (Brooklyn) which is in Bed-Stuy. So I have a beautiful contact in the education segment and someone who will help me to meet the right people in Bed-Stuy. I'm delighted. Afterwards, Jody and I went to lunch at Longchamps but the whole morning, taxi, $2.00 collection, lunch cost us each $7.00. The money goes too fast. But I really feel that this morning was worth it.

On the other side of this page I am going to paste the words of a song that moved me so much this morning I couldn't sing it. You have to hear and feel the jazz-spiritual music to get the full import of it. Make up your own melody and sing it. It's bound to touch you.

Taped to the back of Charlie's letter were lyrics to Billy Taylor's "I Wish I Knew How It Would Free to Be Free," They spoke to our own struggles at the time. In part:

"I wish I knew how it would feel to be free....
I wish I could say all the things I should say.
Say 'em loud, say 'em clear for the whole world to hear."

for the whole world to hear
Rosemary dear
I'm saying what I want to say
FREELY
I LOVE YOU

Charlie

WINONA TO NEW YORK CITY

Enclosed is a Dagwood cartoon. Dagwood promised 3 different people to watch a game with them, all at the same time – so he hides in his closet until the game is over.

11/10/69

Hi dear,

I waited for the mail this a.m., thinking it might contain a letter and new address from you, but it didn't, so I will mail this to Duke's place.

Enclosed please find a moral in Dagwood's plight; rather, not a moral, but a parallel situation – that he doesn't handle right!

Also the program for our first big concert here. Sister Genevieve is greatly talented and a wonderful sister besides. (She is being talked about as a possibility for "sister president" but is perhaps too high-strung, as you musicians tend to be!)

The meeting of some of the English profs at the apartment was fun but certainly not wild in any sense. Mostly a business meeting. In a relaxed setting.

Pam wrote a short P.S. on her last note saying that the trip at Thanksgiving was off; maybe after Christmas sometime. She did not explain. So I am beginning to think about "retreating" at Thanksgiving, where and with whom. (You didn't hear more from Bill M or Joanie [about the proposed Thanksgiving gathering], did you?)

*My spirits are good. I still like my classes. Sister
Lalonde came home from the hospital Saturday, in much pain
and very depressed, but home. I really love her.*

*Must think about getting ready for my next class. I'm
<u>always</u> doing things at the last minute!*

My love, always....

On the back I copied a poem I had written about a pause
in the Vietnam War.

> *THOUGHTS ON THE MORATORIUM – 11/8/69*
>   *gently gentlemen come to peace*
>   *we can not*
>   *err gently so we*
>   *urgently*
>   *urge our gentlemen to be*
>   *gentle men*
>   *gently*
>   *we urge gently come to peace*

NEW YORK CITY TO WINONA

Tuesday [11/11/1969?]

Dearest,

*The neighborhood where I
will soon be living is removed by time
and culture from Alfred Sisley's
[enclosed postcard] "Street in Moret."
When I move over to Brooklyn I'll
take some photos to prepare you for
your Christmas visit. The room is so
dingy I have decided to get it painted before I move. This meant
another hassle with the landlord. He promised to foot the bill if I
would find the painter. Today I got my man and the apartment
will be painted this weekend while I travel to the moratorium in
Washington (and this time I'll be more positive about fasting).*

*Tonight Jody and I saw <u>The Reckoning</u>. It involves the
confrontation of a black pimp and a white Southern governor
(white hair, suit, tie, socks and shoes – so much whiteness
revolting). The truth that comes out in allegory brings home the*

*hypocrisy and racism of the white man. The language is vulgar,
powerful, poetic and brilliant, written by Douglas Turner Ward
who also starred as the pimp, "Scar." I am sure you would find
the "double" theme running through, and if it's still here when
you come we'll see it again together.*

Belinda's letter came yesterday. Her news was: Bernie
[a CSC student and drug user] *is not in good shape, Mike K has
gone to a monastery in Japan, Curt* [Lutheran student center
pastor] *celebrated Sunday Mass with Ed and Walter. Curt read
the Gospel, preached and helped distribute Holy Communion!
Belinda's insights were piercing. "It would seem that planning
permanent careers is a thing of the past. In fact, it would seem
that life is to be thought of not in terms of stability or
permanency. Does the concept of stability have value???
Something for us all to think about."*

*Darling, I miss you. We'll be talking together tomorrow
evening. I need to hear you. The voice is so much more alive
than words on a page.*

*I have had some good talks with John Doar (my boss)
the past two days. He is a strong and positive person. I am now
in charge of the research of eight young people. Obviously he (J.
Doar) has confidence in me. He has warned me that I must lead
these young people and discipline them so that they produce. I
have been successful as the "nice" guy. It will be interesting to
see how I do as task force leader. What a great opportunity to
grow and to serve I have! I can feel my life changing. I find
myself acting much more responsibly, with greater ease. Doar
tells me: "You must make demands on people." "Yeah," I say to
myself, "and first I must be able to make demands on myself and
to fulfill those demands. I remember Professor Frances Fuller
saying that one of the signs of a mature person is to want to do
what you have to do. I feel myself going in the direction of
maturity. Long way to go, darling.*

*At this point I find it hard to put words down, because I
realize that you and I have to face together the question: where
will you stay? I have an extra bed and I desire you, darling, and
I want you to stay with me. But this desire has to be reconciled
with your desires and what we both decide is best. I am very
sensitive to the "cake and eat it" syndrome which I wrote you*

about at great length in one letter. Certainly maturity is breaking that syndrome. Then I know you will want to be with Warren and Nancy, and Pam is all excited, and you will want to write them in advance. Let's talk about it, sweet. This may sound as inconsistent as hell, but I would suggest that you stay with me the 19th and if you want to go to Nancy and Warren's that we go there together after Toby's wedding the 20th. After that we can play the visit by ear and decide as we decide. Here I am trying to reconcile my deep love for you with your feelings and what is best for the growth of our love. I realized it's compromise and not a total escape from the cake syndrome. What say, darling?

I love you,
Charlie

NEW YORK CITY TO WINONA

Thursday [11/13/1969]

Oh Francha dear,

It's late, 9:20 p.m. I'm itching to leave the office, but not before I give of myself to you.

Today has been a frustrating day. I visited a controversial school and instead of finding out all about the problems I was talked to death by one of the teachers. It was like getting a tour in the Soviet Union. I only saw what my guide wanted to show me. But I must admit, the fault was somewhat mine. The teacher happened to be an old N.Y. friend. He talked me to death because he spent most of the time telling me about himself. As we walked from class to class we would peer in for a moment and then walk down the corridor, our conversation unrelated to what we saw. The reason, I'm afraid, was because he teaches band, not academics. He didn't know what was going on. But I admired him for the way he communicated with the students, his interest in them, and his way of giving them a sense of their own dignity and worth. For example, he comes early to school four days a week to give special instruction. He arrives in Bed-Stuy at 7:30 a.m., which means that the alarm goes off in his New Jersey home at 4:30 a.m. That's dedication, ain't it!

The most interesting part of the day was the hour and ten minutes in the lunch room. I found myself exhausted just from watching and listening to 500 screaming boys and girls (5th to 8th

*grade). The life is just bursting out of them. They scuffle, dance,
laugh, cry, look longingly – the whole gamut of human emotions.
What a responsibility for the teachers, and sad to say, dear, the
system is failing. Seven out of ten of those kids will be dropouts
in high school if present trends continue.*

*And that's part of my job. How to reverse the present
trend. It's such a gigantic challenge, that when I came back to
the office, I spent most of my time shuffling papers, trying to
understand the problem, trying to ask the right questions,
restating my analysis.*

*I wish I could be with you tonight. You understand me.
That Dagwood cartoon was just perfect. I'm trying to grow out
of that. But I won't knock it too much because it has its good side
– concern for the other. I wouldn't be in Bed-Stuy if I didn't have
some yearning to be of service to my fellow man. (As I re-read
the above paragraph I realize how tired I am. It doesn't make
sense.)*

*On the subway today I thought again about our
conversation of last night. Let me try to communicate a little
more. I love you, darling. I feel responsible for you. I am
responsible for you. I desire you. I want to be with you. I shudder
when I think of what happened to me in Rochester. My being
with you symbolized responsibility, yet when you pointed a
responsible question at me I wavered. It was an example of
having the "cake and eating it" attitude that is not responsible.
Maybe I'm too harsh on myself, expecting all or nothing at all. I
do think that experience helped me to grow and it showed me the
depth of your love in a way I'd never seen it before. What I'm
saying is, I won't feel completely honest or at ease with you until
I have repeated my love for you and my desire to share life with
you and you have joined hands with me and sealed our lives
together with a smile and a kiss. What I'm also saying is that I
want you to stay with me, that first night and other nights in New
York. I'm saying that I want to respect your feelings, your
desires, your ideals and dreams. We have to work this out
together. Darling, there is no sense in my concealing my
thoughts from you. I am pointing toward that responsible love
confrontation; I am preparing, indeed I am now ready to answer
that question you asked me in Rochester. You are the one, dear. I*

love you so that I want to have you by my side in life. I not only want to show you New York. I want to show you life. Rosemary my Francha, I love you. I want to be responsible for you always. What must be worked out is a time table. How to deal with our folks, our religious communities.

And now dear, I'd better get running along. I loved that part of your letter where things got so uptight that you had to take off your veil and run for a cigarette. I get feeling that way at times too.

You know, I've really cut down on drinking. We've had one bottle of Scotch for over two weeks! It's too expensive and it hinders my proficiency the next day. But I think I've been pushing too hard on this job. I ease my guilt for non-productiveness and avoiding the hard thinking by putting in long hours. This job is too important to avoid the hard things in it. I'll plunge in again tomorrow for all I'm worth. I'm human and I love you.

Devotedly,
Chas

P.S. I'm going to have the apartment painted off white. Will you do the curtains? Will you help me furnish it? Will you help me stock the kitchen? I have gas and electricity now, but no telephone.

NEW YORK CITY TO WINONA

The following note was written on the back of a 3.5"x18" "Peace Now" sign.

Nov 16, 1969

Dearest,
It was great speaking with you on the evening of the Great Day [of the Vietnam War Moratorium March]. *I'm enclosing some souvenirs for you. This is just a sampling of the literature – everything from Women's Rights to Crusade for Christ. I found the postcard in the National Gallery of Art. Appropriately, it depicts the streets of N.Y. at Christmastime. I stood around the altar here at St. Paul's* [the Paulist seminary in Washington] *this morning and thought a great deal of you*

*during Mass. I have come to Washington for Peace and feel a
great deal of peace and love in my heart this morning. I'll be
driving back to NY this afternoon with George H and Duke and a
Sister. Tomorrow morning at 8 a.m. I have my first important
meeting with the Public Services Task Force. We are using all
the ingenuity we have to serve the people of Bed-Stuy. D.C.
seems so much cleaner than Bed-Stuy.*

*Love and Peace,
Charlie*

This letter from Winona to 195 Underhill Avenue,
Brooklyn, was the first one addressed to <u>Mr.</u> Charles Palms at
his new address – no "Reverend" or "Father" included.

WINONA TO BROOKLYN

Nov. 17, 1969

Darling,
        *Today I got your letter of "definite commitment." I have
looked forward to it since our delightful surprise talk Saturday
night, and I was not disappointed. Darling, I love you for it and
I'm afraid I shy away from the big step – the timetable with
ourselves, with our families, with our communities. I thrill at the
prospect of helping you fix up your apartment – our apartment, it
would be then. I'm happy today, and I radiate confidence.
Knowing you are at my side. At the same time, with this same
confidence, I plunge into community affairs and have won the
respect of most of my age group at CST. Consequently, tonight I
was "caucus-ed in" for a capitular* [that is, a voting
representative at the congregation's upcoming business meeting]
*on our first round of balloting. (I agreed, but have told them I
may be on leave of absence.)*
        *In short, my dear, I am still confused on where I belong
at this point in my life. What is "God's will" for me? About my
attitude towards the Franciscans, three feelings emerge. (1)
LOVE – concern for numerous individuals in the community; (2)
JUSTICE – a feeling of obligation to continue to support those
who have given or are giving their whole lives for a worthy
cause; and (3) CONFIDENCE – that there is a place in the
Church of the Future for some kind of religious life: perhaps*

small groups of dedicated idealists who really <u>*can*</u> *witness love to a world of hate and pessimism. Someone has to dream the impossible dream if any Dulcineas are to be realized.*

    My thoughts this far are sorted out. Personally, at this moment, I do not feel attracted to the life of a celibate. I do not believe a promised life of dedication (<u>viz</u>., under vows) has, <u>per se</u>, any more value than a non-promised life of dedication, unless the <u>individual</u> feels he can be more effective and more generous one way or the other.

    This is the way I am leaning. Charlie my darling: I want a life of dedication with YOU. I am <u>*not*</u> *happy in my present state of affairs. Every day I wear the veil I feel like a hypocrite.*

    My next tendency may surprise you a bit, and I wish I could watch your face and hold your hand as I tell you this: I am afraid that my conservative upbringing may boomerang on me. I feel free of the restrictions of the Church <u>RIGHT NOW</u>. I believe in the primacy of individual conscience, but I know that conscience matters shift and change over the years, and experience and evidence around me tell me that after a certain peak in one's life, generally the trend is to gradually revert to more conservative stances and the pull of one's training. My training was pre-Vatican II. (So was yours....) <u>THEREFORE</u>, I would like to talk to you about the possibility of <u>marriage</u>, yes, but within the traditional Church. <u>I.e.</u>, with dispensation from vows and laicization for you. I want to <u>talk to you</u>, because I know it's not that simple, that a principle (<u>viz</u>., a married priesthood) is involved.

    And then we must also think of our families. My own family, I know, would be less unhappy if this were our course of action. We must not think of our families first, but we should consider their feelings as well as those of everyone else we touch in our decision. I will be eager, even apprehensive, until I receive your reaction to this conservative streak in me. <u>BE HONEST</u>, as always.

    I have been forced to sort out a lot of these feelings over the last 2 days, because it finally happened: Lalonde and I were totally and beautifully open with each other. She has been suspecting so strongly that she outright asked me after your phone call Saturday night. She gets <u>really</u> depressed as she sees

*friend after friend leave behind the ideal of the religious life that
she so (I would say) frantically hangs on to. Her faith is strong.
She is <u>lonely</u>. She is sick (her back, her neck).... It has been a
good 2 days of sharings and growing in friendship.*

*Darling, I have been honest in this letter. I hope my love
shines thru it all----*

Francha

NEW YORK CITY TO WINONA
Tuesday [11/18/1969]

Dearest,

*My apartment is almost painted now. I left work on the
dot tonight and subwayed into Manhattan to buy towels and
blankets and pillow cases and a shower curtain and a rug for the
bathroom -- $35.00 worth. And my painters are charging $135,
but my landlord will foot $55 of that bill. I'm becoming very
money conscious. Last week I saved $45! I enjoy getting things
for the apartment. It gives me a feeling of independence and a
chance to risk my artistic sense in choosing colors.*

*I'm enclosing a clipping on U.T. Paranoia! One bit of
charming news. Little Penny made her profession of faith at the
12:05 Mass on Nov. 11. The review of "Stomp" is N.Y. snobbery.*

*We'll be in voice contact tomorrow evening. I really look
forward to that. I'll stay downtown in my office and call you
from there. One of the things we will discuss is Toby's marriage.
The Jesuit friend of Dan's who was supposed to officiate copped
out. Toby asked me today. I said I'd think about it. My tentative
answer is "yes."*

*The job is challenging and I love the area I'm working
in, but I have some doubts about myself as organizer. I don't
seem to be accomplishing much. I can't grind out the reports I
should be producing. But, dear, I'm making a valiant effort. Our
next big meeting is Monday.*

*I miss you my darling. I love you. I choose to stand by
you for the remainder of this life and God willing, forever.*
Friday is our fourteenth anniversary! [Charlie had adopted the
habit of counting every month that went by since his declaration
of love as an "anniversary."]

How are you and how do you feel, dear? How are things going for you?

Devotedly, Charlie

NEW YORK CITY TO WINONA

Sunday [11/23/1969]

Dearest,

I've been trying to write a thoughtful and loving letter of response to your "green letter" [my letter of doubts sent November 17] *but it is taking me too much time and I've been rushing these past two days – meetings and reports and I've just moved into 165* [sic] *Underhill. I slept here last night and this is my first act (after the morning shower) and I have to run to meet Jody for Mass. So as a little Thanksgiving present I send you the enclosed* [the airline tickets for the planned Christmas trip] *– also for light meditation during the retreat. Know that I know of your love and that I stand by you.*

Devotedly,
Charlie

BROOKLYN TO WINONA

Sunday 1:40 a.m. [11/23/1969]

Dearest,

I took possession of my apartment a few moments ago. I took off my topcoat, opened my suitcase and took out my portable transistor radio. It's playing ~~Motzart.~~ Announcer just said Bach. (Sp? I'm too tired to spell.) And now I'm writing you before I go to bed, let me repeat...I love you. And now to the arms of Morpheus (sp again). I'm especially tired because it's so late and I had to carry nearly all my worldly belongings about

a half mile from the subway. One cab stopped, but he wouldn't come in this neighborhood. I said "Thanks a lot fellah!" And now to bed with you in my dreams!

Dear, it's now 7:30 a.m. I just got up for Mass. I promised Jody I'd go with her to Harlem and I have to leave in a few minutes. I have so much to write to you about. All day yesterday, at a legal conference my stream of consciousness was intercepted with reactions to your lovingly honest letter. I didn't get the letter until Friday. I forgot all my keys on Thursday and couldn't get into my apartment or office (until others came to work) so the rhythm of our correspondence was thrown off a day.

Tuesday 7 a.m.

Darling, I began this letter to you three days ago. Since beginning this, I've already sent you another letter with the airline ticket. I was going to begin all over again, but decided to send my scrawl of Sunday. We are going to be on the phone tomorrow, and perhaps much of what I write now will be vocalized then.

Francha my love, my reaction to your letter was mixed. I felt an emotional thump, a kind of emptiness, as I read in the sixth line that you were shying away from the big step. I was looking for definite commitment from you. Yet your love did shine through the letter and this gave me joy and great feelings of affection toward you. I reflected: you stood by me in my anguished moments. Now I had the chance to stand by you in your doubts and questions. And this I do my darling, with happiness and love.

Dearest, I have a great many questions too. Until we have a chance to talk, frankly, I don't know what to do about the timetable. It just takes so darn long if you go through channels. And then to petition for laicization nauseates me because I don't think there is any such thing as being "reduced" to the lay state. I'll always be a priest whether I'm "laicized" or not. And sweetie, I don't worry about my conservative upbringing boomeranging... I feel liberated from so much of it; I'm too old to change back again! I know I can't. I wonder, is it really reverting back that people do, or is it that they find it more difficult to respond as they get older, they don't change as fast as they used to? But I know what you mean by expressing worries about the boomerang. You have to admit, darling, that you're making a valiant effort to live within institutional religious life right now, and this kind of effort brings back a lot of the old rigidities and guilts. Sure they don't want you to leave. And I don't want you to leave me either. We all love you honey, and you have to make a choice.

Now I make my final point, perhaps my strongest. You ask: "What is 'God's will' for me?" You ask it as if it were emblazoned on some great heavenly arch, an arch that each of us has, that it's something that God has for us and that we must discover. No, I'm overstating the case, but I do feel strongly about this. I don't believe that "God's will for me" is something I discover. It's something I do! It's the choice I make. It's the honest responsible decision – that's God's will.

As I reread this letter, I'm not very happy with it. I'm too argumentative – not sensitive enough to your feelings, to the effort you made to be honest with me – not wanting to hurt but not ready to leap – and loving through and through. Well, I love you for it, darling. Incidentally, Toby told me that Eugene Bianchi "remarried" in the Church with everything canonical. So there is something to doing it by the book.

If I don't get going I'll be late for work. Big meeting of public services today. My first lengthy report and set of proposals in education. Hey, I'll send you a copy!

Rosemary, my Francha, I love you.

Charlie

WINONA TO BROOKLYN

Nov. 26, 1969
CST

Darling,

Your return address is not the same as the one you originally sent me. But you have received my letters (?), so I continue to address to 195 Underhill Rd, but will include a return address this time. Please confirm one address or the other??

I told my "Sister companion" to NYC, Sister Assisi, that I would be met by "a friend of the bride." How's that?

Thank you so very much for the airplane ticket and the multitudinous arrangements. I'm spoiled by you, dear. I am getting so excited and impatient for Dec. 19 to come.

And I FORGOT to thank you for the CLEVER anniversary card! I chuckled for five minutes, yes-siree!

Thanksgiving Day

Happy cleaning, dear!

Sister Marya came after supper last night for 4 hours, and we talked and talked. She is definitely leaving the congregation in June. Wants a sabbatical from teaching: thinks she will wait on tables a while.

I'll mail this and join in the festivities here.

I love you.
Rosemary

BROOKLYN TO WINONA

Thanksgiving [1969

Dearest,

I slept late today – 9 a.m. Now I am rarin' to go to start cleaning up this place. But before I do, on this Thanksgiving, I want to express my thanks to you for you. I'm thankful to the Lord too. My existence is a given, my capacity to love is a given (that I must develop), my relationship with you was a happening, a gift, that I am so thankful for. I'm thankful for my job, for the progress I am making in it, for my apartment, for my independence and freedom, for all that friends do for me, for my parents, brothers and sister.... It's endless, darling. So much to be grateful for.

In accordance with Mother's suggestion I called her last night (Dad's club night; she's there alone). She wants me to confide in her about you. For some reason I can't confide completely, but I appreciate her interest. (I'd rather do it naturally, without being pumped.) She sends you her love. She also said that she wished that both of us (you and I) could come home for Christmas. We realized that it couldn't be this year. But I appreciated the wish.

Nancy and Warren were grand hosts as usual. I brought some wine. Nancy cooked a delicious spaghetti supper. But darling, one thing I regretted, after supper, Warren and I talked (serious talk) and Nancy was puttering around in the kitchen with a pie. I wanted her to be with us, joining in. Finally after about forty-five minutes she joined us. It was so much better then. I didn't want it to be just man talk. That seemed old fashioned to me – like the men retiring for cigars and brandy. When she joined us the conversation picked up immediately and this was as it should be.

Another thought or two. On our way to Washington, I was talking about my new experiences. I told George H that I was surprised at myself, because when I was <u>alone</u> in the office and couldn't get an outside line, or dropped an important paper on the floor, or did something annoying, I found myself swearing <u>out loud</u>. George was amused. He remarked, "Good, then maybe soon you'll be swearing <u>at somebody</u> instead of just to yourself!" I enjoyed that insight.

Another thought. Last Saturday at the lawyers' meeting on the new N.Y. law school, as I participated in the discussion, I felt good. The thought flashed through my mind, Why do we have to be committed so rigidly to the institution [i.e., of the Church]? *The vows lock us in. I worked as a lawyer two years before the Paulists, and then left the law for 15 years, to concentrate totally on the institution and the people as they relate to it. Now I'm back in law with a more tenuous relationship to the institution. What's wrong about this? Why not have a freedom to be more or less related to the institution? I might have the job in Bed-Stuy for five years and then go back to a campus as a chaplain! The Church should make it possible for us to have this kind of freedom. It's the only way I can relate to the Church from here on in.*

I really felt for you yesterday when you said you tried to write down what you believed in. I've done it mentally. I talked to Fr. Ben Hunt [a revered seminary professor] *about it. I said I believed in something bigger than myself, a beautiful mystery I labeled with a three-letter word: God. That I believed in the ultimate meaning of life; that I believed in the dignity of my fellow man; that I hoped for the triumph of good over evil; that I believed that man must be authentic and affirm his identity and that no one did this more than Jesus and this was why I am a follower of Jesus and a Christian. There are no higher ideals*

that I know how to live by. Ben felt I was leaving out too much.
He asked me if I believed in Jesus. I was taken aback and halted.
He said the Apostles did. This is what makes Christianity unique.
And he seemed to say that believing in Jesus was a decision to
love – just as I choose to love you, dear,

Always
Charlie

— and what do you think?

WINONA TO BROOKLYN

Nov. 29, 1969

Darling,

        Your "argumentative" letter came yesterday, and it, too,
was honest. I agree with all of your observations, dear, pretty
much. In fact, you misunderstood my "What is 'God's will' for
me" statement. I put "God's will" in quotes just to emphasize
that I don't mean the traditional concept. I mean, I guess: one
must make a decision, and every decision implies a rejection;
one road may be better for me, and I just have to be discerning
enough to determine which road it is. I will eventually have to
"make the leap," as you put it. I will try to do just that over
Christmas vacation. You see, darling, we must make the leap
together, and I think we had better be together and thrash the
whole thing out, and DECIDE, and COMMIT ourselves one way
or the other. The metaphor is maybe like this: my road has led to
a dead end unless I am ready to leap over the chasm into the
brush on the other side; I can't see where that road will take me,
and that's scaring me. But I know in my heart, Charlie, that I
will leap. I can only find the hidden road after I get on the other
side.

        Do you want to hear my creed? It's very simple, because
I have to stop when I get to the contradictions.

        I believe in God.

        I believe that God is in some way a First Cause;
therefore He is my Father; therefore I am a part of God in some
sense, to be more fully realized as I realize my potential.

        I believe from the evidence of myself who am a part of
God that He is a personal, conscious reality, whatever else He
may also be. (Therefore, if one wishes, one can talk to him, i.e.,

pray, and assume that He hears. One cannot assume, however, that He must answer.)

I believe that God is measureless, beyond all human understanding; therefore in His infinite perspective my efforts in themselves are but a "squeak in the universe." (Sister Belinda's phrase.)

I believe that it is in my nature to desire a more complete union with God; to achieve this union I must develop my potentialities as I have received them. I must do this in the context of the Godness around me, and understand that others, as a part of God, have the same obligation. Therefore in reverence and respect we cooperate in the realization of all our potentialities. When I sincerely work at this, I am most healthy and happy and WHOLE.

I believe that: the development of potentialities is a slow and gradual process; in our evolutionary stage our intellect and will are weak and need guidance; God the conscious First Cause provides part of this guidance through exemplary fellow humans who are specially guided by Him to teach us; the one teacher who speaks most to my own potentialities is Jesus.

The contradictions come when I try to sort out the problem of a life after death.

Is God only Goodness?

Can the soul be separated from the body?

Can <u>consciousness</u> continue to exist?

Is all this important??

Chas, I enclose the communal penance service (which lasted 1½ hours, God bless us!) of yesterday. I don't believe one should recite one's sins for the sake of reciting one's sins. I don't know what I believe, but I did not "go to confession." Maybe I will confess to <u>you</u> again, Darling. [I refer to a semiformal confession made to Charlie a few days before we left Texas, when we were enjoying our quiet time together while watching the first moonwalk. Our year of separation was looming.]

I love you.
Rosemary

BROOKLYN TO WINONA
Sunday Nov 30 [1969]

Dearest,

I really miss you. When we talked on Wednesday you referred to a letter of yours that you thought I might have received. Well dear, something's wrong because I haven't got it. In fact the last letter I have from you is the one postmarked Nov. 18. Are the postmen reluctant to serve this neighborhood? This is one fact you learn about poverty sections. All the services break down. The don't-give-a-damn attitude pervades.

Yesterday I had a second lock put on my apartment door and folding gates on my windows. I'm somewhat embarrassed about taking that much care of our security, but there are so many robberies. The former tenant in my 1½ had an electric burglar alarm. Duke was invaded on East 4th Street. (When Duke telephoned the police and reported that a man was on the fire escape, trying to make entry, the officer said, "What's your address?" And when Duke replied East 4th St, all he heard on the end of the line was "Oh crap!" The police didn't think that address was worth the effort. One of the fellows who works with me was robbed last week. Now he has window gates. It's too bad, darling, that our cities seem to be turning into battle zones with certain fortified areas (the homes of the rich) and only certain streets safe corridors of travel. Dearest, this is not Sunday morning conversation. I'll be leaving for Church as soon as I finish this.

How was your retreat? Have you sorted things out more? I'm trying to think, too. The NYTimes carried a column on Bernard Cooke's resignation, which I enclose, and which expresses many of the things we have been considering. [Cooke was advocating priestly ordination for married men and women. He left the priesthood in 1969 and would marry the next year, remaining an active lay theologian and teacher.]

Oh dear, I can't wait to see you. As I see it we have to try to decide about our life together. Can we make that commitment together at this time? Then once that decision is made, the timetable. With some reservations, I agree that our first effort should be to work within the system. But note how

long it takes the Church to grind out its bureaucratic decisions!
Fr Cooke has to wait a year. Dan and Toby are still waiting.
    I saw them both briefly last night. We went over the
ceremony together. They have written some very beautiful things.
I'm skittish about my role in their wedding, but they need me and
are happy and relieved that I have committed myself. We are
going to be very busy preparing for the wedding. There is a
dinner at Toby's on the evening of the 19th. Then we have to be
at the rehearsal at noon on Saturday and the wedding takes
place at 3 p.m. Then we're free to <u>*decide what we want to do*</u>
that evening and from then on. Darling I look forward so to
seeing you.
    Last evening I spent three hours with Lily and Chuck,
old New York friends. They bombarded me with gifts. I have 24
pieces of china, a beautiful green and yellow pattern. Then Lily
noted that my shirt had buttons missing. She sewed on two. Then
Chuck brought out four shirts he never wears. Seriously, I didn't
want them to give me all this. I'm independent and can afford
these things. But when I described my adventures in trying to buy
an overcoat, I left with a coat and a scarf. They are too much.
They love me. I couldn't refuse. I love them. But dear, I'm <u>*IN*</u>
<u>*LOVE*</u> *with you.*

Devotedly,
Charlie

BROOKLYN TO WINONA
Chez Palms →   165 Underhill <u>*Ave.*</u>
              Apt 6E
              Brooklyn, N.Y. 11238

Monday 12:15 a.m. [12/1/1969]

Francha, my Rosemary,
    Now I know where the mail trouble is. I'll call the post
office tomorrow to see if they have any of your letters. It seems
silly that <u>*Rd*</u> *or* <u>*Ave*</u> *can make the difference.*
    I just returned from a school board meeting that began
quite simply as a routine affair, but before the evening was over
it turned into a Black Power rally. I shudder at the overtones of

*violence, but I rejoice at the demand for community control,
because it means community responsibility.*

*You know darling, I cleaned, but it did not become
clean. I had to reconcile myself to imperfection. I spent at least
two hours scrubbing the bathroom. I still have to do the floor,
the rug and the stove. I think I need a new rug. We can decide.*

*Well, now I must go to bed. Big day tomorrow. The
words "I love you" meant so much to me in your letter.*

Love always,
Charlie

WINONA TO BROOKLYN

This letter was returned to Winona and enclosed in the
12/6/69 letter below.

12/2/69

Darling,

*Your letter today tells me that you have heard nothing by
the mails from me since Nov. 18. Was that to Duke's address
still? I am concerned that I have somehow got the wrong address
for your apartment, and now I fear either (1) my letters are lost
forever at 195 Underhill; or (2) they will all come back in a
telltale pile in my P.O. Box 106 – if I put a return address on all
of them. I don't know which would be worse, but I do know I
wrote some heartfelt letters the last 2 weeks. I won't immediately
repeat everything, because I'll send them if they return. (Would
it help to see what's at 195 Underhill? You see how naïve I
am....) But I will repeat one thing immediately: I LOVE YOU.
That has been a consistent theme.*

*My private retreat was a hard experience. It meant time
to think and time to face up. I know I can't go on like this in
partial commitment. I wrote that to you, too. Christmas vacation,
with you, will be a time for decision, a time for total commitment
one way or the other. But it has to be a decision made with you.*

*I also wrote you my creed, and was almost amused
yesterday to receive yours: practically identical concepts, dear –
different words but the same basic ideas.*

I fear for you when you write of robberies and locked doors. I cry for what man has done to man. I grew up in a house that was never locked, even when we went on vacation. That seems almost unbelievable. And it is still that way. My cousin laughs to remember the night he decided to stay with my folks overnight. It was late so he crept into the house quietly without turning on lights, and crawled into bed. The next morning he woke to find a deserted house: my folks had moved back to the home farm!

I love to hear your reactions to things, like Nancy the old-fashioned wife puttering in the kitchen. You write such beautiful letters, dear. And so often. You put me to shame.

Your report from Bed-Stuy was ever so impressive. And massive! I wonder that you don't get more discouraged. Do you still feel that such organizations as Bed-Stuy in the long run do more harm than good by supporting the existing power structure? Maintaining the <u>status quo</u>? I was reading from <u>Main Currents in American Thought</u> by Vernon Louis Parrington tonight, and his concluding remark (in an intro.) reminded me of one of yours: "Education begins to fail – except education to individualize and to summon forth the potential intelligence of the younger generation."

I have spent many beautiful hours with Lalonde lately. She is so very BEAUTIFUL. Questioning. Supportive. Understanding. Loving. She asks me good probing questions and makes me think more carefully and deeply. My answers sometimes disturb her: she doesn't, for example, believe that a vow is a "squeak in the universe." She believes in the hierarchical Church and in Jesus as God. Etc.

On Thursday via phone, I will try to catch you up on dangling issues in our broken correspondence. That must be painful for you – if you look for my letters as eagerly as I look for yours.

I <u>so</u> look forward to Dec. 19. It sounds as if Toby will keep us busy till the evening of Dec. 20.

Have I told you lately that I LOVE YOU?

Happy Advent. Happy waiting.

Francha

WINONA TO BROOKLYN

The following was written on a homemade Christmas card, reading "GOD WITH US" on the outside, and excerpts of Ps. 26 inside: "This I believe:/ I shall see/ the Lord's goodness/ in the land of the living. / Hope in Him. / Hold firm/ and take heart. / HOPE IN THE LORD."

12-6-69

Dear Chas,

This is my Christmas card this year – by making my own I can at least be sure it conveys what I feel this Christmas. I am trying to say that Jesus, whatever else he is, is a promise, a reason to hope, a reason still to believe in the dignity of man and in his progress.

I enclose the ballet program – very amateur but including the little kids who take ballet here. It was enjoyable and began to get me in the Christmas spirit.

Georgia wants ideas for her wedding ceremony. She knows what she doesn't want but doesn't know what she wants. Any suggestions?

I scrubbed my room today and thought of you.... I think of you often; do you know that?

Your address remains a mystery to me. On the phone you swear it's 195. On the letter you write 165. I double-checked, dear. So I'll take your oral word for it.

I love you.
Rosemary

BROOKLYN TO WINONA

195 Underhill Ave. Apt 6
Brooklyn 11238
Friday Dec. 5 [1969]

Francha, my Rosemary

When I returned last night, your beautiful letter of Nov 29 was tucked snugly in my mailbox. I awoke at 5:40 this morning, and couldn't rest any longer until I had reread it.

I did misunderstand "God's will," but in a way I'm glad I did. It drew forth such a sound response from you. And I was able to air my hostility to the traditional concept. I just caught myself drawing a deep breath, as I am about to put down "we must make the leap together." To try your metaphor, I think I've taken the leap, I'm in the air, I haven't landed yet and don't know what's on the other side, but I'm experiencing the thrill of being in the air, free, and I'm reaching for your hand to pull you along with me.... and Sweetie, in my heart I realize how much our relationship has been a reaching and a touching of each other that has already brought us a long distance together. Come, fly to New York, Darling!

Your creed, my sweet, is profound. You do me credit when you liken mine to yours. It livened my faith to read of your faith. Yet I do agree, there is a fundamental identity of approach. You have expressed it much better than I. One question I have, which has plagued believers for centuries: What does "guidance" mean, and what does it mean to be "guided" by God? I agree, the one teacher who speaks most to my own potentialities is Jesus. At this point, "guidance" to me means self awareness of the best that's in me and the courage to live it out. Others become my teachers when I see them living out the best in themselves (Martin Luther King). You are going to deny it darling, but one of the most beautiful and attractive qualities you have is this courage. And you wouldn't be at St. Teresa's now if you didn't have it.

Is God only Goodness? Goodness is an abstract idea. This "greater than I" must be more than an abstract idea. I can create abstract ideas. Where does goodness come from? It's a greater mystery than evil, because without it evil has no meaning.

Can the soul be separated from the body? We are separated from each other. Our bodies do not touch. We communicate in spirit. We long to touch. Spirit and flesh can be separated but they were not meant to be so. The Greeks have really fouled us up with the ideal that nobility resides in the spirit which strives to escape the fleshy prison.

Can consciousness continue to exist? Darling, you just keep wondering.

Is all this important?? It is to me, to you.

And now dear, I'm eating a little breakfast. I have Danish coffee ring and some instant coffee. I'm not going to get

any other supplies until you come. Yesterday I bought my
"silver" – for 70 cents at the St Vincent de Paul thrift shop – two
knives, two forks, two tablespoons and two teaspoons! I would
like to get a set of stainless steel flatware. We can talk about this.
My dishes are beautiful, as I wrote the other day.

    Had a fetching note from Ed yesterday. [He suggested]
ways for us all to spend time together in Austin.] *I guess the*
easiest and clearest thing is to enclose it. I'm all in favor of the
fireplace, provided we can get to the Church [for Georgia's
wedding] *on time. Why don't you communicate your response to*
Eileen? I'll write Ed of my enthusiasm and they can decide
where to be with us on the 26th! (Georgia knows we are flying
down together!)

    And now I'll get this off to you. Even before I started
writing this morning I read Isaiah 49, following, or rather, being
with you in the office. I'll leave you with the last lines of the
hymn in the communal Penance Service. It's how I feel, early
this Friday morning. "You fill the night with your quiet and your
deep love."

                                   ♫ *Charlie* ♫

WINONA TO BROOKLYN

                                     12/9/69

Dearest Charlie,
    I like the extension of the metaphor. I like your
confidence in me. I hope to live up to your confidence as we <u>leap</u>
together.

    Sunday I bought some nice warm long snow boots, and I
feel a little <u>mod</u>*. And* <u>nobody</u> *has made any snide remarks!*
Tonight after supper 2 other young sisters and I went playing in
the glittering snow that has been falling for four days. With my
new boots I felt snug and <u>smug</u>*.*

    "Can consciousness continue to exist? Darling, you just
keep wondering." Did you intend a pun, or is that what your
grandmother meant all along? At any rate, with the double
meaning it's the perfect answer to my query. And you have said
that your grandmother's beautiful spirit still lives for you. You
felt it especially when you reread her letters.

*Georgia wrote, asking for ideas for her wedding liturgy.
She said she had asked you for ideas, too. Today I sent off 3
beautiful songs: Psalm 127 – "The Olive Branches" – and 2
about love by Tom Parker. I suggested she ask Ron S to come,
and Barb. I also sent a few other suggestions for the liturgy, to
bring in her two young sons, etc. I imagine you have lots more
ideas. I hope I remember to ask you when you call.*

*Ed's fireplace idea sounds ideal. But won't you have
practice or some kind of rehearsal to go to? I'll write to Eileen
tonight.*

*Did you get the letter in which I told you that at the
airport you must be a "friend of the bride's"? In fact, I'll hardly
remember your last name, so don't talk about anything but the
weather, the plane ride, and the awful traffic in New York! Sister
Assisi just told me tonight that her sister may not be able to meet
her at 1:47 p.m., so she may go by herself or may just wait at the
terminal. I did NOT offer to take her anyplace. She lived a year
in NYC, so I won't worry about her. (And I don't know you well
enough to ask you to go out of your way!)*

*My letter, I think, conveys my rising excitement, rising
spirits. It won't be long, darling! Love, Rosemary*

BROOKLYN TO WINONA

December 9 [1969]

Dearest,

*I hope we have our communication problems solved. The
mail here is pretty bad. At Thanksgiving I sent a $50.00 check to
my Father to cover my telephone expense. The letter also
included sentiments of love and prayer. Last night I called
Mother and Dad. Toward the end of the conversation it became
apparent that they hadn't heard from me at Thanksgiving – for
the first time in our lives! Mother shed tears! Then it all became
clear. The mails had failed! I stopped payment for the original
check and sent another tonight. They were so thankful that I had
thought of them and expressed my love – and prayer – even tho
the original letter never arrived.*

*I meditate in the mornings before going to work. Today,
it seemed clear that in spite of Bill M's and Toby's
antinomianism, I think it important to go thru channels. But*

*dear, it takes so long. As I've indicated in our telephone
conversations, I'm fighting to have a Puerto Rican secretary,
because I made a commitment to her. I asked myself this
morning, why is my commitment to her so sacred and my
commitment to the community one that I am ready to avoid? I
felt that my commitment to the Church and community is not
irrevocable and the way to acquit oneself is through the proper
channels. But if ∔ we decide that the procedure is unjust, then I
would feel justified in acting extra-legally. This is one of the
things we must talk over. With Toby and Dan, I feel I am
witnessing to their decision. I don't want to make an issue of my
role in their marriage.*

*Darling, I need you, this apartment needs you. And you
know, our time together is going to be so short! I have found,
darling, that changing environment does not change problems. I
need to communicate with you. I need your honesty and
confidence. At times, my act of faith is in the mystery of God
within.*

*The other night I stopped to help a helpless man in the
subway. I talked a little with him. He was 31. He asked me thru
his glassy eyes, if I wanted to kill him. I said "No" – that I
wanted to help him. Then he said, "Take me to your home!"
Sweetie, I was late for an appointment, and I couldn't do it. That
is, I didn't have enough expansiveness. But his plea has haunted
me. All I did was help him relieve himself in a drain in the
subway station. Ye gods, what a life!*

*Darling, I love you and need you. I can't wait to see you.
Please, we need time to relax and talk. Despite the exciting
attractions of New York, don't let me compulsively take you
places. I want to take you into myself!*

Affectionately and devotedly
Chas

WINONA TO BROOKLYN

12-11-69

Dearie,

This enclosed letter [my 12/2/69 letter included above]
*came back today, so I opened it to see what it said! It's a good
letter, so I'll send it on to you.*

I have a final to make out today yet, and a final lecture-review. So this will be just a note.

There is a concert tonight (Thursday) at 8:00, and I have invited my brother [Michael, attending Winona State College], *so I don't see how I can be here for your call. I will try later to get your new telephone number – but it's a long shot. Otherwise I will just have to leave word to try at 11:00 p.m., or miss you. Unless you leave your number. SORRY.*

In just a week I will be on my way to see you!! Hurray! I love you.

Francha

BROOKLYN TO WINONA

December 13, 1969

Dearest Francha, my Rosemary

I got up early this morning to read "our office." In Paul's second letter to the Thessalonians, assigned for today, there is a beautiful passage which echoes the prayer in your Christmas card. "May our Lord Jesus Christ himself, and God our Father who has given us his love and, through his grace, such inexhaustible comfort and such sure <u>hope</u>, comfort you and strengthen you in everything good that you do or say" (2 Thess. 2, 16-17).

In addition to the Bible, I have been reading Martin Luther King's sermons. One theme that comes through again and again, like the dominant melodic strain in a symphony, is love. MLK writes: "Love is mankind's most potent weapon for personal and social transformation." And again, "Love is the most durable power in the world. This creative force, so beautifully exemplified in the life of our Christ, is the most potent instrument available in mankind's quest for peace and security."

As I think of Christmas I am filled with love. As I think of our Christmas together, my heart wells up with love. I will be sharing all that I have and am with you and you with me.

And I am abounding in hope, because in loving you, my dear, I have seen "the Lord's goodness in the land of the living." Welcome, and peace.

Your devoted, Chas

WINONA TO BROOKLYN

This letter is written on the back of a *Messiah* program.

12-14-69

Dear Charlie,

I'm getting more and more excited! I can't seem <u>too</u>
happy about <u>leaving</u> here for Christmas, but I REALLY AM – not
so much about leaving here as going to where YOU ARE.

Finals begin tomorrow, and I have just about everything
I can do done before I give them, so that I can get the grades in
on time – i.e., before I board that train. All is going on schedule.

My folks are coming to pick up brother Mike on
Wednesday afternoon, so I'll see them then and send a couple of
presents home. I planned to go home last Sunday and got snowed
in. So I never made it home.

Kathy wrote, wishing us both a happy holiday together.
She says her neighbors, seeing the McKays' daisy mailbox,
painted theirs a shocking pink! They will drive up Christmas Day
to Minnesota, and back again the next Tuesday. So I will miss
them. Well, one can't have everything!

Today I heard the MESSIAH program and attended the
Christmas faculty-student banquet and dorm Christmas Open
House. All was fun. Now I am relaxing by the record player in a
parlor all alone, trying to finish up Christmas cards before the
onslaught of Final Exams tomorrow.

Darling, my next communication will be in person!

My love, always –

Rosemary

BROOKLYN TO WINONA
Sunday evening [12/14/1969]

Hi darling,

I have a telephone, but I'm not getting any dial tone, and
I don't get any ring, and when I pick up the phone I sometimes
talk with the person using the pay phone a few blocks away.
Everything is such a battle in New York. That's why I worry
about meeting you and insist that you go to the American
Airlines ticket desk if, for some failure in services, I don't get to

your gate on time. As I recall, the building you will arrive at is totally devoted to American. Be sure to call when you get to Chicago to make sure your ticket is OK. In fact it would be good to contact AA from Winona just to double check. I don't think you'll have to call long distance.

I forgot to give you my telephone number, but I can't be sure, because I've never heard it ring. So take this provisionally. [He provided a seven-digit number, which proved to be correct.]

I'm very excited about seeing you, dear. I'm going to hate faking indifference when you arrive. I want to kiss you. But you have to blame your own generous heart for my restraint.

When I wrote "you just keep wondering," this is what my Grandmother meant all along. I always felt she was so sure, and that quote made me realize she had been, like us, a wonderer.

What I may say to Sister Assisi is that I have to wait to meet another plane. Then we will wait for another plane to arrive, so that Sister Assisi can sail on her merry way. How does that sound?!

I'm so anxious to see you darling. I hope we have enough time to relax and take it easy. I don't want to make this a sightseeing tour. It's <u>insight</u> *and enjoying each other. Yet I want to show you so much. You love to see things and experience things so much.*

Blessings, dear, and love – always
Charlie

BROOKLYN TO WINONA
Monday letter No. 2 [12/15/1969]

Darling,

Your arrival is heralded by an avalanche of letters, and beautiful ones too.

Your personality is like your unlocked home, open and trusting and generous.

I enclose a leaf from my tree, planted in Brooklyn.

I look forward to greeting you and being with you.

Love always,
Charlie

Charlie and I were united in New York on December 19. We went to dinner at Toby's, a kind of rehearsal dinner; and we traveled to Tarrytown for her wedding the next day. I stayed a few nights with my loyal friends Nancy and Warren, but spent Christmas with Charlie.

 This note accompanies Charlie's gift to me – a platinum Tiffany "engagement" ring. He had hidden the ring from potential burglars by burying it deep inside his refrigerator.

Christmas 1969

My dearest
My gift to you is simple, yet beautiful.
It may not be something you can use right away
          but I'm sure that some day soon you will;
          and even though it's not very practical now
          you can treasure it always.
I give it as a symbol and pledge of my love
          only you, only both of us together,
          can give it its full meaning
                    Much of that meaning has been given already
                    but there is so much more....
And isn't it exciting, the way we've begun!
I love you Francha, my Rosemary
          Always,
          Charlie

The ring, as an engagement ring, represented our private but firm commitment to each other. From this point on we would separately seek our leaves of absence and dispensations from our religious vows and move toward our marriage.

After several wonderful days together, in New York City and in Austin, Charlie returned to Brooklyn alone while I stayed on in Texas for another ten days.

BROOKLYN TO AUSTIN

December 30 [1969]

Dearest,

I hesitate to write because all that is in my consciousness is the overwhelming loneliness and all I seem able to say is how much I miss you. That seems so self-centered, doesn't it? My preoccupation is feeling sorry for myself. So much for my raw humanity.

But when I returned to the apartment the light was still on, the dishes still in the sink – two cups, two glasses, two plates. The curtains and bedspreads, rather than pleasing, were painful. They reminded me too much of you. I'm sitting in the chair that you sat in to sew! This apartment is so empty without you.

I'd give anything to know what you and Ed talked about last night. I'm glad we spoke together. I'm embarrassed that my drinking was so noticeable. It's one of the hazards of living alone. "It is not good for man to be alone" is so meaningful to me now. In these weeks of solitary existence I am coming face to face with myself in a new way.

Today I'm taking the ring back to Tiffany's to exchange it for a size 5. I'll keep it for you. It occurred to me that if you wanted to wear it I could have it put on the golden chain, and you could have it close to your heart. Two circles, expressing infinity, inseparably entwined, symbolizing our love. I'm afraid, though, that the chain is too light to bear the weight of the ring.

I love you my dear. These past few days were so WON-DER-FUL!

Call me soon. I need to hear your voice.

Today I'm launching a new investigation into the mental health facilities, or rather lack of them, in Bed-Stuy.

Devotedly,
Charlie

BROOKLYN TO AUSTIN

December 30 [1969]

Dearest,

Just hung up the telephone, re-arranged the photos in our album so that you are pointing toward me (in a blanket). I'm enclosing a check for $50, which I hope carries you safely back

*to Minnesota. But if there is any trouble, please don't hesitate to
ask. What's mine is yours. It was just <u>wonderful</u> laughing with
you tonight. 1970-1980 will be our decade of development. I'll
be in touch with you darling. I love you with all my heart. Happy
new year.*

Devotedly,
Charlie

BROOKLYN TO AUSTIN

Saturday
January 3, 9 a.m. [1970]
Darling,
          Larry G [a University of Texas professor and friend]
*spent thirty-six exhilarating exhausting hours with me. He
arrived at 1:30 a.m. on January 2. We talked (he talked) until 3
a.m. Then we got up early the next morning and I took him to
work with me. We toured Bedford-Stuyvesant. His anger at the
conditions deeply moved me and helped me to <u>feel</u>. Then we went
out with a <u>Time-Life</u> editor friend of his last night and didn't get
back until 1 a.m., when again we talked until nearly 4 a.m. Larry
has the stamina of the Texas football team. He had my back
against the goal line, and except for twice during the evening
when I fell momentarily asleep, I stayed with him. I'm better in
the morning than he is.*
          *I hated to be out as late as we were last night because I
had hoped to hear from you, knowing you were with Dolores* [the
poet Jerry's friend] *and John and the children. I can especially
see you with little Emily and Laura. You are so beautiful with
children, darling. I hope that you'll call today.*
          *At nearly 3 a.m. this morning Larry and I got talking
about my loneliness. I said I was in love and was going to write
the Paulists. I didn't tell him "who." He didn't ask. I don't want
to speak openly until certain steps have been taken. Darling, I
love you with all my heart. The <u>Time</u> editor had a girl with him
who joined us for the evening. I couldn't take my mind and
imagination from <u>you</u>. She reminded me of you in her slim
beauty. I kept seeing you all evening.*
          *I poured my heart out to Larry about the frustrations of
my work. He was understanding/helpful. He feels that the*

seventies are going to be violent no matter what we do. That at the present time the poverty programs are merely a Band-aid on a cancer. What we need is a massive financial commitment (in the billions) and the country won't be ready to make that commitment until there has been tragedy. Then, he says, we will need to know how to spend that money that is given to heal the wounds. So my primary task at present is to learn from failures and be ready to use the forthcoming $ commitment where it's needed most. Larry has a rationale. It's pessimistic. I don't know how accurate it is. I do think he's right abut two points: the $ we need is massive. The thirteen million we have asked the Office of Economic Opportunity for is a drop in the bucket. Secondly, it takes something tragic to make this country move, e.g., the passage of an open housing law after MLK's death. Larry encouraged me by saying that I was sensitive and human and "non-bureaucratic" and was needed much more here than in Texas. He also made some good suggestions for our program. For example, he urged that we convert some of the unused storefronts in Bed-Stuy into residences and develop a "model landlord" program, treating tenants with the respect and dignity they deserve. Secondly, pointing out that the real power is the corporations, he suggested that we get young corporate executives to work with us with the hope that they will see the poverty and needs and commit their corporations to Bed-Stuy and open up job opportunities.

    I didn't see Joe or any of my Paulist classmates on New Year's. I had hoped to discuss with him the procedure I must follow in writing Father Fitz. My next step is to consult Joe who returns Monday to Queens College.

    Darling, I love you. I really feel your presence and love, even tho lonely to <u>see</u> you sitting in that empty chair opposite me. The curtains and bedspreads look great. I'll have to sew where those safety pins are, tho.

My love, love
Charlie

P.S. I'm not smoking!

AUSTIN TO BROOKLYN

This letter is written on the back of minutes of the
Catholic Student Center faculty-student advisory board.

Jan. 5 1970

Darling,

*I've been having a great time in Texas – so much so that
I hate to go back to Minnesota. I am more and more convinced,
dear, that my decision to leave is the right one. I act freer,
happier, more lively here (and in New York!) than I do in
Minnesota.*

I went to Midland [where Dolores lived] *via Greyhound,
and during a layover in Abilene walked around a few blocks. I
felt happy, and decided to experiment with smiling my happiness,
and "howdy-ing" the people I met. 100% of them responded
likewise. I got back on the bus glowing. But I couldn't help but
compare Texans with New Yorkers. Sorry about that.*

*I got back from a <u>very nice</u> stay in Midland at 6 a.m. Ed
and Eileen met me and then we all went back to bed (me on the
sofa ☺). Today I'm chatting with Georgia & others at the CSC.
Tonight dinner at Bonnie's; tomorrow I see* [dissertation advisor]
*Prof. Jones & dine with Elaine and Mary C; Wed. I drive to San
Antonio to see Naylor Publishing Co.* [about Jerry's poems] *and
then dine with Georgia and Ron; Thurs. I see an Austin printing
co. and eat with* [Paulists] *Ed, George L, <u>et al</u>. and go to the
ladies'* [ecumenical] *dialog group. Friday morn I fly home.
(Home?)*

[Jerry's artist friend] *Marilyn Todd came thru Midland
and we worked hard doing the book – figured out how many
pages and which poems and where* [Jerry's mother's]
*illustrations would go. All 3 of us (Marilyn, Dolores, I) are
excited. It should be a good book. Marilyn spoke so highly of you
I almost burst my buttons but managed not to confide in them.*

*Under separate cover I hope will arrive a cylinder of
goodies – a Corita poster Dolores gave me, and 5 India ink wash
drawings by Meg McCarty which I like and decided not to return
to her ☺. If you like them, I visualize all five of them framed in*

black and hung artistically on that huge blank wall above your bed.

I will call you late tonight – and often. I'm so glad you finally have a phone!

I love you, dear, and miss you terribly.

Love, Francha

Many of the next letters record our concrete actions to carry out our commitments made over Christmas. Charlie started his process of applying for a dispensation from his priestly vows, and I applied for a leave of absence and began looking for a teaching job somewhere near Charlie.

BROOKLYN TO WINONA

January 10, 1970

Dearest,

It's now 5 p.m. I've been in my office for 3½ hours. I want to reach out to you from my thoughts in this letter, then do some shopping before the stores close. I've been trying to break through a barrier, plotting my work so that it will be more productive. It seems that most of what I do is shuffle papers and gather information that I cannot use in a practical way. I studied the hospital problem for a couple of hours and suspect that there are many unanswered questions in the Catholic Medical Center's lustful eye on the Triboro Hospital now operated by Long Island Jewish. Maybe I can help CMC find their needed beds without having to wrest control over Triboro. I hope so. Another plan I have is to look for government programs where money is available and then devise a program for Bed-Stuy. This assbackwards attack was suggested by the consultant who shares my office with me. I'm going to come back tomorrow and begin that search.

George L spent the evening with me. I really enjoyed having him and cooking for him. He washed the dishes. We talked at great length. He seemed very grateful that I had taken the interest in him. He explained his job, and I told him that he understood what he was doing much more than he would admit to me. I explained my work and he acknow-ledged its

*frustrations. We both really enjoyed talking to you. Ed and
Eileen called later.*

*Your letter and the prints delighted me. I can just see
you walking down the streets of Abilene saying "hello." It makes
me feel so good when you tell me how much you love me and
miss me. I can feel your love, darling. It strengthens me and
gives me something to be thankful for, to live for and to work for.
I feel so close to you. One little incident of our visit that means
so much to me was your complete openness, as signified by the
incident that morning when I flushed the toilet and told you that
you had to hold the lever down a little longer. I can't tell you
how deeply that little exchange touched me and brought me
closer. Isn't that kind of crazy?*

*On the next page, I'm going to list the colleges in no
particular order, and I presume you write to the head of the
English Department. I'll use a separate sheet.*

*Yesterday I took the first step. I talked with a priest at
the Chancery for about a half hour (by phone) and will soon be
in to see him. I have a formal appointment for January 23 at 2
p.m., but I'm going to see him informally before that date. It's
not an easy thing to do, but it's the direction I've been moving
toward for two years. I know it's going to be hard for you too,
darling. Courage. Love.*

LOVE LOVE Charlie

P.S. How is Lalonde?

WINONA TO BROOKLYN

Enclosed is a recycled card: "When you left... [picture
of little girl with her pajama-bottom flap open] ...the bottom fell
out of everything! Miss you!"

Jan. 10 [1970]

Dearest Charlie,

*My mind just isn't on my work – it's on you! This is a
note to tell you so.*

*I know I showed you the enclosed card before, but it's
worth a re-run because it captures how I feel.*

*Sister Assisi was terribly disappointed not to get hold of
me in NY – she called the dorm number and asked for me, not*

Nancy and Warren. She left today for her new "mission" – I was glad to be here to send her off.

I slept 11 hours last night! I'm trying to get rid of my cold. At least the house is warm – everything is so drafty in Texas. I just missed the cold weather here – minus 60° wind chill!

Do you hear from Toby?

The picture enclosed is from Dolores to me and I contribute it to our photo album. Kinda small but kinda cute.

I just sent Warren and Nancy $10.00 to help cover a telephone call I made and the rent of the rollaway. Or for them to buy TV trays if they wish.

I bought $10.00 worth of groceries, rug shampoo, and gasoline while at Eileen's, and left her $10.00 more to pay for telephone calls (2 to the Naylor Co., one to Laredo). I ate there very little, since I was invited out for almost every lunch and dinner. (I enjoyed my popularity!) I also did some laundry for her.

And still I had enough money, although your extra $50.00 put me at ease. I'll save it for our next rendezvous ☺.

We get Feb. 20 off for some unknown reason. And a 10-day spring break which might be a good time for interviews in the East. (Holy Thursday through Easter Week.)

I'll call tomorrow. I want to call tonight, but it's an expensive addiction!!

Love – love — love,
Francha

BROOKLYN TO WINONA

Charlie enclosed three New York Times articles: "College Language Posts Hard to Find," 12/29/69; "Suddenly Ph.D.'s Are 'A Glut on the Market,' " 1/4/70; and "Columbia Accused of Bias on Women" – i.e., in hiring practices, 1/10/70.

January 12 [1970]

Rosemary, my Francha,

Darling, the next time we talk we'll have to have a good connection. It was so frustrating to strain for understanding. I couldn't enjoy the sound of your voice. It's easy to get another connection, darling, and believe me, it's worth it. I have to call the telephone company today to complain about my bill.

I'm enclosing the promised newspaper clippings in this letter. I don't want you to be discouraged by them. If I were you, I would write all of the colleges that I sent you. Many of the schools are not "plums," and I just suspect that qualified professors are hard to get. Then you have to be interviewed! It would seem you would need at least a week here for that. When should that be planned? Easter sounds reasonable. But I don't know if I can wait that long to see you. Will have to keep planning and talking about it.

At the moment I'm cooking breakfast and writing this over the sink. Water is dripping intermittently from the tap. A little roach creeps stealthily along the top of the sink panel near the stove. The egg water is simmering, about to bubble any moment. I just turned over the toast to the white side; one side a little too brown. I ate a beautiful golden brown pear this morning. I wish you were here beside me. That pear reminds me of your golden brown hair. Now the water is boiling. There was no hot water in the shower this morning so I was ascetic and took a cold shower, gasping as I felt the shock of cold.

My darling I love you. I look forward to Wednesday evening and a solid connection. We will continue to plan. I hope your first days of class went well.

Devotedly,
Charlie

WINONA TO BROOKLYN

CST, Jan. 13, 1970

Dearest Charlie,

The list of colleges came today, and thank you very much for all your research. I'll find out the procedure and begin writing letters as soon as I have time, probably sometime next week.

This weekend I'm going home to tell my folks about Christmas vacation, about the leave of absence, and about whatever else seems best at the time.

My spirits have been so high since I returned. I think I know what the difference is: I am committed once more to a person, and that person is you. I'm engaged to be married! This year I have been committed to a job, yes, but that is different from this. I am still committed to a job, but now I also know where I'm going. Wow! What a difference in me! One thing that surprises me about it all is that I no longer fear so much the disappointment I will cause to my sisters and my family. I think that is because I am so happy myself that I feel I can convince them that it is all for the best. I no longer feel close to tears when I think about the break.... as I did so often during the first semester.

Both our mother general and our college president have been gone since I returned. I shall see them as soon as it is feasible. Then we can be making the step together.

Lalonde is not well at all. Her doctors finally found the source of the trouble: her fifth vertebra (in the neck) is deteriorating. Yesterday she came home in a Peterson brace, which gives her painful traction all the time. Even when she tries to sleep. On top of everything else, her father, who has been dying of cancer slowly, has recently gone downhill fast. I will tell her you asked about her.

I fought the desire to call you tonight. Discipline!

My love, dear Chas –
Francha

BROOKLYN TO WINONA

Enclosed with this letter is an invitation in the form of a memo, inviting twelve people from Charlie's office to a Martin Luther King Day party at his apartment.

Martin Luther King's birthday
1970

My dearest,
I've just come back from the conference we talked about last night. The words that have been coming back to me again and again all day are yours of yesterday -- "I'm committed to

you." And I respond – "I'm committed to you." MLK's quotes are on my walls; yours are in my heart.

The conference today was about as frustrating as our *RWA* [a group of chaplains of religious student centers] *meetings of last year. Some of the key institutions of Brooklyn, schools, hospitals, businesses, wringing their hands: "How can we get together?" yet realizing none can give up its identity or autonomy. At least there is effort to form a kind of coordinating council to exchange information and ideas. One of the participants pointed out that though our institutions are located in a black community, no one of the community was present at the conference. It was lily white because the institutions are lily white.*

I learned one thing. In my public service area I should (1) pick a project that fulfills a need (2) that is easy to do fast (3) that will make a big splash – so as to keep our hopes up. Now I've got to rack my brain for that project.

Irma and Sherry who are doing the cooking for the party should have been here at 2 p.m. (I gave them my keys), but it's now 5 p.m. and no sign of them. I'm just hoping my party comes off. I know them well enough to be confident. Larry G, when he was here, said that he told the Vista workers that if they worked for three months and made one friend, they had made great strides. I think I've done that. One of the speakers today said, "It's not institutions we are blocked by; it's people. We get things done through people." I'll have to get to know more people in strategic places.

I am committed to you, Rosemary my Francha.

I think of your going home this weekend and how difficult it's going to be for you. We're alike in so many respects – one of which is our love for our families and friends. It's hard for us to do anything that hurts others. I also think we're both naïve and idealists, but I think you are more of a realist than I am. I can't prove it; it's visceral.

Irma just called. She'll be here in a little while.

I'm committed to you, darling. I'm leaving your picture out, but putting our photo album in my drawer with its new addition.

*You are fantastic with money. I'm too extravagant, I
know. Must be part of a need to be loved. How you did all you
did on the money you had – plus your thoughtfulness to Eileen
and Nancy and Warren – is something I need to learn.*

I love you with all my heart, Rosemary my Francha.

Devotedly,
Chas

WINONA TO BROOKLYN

1/15/70
Birthday of MLK

Dear Charlie

The news clippings arrived today [about the scarcity of
jobs in academia] *– thank you very much. They convinced me
that I had better write to <u>all</u> the addresses you sent me, and then
hope against hope for some sort of miracle!*

*When I call I will read you my letter of application, for
your suggestions. It sounds rather dull to me.*

*I write on the back of my "purple letter" for this week –
thought you might like to re-live some of my New York
experiences with me! I'll send the Christmas one along, too.*

I think I <u>can</u> use the 5x7 photo on the dresser of me [to
reproduce for inclusion with job applications, a customary
practice at the time]. *Can you part with it for a while? If you can,
you will save me quite a bit of money, if all works well. Will you
send it to me – pronto? (It will also save time and the muss-and-
fuss of getting one taken <u>sans</u> veil without raising all sorts of
questions.) Thanks, dear.*

*I heard from Toby today, too, reminding me that a year
ago she met me. Her parting words were: "Be good to Charlie.
You, too." I can barely read her writing, including the return
address. Send it to me sometime if you can read yours!*

*I keep thinking of your MLK Party and wishing I were
there.*

*I'm very happy, dear. Not even very scared about the
weekend and telling the folks. Actual grace?* [I refer to the
Church teaching that God provides the help one needs as it is
needed. I would be telling my parents that I was applying for a

leave of absence from the religious life.] *Or "fools rush in where angels fear to tread"?*

I love you! Rosemary

WINONA TO BROOKLYN

1/19/70

Dearest C –

Enclosed comes from <u>U.S. Catholic</u> [an article on a Minneapolis financial counseling center and bank] *which I'm not sure you receive at 195 Underhill, but I want to be sure you see the article. Sounds like a great idea, one that Bed-Stuy might consider, one that maybe all those lily-white institutions could underwrite?*

Thank you for your letter with the memorandum invitation. Clever! Sorry I couldn't attend!

It's 27 below zero here today. Everyone is ready for a January thaw. Flu is also prevalent. Sigh....

I love you so much, dear. I thought about you with longing for a long time before I slept Saturday night. (It probably kept me awake!) Were you thinking of me? I miss you so much.

I got a great letter from Larry K over the weekend. He and Margie are excited about me "leaping over the wall" and want to talk to me about it. I assume it's positive excitement. (?) At any rate, they invite me to Utah [where Larry as a conscientious objector was assigned to community service; he had married Margie in 1968].

---- Must run. Love you.
Rosemary

BROOKLYN TO WINONA

Monday January 19 1970

Dearest

I wish you were next to me now. I wish I could look into your eyes as I confide in you. I had a lot to drink yesterday, my dear. I was ridin' pretty high when you called. I took Fran [a visiting U of Texas student] *to Mass and to lunch and put her on the bus. Then I saw Jody (she flew to Israel today with her boss) and ended up with Jim G, a fellow I was in the seminary with who works as a bartender on York and 1st Ave. I had something to drink at all those stops. I was late getting back, too late.*

I spent about five hours in the office on Saturday trying to think of where I should concentrate my energies on the job. What could I do that would be productive? I gave birth to nothing. I had a kind of feeling of fright that I couldn't think of anything. At the same time I worry about myself. Too much. I should be spending my energies on the people of Bed-Stuy, not on the inner workings of C.P.

This morning I had to force myself to come to work. I left for work deliberately much earlier than usual. I wanted to face that desk again. I fought the temptation to give up. I plunged right in. I called Jody up to say goodbye. I talked to her about yesterday and about the job. Jody was concerned. She is aware of my problems of confidence. Being a first cousin, she shares some of the same family traits. She knows about me. I have no in-love-ness about Jody. She's just a damn good friend. I've told you much more about myself than I've ever told Jody. You have seen me in much more difficult straits than Jody has. I've been at my lowest with you, darling, and you have LOVED. You have no idea how much this draws me to you. And it's also one of the principal reasons I miss you. The other principal reason is: I miss holding you and loving you. At any rate, there are forces within me that I don't understand. I don't believe about me what you believe about me; what John Doar believes about me. I can bounce around the office with humor, and no one would expect the fragility that I carry within. I want to do something about it. I made an appointment with a psychiatrist for Thursday. He is Dr. Dotolo, a Catholic, and Lily's psychiatrist. I haven't told you all about Lily, but you know that we have been friends for years. I was upset at her when she encouraged her husband Chuck to write Toby about my part in the wedding. But now, that's over with. Lily told me when I first came to NYC this time, that if I ever wanted to see anyone, Dr. Doltolo would see me. I'll see him Thursday.

Why am I telling you all this? Because I love you. I risk making you worry about me, but I feel that our love and future together demands that I am honest with you as I always have tried to be. I'm telling you because I love you and want to share

*everything with you. Not just the good times, but the difficult
things too. And it's so hard to write about it. As I said at the
beginning of this letter, I wish you were right next to me.*

*The great thing about today was that within an hour and
a half I had my project planned – a study of the educational
needs of the young people of Bed-Stuy in relation to Brooklyn
Prep, a Brooklyn school that will be closing in three years
(Jesuit operated). As I look on this project now, it seems so
obvious. I should have thought of it days ago. I look forward to
coming in this office tomorrow, and rolling up my sleeves,
because I have something positive and worthwhile to do. The
next thing that was great about today, I had my weekly public
service staff meeting, with ten people in attendance, and the
meeting went off beautifully. It was productive. I announced my
school study. We talked about other possible projects for the
people of Bed-Stuy. It was great, that's all. But what a sweat.*

*Regardless of the greatness of today, I'm still going to
see Dr. Doltolo. If I can't crack those fears, at least I want to be
able to understand them so that I can live with them, so that you
can live with them. I just hate to show my fears to anyone. I play
the "solid" role so well.*

*Under separate cover I'm sending back your picture.
How I hated to take that off my bureau. I just love that shot of
you. And sweetie, I don't think you can get that color shot
reproduced. At least, I remember when I worked on the
magazine we could never reproduce a color photo in black and
white. Maybe that's just regarding publishing. If you need any
dough, I can pay the photographer.*

*Wednesday is our anniversary. It's also the anniversary
of Marie Louise of "You just keep wondering." She's part of our
lives. You know, at the MLK party, her words caused more
comment than the MLK quotes I had on the walls.*

*Darling. It's late. I'm still at the office. 11 p.m. I'm
going home now, loving you and missing you. I look forward to
your Wednesday call. I'll be going to Steve and Jean Smith's for
dinner tomorrow evening.*

*Devotedly,
Charlie*

BROOKLYN TO WINONA
F: I'm coming to you!
C: I'm waiting!

Wednesday Jan 21 [1970]
"our anniversary"

Dearest,

When we parted, electronically, this evening, I finished the <u>U.S. Catholic</u> article on the financial counseling center and bank. It was terrific, and I plan to circulate it in the office. We do have something akin to it – a mortgage pool. About 35 banks have contributed capital, so that people of the Bed-Stuy community can borrow money at a low rate of interest, refinancing debts that they are currently paying off at a higher rate of interest, or perhaps remodeling a home or even purchasing one. We are with Minneapolis in principle; perhaps we can learn something from their unique application of it!

It was just great talking to you tonite. I felt your "I'm coming" in my whole being, physically! You are good for me. I hope you get over that cold soon! I forgot to say we had 2" of snow here and the weather has been bitterly cold!

My private office line means you can reach me anytime (if I'm there) without going through the switchboard.

Did you see the courageous statement by the Dutch bishops? [The Dutch bishops informed their priests that the Vatican offered no hope that the requirement of priestly celibacy would be lifted any time soon, and the bishops were committed to obedience to the Pope.]

I LOVE YOU DARLING AND I'M WAITING......

Devotedly,
Chas

BROOKLYN TO WINONA

Enclosed in the following letter is a New York Times article, "Dutch Bishops Ask Celibacy Change," Associated Press, 1/20/1970; and the front page of the New York Times for 1/22/1970 with two side-by-side articles: on detention centers being over capacity and on the family as an all-important

essential to human survival. Charlie commented in the margin:
"What a juxtaposition!"

Thursday [1/22/1970]

Darling,

    *I just bought a chicken pie and some Danish vegetables.
They are thawing out on the stove. I'm home early. It's 6:50 p.m.
I miss you. I love you.*

    *I spoke to Dr. Doltolo today. He took my vital statistics.
He asked me some questions like: "How do you describe
yourself?" I answered, "A nice guy, but nice guys don't win
ballgames." We talked, I talked for an hour, spouting my
anxieties. I told him, "I know there's something good inside; I
want to find it." He said he would like to see me next week, and
weekly for a while. He said there must be a problem or I
wouldn't be in his office. He said it's like a jigsaw puzzle, and if
I can keep talking we'll be able to get out all the pieces and then
put it together and both of us see it.*

    *I went back to my office and spoke with John Doar for
almost an hour. I told him I was anxious to produce something (I
didn't say the anxiety had precipitated my visit to Doltolo). John
said, "Yes, we've got to get off paper and into action." He
criticized my approach to the school problem, told me to hold off
on the hospital problem, and got interested in a suggestion for a
center for alcoholics that I proposed. As our conference
concluded, he said, "You're doing a fine job." Inside me my
feeling was "bullshit!"*

    *Sweetie, I'm going to get at the root of this thing. As I
sat there with John, as strong and self-assured as he seems, I
felt, "You must have your hang-ups too, John." In fact when I
mentioned a visit to a competing corporation in NY (the Vera
Institute for Justice), John seemed a little defensive, explaining
that "they" had a much more professional staff.*

    *John asked me what I thought of a young lawyer who
works part time for me. "Does he have any sense?" I said I
thought he was intelligent and resourceful. John smiled and said,
"And the greatest of these is charity." John thinks the young
man is scatterbrained. He isn't perfect, but he is helpful to me
because he sees so many implications in things. I couldn't*

*criticize him to John. I felt a loyalty to him. I guess I wish I'd
been able to say to John – "That's an irrelevant question," or
"That's for you to decide; he's helpful to me."*

*Maybe these points don't seem so serious to you darling,
but my inability to be straightforward – i.e., risk his displeasure
– just breaks me up.*

How are you feeling? I have a mental picture of you
[putting in a phone call to Brooklyn] *wrapped up in three
blankets, huddled in a closet. I'd love to be cuddled next to you.
I'd love to catch cold from you. I've given you plenty of mine –
remember last year?*

I wanted to tell you I'd heard from Susan [a funny, wise
U of Texas student who worked in the St. Austin rectory], *so I
put this pad down and opened the beat-up package. It was hard
candies – the kind I loved to steal from Georgia's cubbyhole.
And in the package was the enclosed letter which is worth 100
times more to me than my $25 visit to the psychiatrist today. I
enclose it, because maybe it explains better than an M.D. can
what's happening to me. I'm much more hopeful. "I'm coming"
too, darling.* [In margin: *"P.S. Letter not included."*]

*I love you so Francha, my Rosemary, because you stand
by me. You love me – or you see me, my ups and downs – and
trust on, trust on…… God, how that makes feelings stir and
tears well up. I feel you give me so much more than I give you
(but there I go again, damn it!).*

*I noticed that Washington's birthday is on a Sunday. If
we get Monday off, do you think we could meet? What about
Chicago? Or Mary B's in the Twin Cities? it would be expensive,
but I just believe our seeing one another is something we can pay
for $$ in later life. I'd rather ride the edge of the expense line (?)
and live for my love of you. I'll check on our office policy
tomorrow and mention this on Sunday when you call.*

*Love you dear. You were beautiful on the phone last
night.*

Devotedly,
Chas

MORE

*And darling you were sweet to call tonite. You "came"
close to me. I just wish that when I take your advice in a few*

minutes and hop into bed, that I could hold you tonight. I long
for you close to me. Love you, love you,

Charlie

WINONA TO BROOKLYN

A little cartoon is glued to the top of this letter: Charlie
Brown is hanging upside down from a tree, with a kite doing the
same: "On certain days it is best not even to get out of bed."
Also enclosed is a note from Ed V, my Jesuit seminarian
friend, dated 1/18/70, quoted in part here:
You spoke of a 'break' from a community for Charlie.
What group is he with? Then you spoke of a leave of
absence for yourself. And then you spoke of laicization
for him. Is it possible for you both to continue some sort
of relationship with your communities? And even more
interestingly, is it possible for him to continue as a
priest, somewhat as Barney [i.e., Bernard] Cooke is
trying to do? I really think we need priests who ask to be
dispensed from celibacy, but also want to continue to
pray and practice as priests. This is the way to get a
married clergy. Barney sees his move as helping the
Church. Perhaps Charlie could gear his move the same
way.

1/23/70
Thank God It's Friday

Dearest Charlie,
        It's 10 o'clock and I'm trying to clean off my desk and
then my bed before jumping in! And I'm missing you, dear. (But
I'll try not to call!)
        The above cartoon was given me as a get-well-wish the
day I was down with the flu. Sister B was the thoughtful one.
        I sent the picture off to the mail-order house today.
Here's wishing it a safe journey. Thanks (again!) for the offer of
cash. I'll let you know, dear, if/what I need.
        Something unique and disgusting is happening in my
convent home: money is disappearing. The <u>*superior*</u> *was missing*
20 bucks today. And there have been 4 or 5 similar cases <u>*I*</u> *have*
heard about.

Judy (first cousin) and fiancé Hamdy (Muslim) came for supper tonight and met the lovely young sisters who will sing for their wedding Feb. 7. It was a fun thing to do on a Friday night.

My students, I fear, are getting a little frustrated with the "double motif" research paper. I hope I'm not being too ambitious. In desperation I offered to put the first chapter of my dissertation on reserve for them, and that appeased them, at least momentarily.

Good night, sweet love – Francha

WINONA TO BROOKLYN

I began this letter with two quotations from Carl Sandburg. The first is a comment on "creative solitude" – how productivity can arise from loneliness. The second is his poem beginning: "love is a deep and a dark and a lonely."

CST, Jan. 25, 1970
1/26/70

Darling,

I was (for some reason!) reminded of you as I prepared for a Sandburg class today. The above quotes are meant as encouragement.

I was nervous last night on the phone — I suppose you could sense it. I was squashed into the blanket closet (curses on our Alverna telephone system!) next to a bedroom (or several of them) at a late hour when all was quiet except me. Alas and alack....

I love you, dear.

Rosemary

P.S. Your yellow letter was in my mailbox when I came over this morning. You described your interviews with Dr. D and Doar. I can feel your frustration, dear, and long to be with you.

My free day is Friday, Feb. 20, so if you get Monday off, how does that help me??

When are you going to Detroit? Shouldn't you do that soon?

Have a good day—

R

BROOKLYN TO WINONA

Monday [1/26/1970]

Darling,

 I'm at work, on the phone. There are so many "hang ups" on this telephone system that I have a chance to jot a few lines.

 Wouldn't it be a good idea to include a sentence [in the job application letter] *describing your thesis? I would think your thesis topic would be of interest to a department head.*

 Now the working day is over. In a little while I'll be off to an old law school friend's home – Jack M. He and his wife Sally live on 86ᵗʰ St. Jack was on the Law Review at Harvard and has been working with one of the best law firms in New York for fifteen years. Jack and Pete T and Bill G and I used to go to daily Mass during Lent. All of us were members of the St Thomas More Society. The Catholics stuck together at Harvard.

 I filled out my insurance forms this afternoon. We get life insurance free – part of our fringe benefits. I named you as my beneficiary. Not that I want you to feel morbid; rather, loved. You are closest to me now.

 I studied the health problems of Bed-Stuy today and made an appointment to see about a center for alcoholics, a mental health facility and an ambulatory medical center. I've got to get off the paper and into action.

 The course at the art museum was enticing, but I decided I'd better stick to the courses at the New School and perhaps take advantage of the art course at another time. I think three courses and a job would be too much. I'm afraid I wouldn't enjoy it.

 Just called the airlines and made a tentative reservation for Chicago on the GW Birthday Weekend. It's $107.10 round trip. Minneapolis is $142.80 round trip. It's not certain that we have that Monday off, but I'm planning on it. I was told, "If the city has it, we have it."

 Darling, this carries all my love.

I love you
I'm coming to you
Charlie

BROOKLYN TO WINONA

Friday [1/30/1970]

Hello sweet love!

Your Sandburg quotes touched me and I am reminded of some lines from Robert Frost that Dr. Tom Dooley loved. The poem went something like this:

> *"The forest is lovely, dark and deep....*
> *and I have promises to keep....*
> *promises to keep...."*

Today I see Dr. Doltolo. I don't want to go (I feel uncomfortable), but I will make the effort five or six times anyway. I have no confidence in him yet. I'll keep you posted on our conferences.

This evening I have dinner with Lily and Chuck. (Lily recommended Dr. Doltolo in the first place and will be pumping me about how things are going.) Sunday I will have lunch with Jody who has just returned from Israel. Sunday night I'll be waiting for your call. Lots to talk about.

My physical exam is scheduled for Friday, February 13. I am going to the Strang Clinic, recommended by our office manager. The exam costs $50 but Blue Cross foots part of the bill because I go into the hospital for a few hours. Blue Cross would not pay anything if I visited the doctor in his office. I've discovered that the clinic is a "cancer detection" center. Part of it includes a proctoscopy and I have to give myself an enema the day of the exam. I don't know how I'm going to accomplish that ordeal. I dread the probes.

One thing about living alone, darling, is: Suppose I get sick! I'd really be in tough shape. There is no one that I know well enough in the apartment building. Maybe I could ask the super to bring me food. Thank the Lord I've been healthy enough so far.

I'm enclosing some pictures you can keep (I had two sets made). I love the shots of you smiling in the chair, sewing the bedspreads. Your smile penetrates my inmost being and makes it easy for me to smile. Note the details in the picture: our

*photo album, the little glass you gave me for Christmas, the bag
I spilled glue on, a little piece of "You just keep wondering."
That day was so much fun.... just being with you.... we didn't go
out until late afternoon.*

*You have a good photo of the rose of sharon tree. I
planted two of them in front of my parents' house last August.
One is you and the other is me. Rose(mary) of Sharon and
Charlie of Sharon. Mother and Dad posed in front of our house.
I remember Mother saying to me, "Don't think I don't know why
you're taking these pictures!"*

*Georgia, now in Louisiana, sent some beautiful color
photos of you* [from the farewell party for me at the Catholic
Student Center]. *I love them. I love you my darling. I hope we
can be together on that February weekend. It's worth it even if
you have to leave on Sunday night. And now, breakfast and off to
work.... lovely, dark and deep.... love... and promises to keep.*

Devotedly Chas

WINONA TO BROOKLYN

January 31, 1970

Good morning, darling!

*It's (late) Saturday morning, and I'm just getting started
at 10:00. I want to share some thoughts of poet Wallace Stevens
with you before I file the stuff away. I was reminded of both you
and Belinda by some of these quotes, and others I just want to
share with you.* [I copy about a dozen unconnected sentences.
Three examples: "It is the belief and not the god that counts."
"Poetry is a pheasant disappearing in the brush." "Death is the
mother of beauty."]

*(Remember the poem of Pierre Charles on real flowers
versus paper ones?*

*And now for a report on recent events. . . . Yesterday I
spoke with both the dean, Sister Margaret B, who shed two tears
(and triggered a few of mine), and my department chairman, Mr.
Goodreau, who said it was sad, that he wished I would not feel
as if I had to leave CST because I was leaving the Franciscans,
but he could understand that some would not like the idea of me
staying on here. It was a good day, but I always feel so tired out*

after the strain, which, I guess, is mostly on the subconscious level.

Joanie came back through last evening. She had a great time in Chicago — she misses the metropolitan excitement. She expects Bill M Monday evening, will meet him in Waterloo [Iowa] Airport. We had a very good talk. Seems like we communicate more this year than ever, despite our infrequent visits. We share a lot of common experiences. That's what she misses most in Decorah – a commonness of background with the friends she has there.

Bill and Joan will try to get to Winona for dinner Wed. or Thurs. If they do, we'll try to catch you at home and give you a buzzzzzzzzz.

I love you, dear. I must go now and write to the U of Texas Placement Service. Love,

Rosie

BROOKLYN TO WINONA

Sunday [2/1/1970]

Dearest,

Last night I really wanted to call you. Yesterday morning I took the next step. I wrote [Paulist President] Fitz. I'll read you the letter tonight when you call.

I wrote the letter effortlessly. I was surprised it came so easily. Mailing it later in the day was the difficult thing. The experience taught me about myself. The trouble with mailing it was fears of not being liked, of loving approval. It indicated so much about the way I have succeeded in life – on being the nice guy, on fulfilling others' expectations of me. Even on the job I catch myself. "Am I doing this report to please John Doar or because I really think it's the right thing for the people of Bedford-Stuyvesant?" I can't abide that sycophant modus operandi. It's one of the big things I hope Dr. D helps me with. It's crucial to my life, darling, and my love.

The letter to Fitz was not written because of fears about what parents or Paulists would think. It expressed what I felt deep down. That's why it came out so easily. I wasn't thinking about how others would react so much as where I was really at.

And something else that is deep within me is my love for you. When we are together, my love expresses itself as effortlessly as that letter was to write. Somehow you have penetrated to that inner me, and love what you see, and I intuit your love and love you all the more. I haven't been able to penetrate me the way you have, and so, since I am not so sure about what's inside, I go through life conforming myself to others' expectations because this gets approval and reassures me about myself.

This self analysis is not excitingly new. We've discussed it before. I think I understand it better now and therefore will be able to cope with it better. One of the good things about living alone is that there is no one around to approve or disapprove, so I am face to face with the inner man. I remember Belinda's statement, "[The sacrament of] Penance is self acceptance."

I want to finish this letter with some fun. I couldn't resist clipping out the enclosed New Yorker cartoons. I know you will laugh. [They depicted phone service in NYC; studying urban problems; telling a bartender one's problems; and nuns with knee-length skirts standing next to women with to-the-floor coats.]

This coming week I start night school. I decided not to enroll in the painting course – too much of a bite into my time. Perhaps what I should have done is give up the New School course, and just take the art to give greater balance to my life. I'm deluged enough with the problems of the city.

Georgia and Ron have moved to La. Ron has the job he wanted with Trunkline, a pipeline division. Georgia seems very happy to be in a "family" again. She says that you and I are welcome any time. Ok then dear, when do we go! Marilyn P, an attractive divorcee, is the new executive secretary [at the Catholic Student Center]. *She used to come to Mass at the Center occasionally and I had one long talk with her. It will be interesting to see how things develop there. She's a warm person and not aggressive. Let's keep our eyes on Walter!*

Rosemary, my Francha, I love you. "Hang in there," as John Doar says. I miss you, sweet love.

Devotedly
Chas

BROOKLYN TO WINONA

Wednesday [2/4/1970]

Dearest,

    I love you. I expected this to be a cheery letter, but brother Bob called up this afternoon to say that Dad was in the hospital with a blood clot. All he could say was that Dad was sitting on a chair saying the rosary and something happened. I've been distressed since I heard the news – worried about Dad, about Mother. I've been tormented with guilt feelings because I read my letter to Fitz to the folks on Monday night, and they were loving, but audibly upset. I'm going to telephone Mother in an hour. Then we'll be talking later tonight. I've been praying, darling.

    Tony [an ex-priest friend] *happened to call up this afternoon and I told him what happened. He's coming over to see me at 11 p.m. after I come home from school. He was very helpful.*

    Cousin Cleve called last night. I told him of our Christmas plans [for me to visit Detroit to meet Charlie's parents]. *He said, "Can you wait that long?" It's awfully long, darling. I loved his spirit. I plan to see Cleve Friday. Bob didn't think I should come home. He advised me to wait and keep in touch.*

    I have another college for you to apply to, Baruch College. They said you don't have to send a picture, but urged that you make application.

    I'm enclosing Dolores' poems, which don't make much sense to me. I guess I think they reflect the troubled psyche, and I shy away from analysis at this point. I think of Wallace Stevens' line, "Poetry is a pheasant disappearing in the brush." I would like poetry also to be a pheasant taking flight!

    I wish I could touch you at this moment, my Rosie. I love you. Can't wait to hear your voice tonight.

Devotedly, always,
Charlie

BROOKLYN TO WINONA

Saturday Feb. 7, 1970

Dearest,

    Rosie my dear. I've been thinking about you all day. I've been thinking about that night, or was it morning, when we were next to each other and repeated the words of the marriage promises to one another. Cleve keeps asking, "How can you wait?" It's because I feel we're already married. We are responsible for one another. We are working out our lives together. We know each other completely. We love each other. SWEETIE, WE ARE TOGETHER!

    Dad is better, darling. I haven't spoken to him yet and probably won't for a while. I call every day, usually speaking to both Bob and Mother.

    I have another name for our wedding list. Cleve. He says no matter where it is, he wants to be there. He's so anxious to meet you.

    I spent an hour with Dr. Doltolo today and for the first time I got a little light. I spent the whole time discussing my relationship with my father. He says he thinks the problem is that I confuse my conscience (a rigid one that I've absorbed from my father) with my identity. If I understand correctly, he says that my conscience is not mine, but a given; that in rejecting this conscience, I've been rejecting myself. I don't love this conscience which has been formed out of love and respect for my father because it's not mine; therefore, confusing my conscience with myself, I reject myself or rather can't love myself. I'm oversimplifying, but the theory does make sense. I'm sure there are many more things to be explained, but I can understand what Dr. D is driving at. I can't go through life pleasing that conscience formed out of devotion to Dad. I have to have my own values, confidence in my own power to make a conscience. As Belinda would say, "I understand this intellectually, but psychologically, I remain confused by the me that's been ingrained by my parents." I think Dr. D is going to be of immense value.

    Tonight I'm going to go out with Tony and the other priests and their friends. Tomorrow I'll see Jody and Cleve and

*tomorrow night we'll be on the phone together again. I look
forward to talking with you.*

*Bill M called and I told him about my letter to Fitz and
about us. You were thoughtful to let me do the telling. After Bill
hung up, I called Eileen and Ed. I gave them the same news.
They were happy for us. Ed is going to talk to the Paulists about
living away from the Austin house next year. As far as I know,
Ed and Eileen have no firm plans. Ed's folks had been in Austin
for a ten-day visit. Did I tell you that the [senior] Lundys sent me
$5 for Christmas? I told Ed about Dad's illness. He was very
understanding.*

*I love you, Francha my Rosemary. I can't wait to see
you over the Washington birthday weekend.*

Devotedly,
Charlie

WINONA TO BROOKLYN

Enclosed in this letter were a carbon copy of my job
application letter, my curriculum vitae, and Charlie's letter of
recommendation. (See Appendices.)

2/9/70

Dear Valentine,

*I am so very busy these days, and even emotionally
exhausted, that I fall into bed and drag myself out of it and never
do seem to get to writing to you. I didn't want to just send these
carbon copies without even a note, so that's why the delay. Even
now I'm sneaking this note in between conferences with 70 (!)
freshmen on the progress of their research papers.*

*I have sent 8 letters of application, 5 on Feb. 6 and 3 on
Feb. 7. My pictures still have not arrived. It takes me 20 minutes
to type a letter, and the 20 minuteses are hard to come by!*

*I'm not complaining! The weekend at home, for example,
was time-consuming but well worth the time, for my parents'
sakes and my own. And it was good to meet the Harmony priest
Father Woodford, as I told you on the phone. I hope to tell him
about us and have him help out when the time comes.*

Love, R

BROOKLYN TO WINONA

Tuesday
Feb 10, 1970

Darling,

*I called Mother last night and had two great pieces of
news: (1) Dad is coming home from the hospital tomorrow; (2)
he wants to talk to me. Did I tell you that even though Dad had a
telephone in his room, Mother (and Dr. Doltolo) thought it better
that I not contact him directly – only through Mother. She
suggested that I wait to call until he gets home. I told Mother
that I would sleep well last night – and I did. Almost overslept!
And I went to bed at 10:30 p.m.*

*While I was showering this morning, I remembered a
scene from a dream. Remember, today I'm going to the Brooklyn
Chancery to my "interview." The scene: I had returned to the
seminary. It was crowded, lots of young happy people who knew
me, but I didn't recognize them. They were milling about and I
was making my way through them, hastily, embarrassed I think,
too, because I knew I was not part of that life any more, but they
didn't. And the seminary didn't look like the seminary; it looked
like the Country Club of Detroit (that I once was a member of,
and thought I could never resign from). I made my way into the
lobby. There seemed to be a dance scheduled for the evening, the
lights were on but the large ballroom, which you can see from
the lobby, was clear. I had my long maxi habit on and I made my
way upstairs to the balcony overlooking the dance floor. There I
met a couple, my age or a little older, conventionally dressed,
with whom I was engaging in friendly conversation. I don't know
who they were, maybe I'd just been introduced. All I remember
saying was: "I don't know why I'm dressed like this!"*

*Fitz is away, but I received an understanding letter from
Fr. Johnny C, his assistant.*

*Dearest, I love you. Can't wait for you to come. It's a
cold, windy, rainy, dark day, but there is sunshine in my heart. I
love you.*

Chas

BROOKLYN TO WINONA

Lincoln's Birthday [February 12, 1970]

Dearest,

I talked with Dad today. He sounded great. We laughed a lot. He was worried that I would make a connection between my announcement and his blood clot. He insisted it could happen to anyone, even at age 25! I got such a good letter from Fitz that I read it to him and Mother. Here are some excerpts:

You are quite right in thinking that I would have hoped for a different solution of the problem but it is your life and you must make the ultimate decision. I can testify that you have given it long and serious thought and have followed all of the recommended steps in reaching your solution. I am happy to hear that you are contented in your work and I am sure that once the dispensation has been granted you will be able to give yourself whole-heartedly to your future vocation. Since I have never met a Paulist who was not on friendly terms with you I am sure that your relationship with the Paulist community will always be a happy one.

I am enclosing the check to the Minnesota AAA. I'm glad it's not AA! How I long to see you.

Also enclosing a little Valentine. I think it's a poem. Is it?

All my love to you Francha, my Rosemary.

Chas

<u>*talking to my love on the telephone*</u>
"Will you accept a collect call from Rosemary?"
The question sends a little impulse of electricity
  through me.
You say "hel-lo" in a musical way
We make a connection.
I laugh a lot
You ask questions – so concerned about me.
My sentences rush excitedly on,
not like sheep anxious to get back to the barn,
following one another in orderly fashion;
but like big salmon, swimming against the current

and jumping
in the white water.
I sometimes even forget to ask you how you are – except
lately.
As we talk, something opens at the vortex of my being
like a flower opening up to the sun
I feel warm and good.
You know, I like to talk to you on the telephone
Happy Valentine's darling

BROOKLYN TO WINONA

Taped on the back of this letter, from the local church bulletin: "What is temptation? Once we have made our choice and been committed to the kingdom of God, we are tempted to waver in our resolve and to look for happiness in the world and in ourselves [emphasis added by Charlie]. And we want to do this thing without renouncing the basic commitment. We try to compromise and blend two loyalties in spite of our Lord's warning us that we cannot serve two masters."

Sunday
Feb. 15 [1970]

Dearest

It was so wonderful to hear your voice last night. I was lonely and thinking of you. It's the first time you called me apart from plan and I'm so glad I was here. Keep my life full of good surprises like that, darling.

I just returned from church at nearby St Teresa's. It was a sad little folk Mass. The lower church. Three kids about 13 or 14 on electric guitars. They played well but got very little response from the sparse congregation – blacks, a few old whites, all of us islands, we were so distant from one another in the pews. Venerable old ushers took up two collections. A black Haitian priest celebrated and preached. The thing that made me saddest was a notice in the Sunday Bulletin – over.

Darling! No wonder I have an identity problem!

I've been raised on this stuff, and my parents too. This is not Christianity – the Gospel, the good news is: "I am somebody!" Christianity will [not] have its impact until it is a congregation of somebodys!

I have been reading the Feb 11 National Catholic Reporter with careful interest. There is a good discussion among Groppi, Dunne, Neuhaus that begins on page 1. But also of interest is a long article on Thomas Merton in the Lenten Book Report. The ideal of the Trappist life is presented as: to be conscious of one's true self in the presence of God. This is beautiful. Merton's life is described as a search for identity. OK, fine—mine too. Merton's basic view of the relationship of man to God is described as:

(1) *"God utters me like a word containing a thought of himself." OK.*

(2) *"A Word will never be able to comprehend the voice that utters it." OK.*

(3) *"But if I am true to the concept that God utters in me, if I am true to the thought of him I was meant to embody, I shall be full of his actuality and find him everywhere in myself, and find myself nowhere. I shall be lost in him." NO!*

Darling – this causes me to rebel! God does not want me to be lost in him. I am made in the image and likeness of God. A little lower than the angels. If I am lost in anything, anyone, I am nothing. I am something! This is the Gospel. This is what I need so much! It's the same thing the black people are going through!

Enough – I look forward to seeing you so, Francha my Rosemary. The pictures are all framed, we can hang them together. There are lots of new photos in our album. The bedspreads need some stitching – and 195 Underhill needs loving and living, which we will give it. There are lots of things to do in N.Y. but no plans until we talk out what we want to do. There are the schools to see and visit.

Darling – you have real daring and guts and determination in you. I love you.

Devotedly,
Chas

I took advantage of a one-day holiday over Presidents' Weekend and flew to New York for a quick reunion.

CHICAGO TO BROOKLYN

This is a postcard stamped "O'Hare Airport, Feb. 22, 1970." I wrote a thank-you note to Charlie back in Brooklyn.

BROOKLYN TO WINONA

Monday [2/23/1970]

Darling,

The silence. Your absence. Part of me is missing. I know I shall adjust to your not being here. But it is not good for man to be alone. The self-doubts and the emptiness. I counter them by my act of self-faith (God within) and my trust in you.

Kathy called last night. She wanted to reach you because your brother had tried to get in touch. I gave Kathy your schedule and I hope everything works out without embarrassment. I'll find out Wednesday. Kathy sounded terrific. She really understands what we are going through – I could tell by the warmth in her voice.

I've been lounging around the apartment all morning – reading NYT, cooking breakfast. I called Tony and talked to him for about an hour. We talked about the addiction problems in Brooklyn, the legitimacy of my job. Tony knows the score. I expressed my doubts about any real good that could be accomplished. He said he thought it better that a sensitive person be in my position, than an opportunist. He urged me to stay and to do what I can even though it doesn't seem like much. I felt better. Darling I love you. I miss you terribly!

Devotedly,
Charlie

WINONA TO BROOKLYN

Monday p.m.
Feb. 23, 1970

Darling

End of a teaching day. It was hard to get back in the swing of things – boring classes both from the teacher's and students' points of view.

Sorry the photo is slightly beat up. The smaller ones are very nice, though, don't you think? You can keep them if you wish. I have plenty – got 18 colors ($2.25) and 32 black & white ($1.00). (A real bargain.)

My policy now is to tell people who ask where I went that I went to NY checking out schools. 3 good reasons: (1) friends there; (2) tuition-free schools; (3) about the only place in

U.S. with job openings! Sounds convincing and (what's more) is
TRUE!

> *I must run to Mass – am already late.*
> *I love you. Kathy enjoyed talking to you, she said.*
> *Lalonde did call – that was the call we didn't answer*

Saturday! In fact, she tried 3 times. Good thing no emergencies –
she was just lonely.

Bye—
Rosemary

WINONA TO BROOKLYN

I enclosed a widely circulated CST campus letter to
"colleagues" protesting the trustees' decision to switch to a
three-term calendar without input from the academic body; it
was signed by two professors. The financial difficulties and new
leadership at the college have added a level of stress to life on
campus.

Wed. a.m.
2/25/70

Good morning, dear!

> *From 40° to -7° in a few hours. Our spring fever was*
nipped in the bud.

> *I miss you so very much, darling.*

> *I finished Hemingway's* The Sun Also Rises *just now. I'll*
send you some stuff on it as I get it prepared for teaching.
Meantime, do your homework! I'll also enclose the class
schedule for the semester.

> *The letter enclosed summarizes the present feeling on*
campus. Too bad. Really too bad. Faculty morale is low.

> *Got 2 letters today: (1) Mrs. McCarty says "Go Ahead"*
and God bless me. She'll send $250 whenever I say [in our
effort, ultimately failing, to self-publish Jerry's book of poems].
(2) [U of Texas CSC student] *Jim J just finished Navy boot camp*
and is off to Maryland.

> *What's up with you?*
> *I love you.*

Francha

BROOKLYN TO WINONA

Charlie enclosed a memorandum-style invitation he had received, to a party "to honor one Charles Palms on the occasion of 'the 5th month of the Public Services Program.'" He also enclosed an article about CUNY and SUNY reporting a big rise in student applications, giving us hope that there would be job openings.

Thursday [2/26/1970]

My dearest,
Your card written above my old "water Wonderland" [of Michigan] *really touched me. Especially the line: "I depend on your love – on you – on us." And you were so right last night on the phone – that we experienced something very beautiful this time – our need for each other.*
The emptiness in the apartment on Monday was almost unbearable. I called your name out loud three times – just to hear it – to – I guess – invoke your presence.
If we miss on Sunday and you call Monday night, I will be at the meeting of the Chum Chum Club. (See enclosed.) Please call collect and I will charge it to my Underhill number. My staff very cleverly invited me using my memorandum style.
I'm enclosing an article which indicates why you will be needed here. The attendance will be mammoth. Here are some other schools you may want to write.
The New School.... – This is where I've been taking classes. They teach English as a Second Language to minority and foreign youth.
St. Joseph's College for Women....Brooklyn
St. Francis College.... Brooklyn – You liked this -- remember?
This carries all my love Darling.

Devotedly,
Charlie

WINONA TO BROOKLYN
2/26/70

Dearest Charlie,

Another fairly good day today – the worst hasn't hit yet, I guess, or I misjudged. Those who know about my impending departure are loving and good-natured indeed.

Our president formally apologized this p.m. to the faculty for the recent uproar and just grievances. It was very dramatic and must have taken gutsy humility.

Dearest, I miss you so much. I think about you so much that I have almost forgotten to keep my guard up. It would be so easy to say, "Charlie lives in a place like that," or "Charlie took me to hear Mayor Lindsay," or the like. Some day soon, dear, this schizophrenic stuff will come to an end. Soon. Soon.

I'm working tonight on an outline for discussion of The Sun Also Rises. If I can't animate the class with this book, I may lose my last chance to save the course. They really are unmotivated. (The freshmen compensate, however!)

Would you believe – I LOVE YOU!

Rosie

Charlie asked Harvard Law School about acquiring a Juris Doctor degree, and learned that, in effect, his LLB degree was equivalent to a JD. Harvard required only a small fee to change its records. Thus Charlie's ironic signoff below.

BROOKLYN TO WINONA
Saturday [2/28/1970]

Wow darling,

How are you? I've been knocking myself out for the past 3 hours, finishing my analysis of the drug proposal. I hope to have it done by Monday. So many little odds and ends. Like every other need, services for addicts are not nearly adequate in Bed-Stuy.

I'm glad to have the photo back. The smaller ones were a delightful surprise.

Had a good session with Dr. Doltolo yesterday. I have a great deal of trouble doing the "shoulds" and the "oughts." Anything imposed from "above." I want to do something for the *people of Bed-Stuy, but this drug proposal has been on my desk and in my briefcase for nearly three weeks. I was asked to make the analysis by someone <u>above</u>. I have to make a tremendous effort to get the job done. It's a constant battle with myself. Dr. D sees this as a deep-seated rebellion. The only observable manifestation of it has been my experiences hitting the bars along Flatbush* [the usual route home from his office in the old Granada Hotel], *a self-defeating activity. My anxieties have been escaped through alcohol, which is no escape, and only contributes to my feelings of self-reproach.*

Even before he suggested this analysis, I told Dr. D that I was thinking about giving up alcohol – that it would be a good way of facing up to myself. Dr. D left it up to me, whether I wanted to give it up in toto, or just to take, say, one drink. As a matter of fact, I haven't had a drink since Thursday. I'm going to a colleague's house for dinner tonight (he is a part time staffer for me) and I plan to abstain there too. When I see Jody tomorrow, I don't know yet what I will do. Anyway, Dr. D wants me to face up to my anxieties. He wants me to reflect upon my experience in facing up to Charlie. Last night I warmed up some lasagna left over from Harry and Aurelia's dinner. I drank ginger ale instead of Scotch or wine. After the dishes, I started reading and fell asleep as usual in the chair. I was in bed before 10:15 p.m., so far no difference. I'm interested to see what happens. I guess I keep wondering, do I have to be this abstemious?

Dr. D also urged me to get a project done; to see it completed. This is pretty tough, with my job. Projects have to be cleared through so much bureaucracy. But Dr. D feels that accomplishing something will raise my level of self-esteem. I know he's right.

Apologies for so much baring of my psyche. But I know you are interested. The thought of how we supported each other during your visit really comforts me. I think of you heading home this weekend. I hope you don't have to disclose anything that will hurt; that you can keep telling as it is, by degrees. My love to you, darling. I'll be waiting for your call, Sunday or Monday.

Your ever-loving juris doctor,
Charlie

WINONA TO BROOKLYN

I enclosed this just-for-fun "memo," purportedly from
Pope John XXIII. I typed: "To our faithful servant C.L. Palms –
the papers are on the way. Best of luck in your search."

Mar. 2, 1970

Dearest Charlie,
*   March came in ambiguously,*
with a beautiful 5-inch snowfall that was
soft and warm but inconvenient. Lion or
Lamb?
*   I send you a few goodies*
[photos]. More will come. It was fun
looking at hundreds and hundreds of
photos with Mother. I promised I would
help sort them and "album" them some
time soon. They should be labeled
before there is no one who remembers who was who.
*   My parents will be driving to Phoenix with some of my*
aunts and uncles on a little 2-week jaunt. My father enjoys this
jaunting a lot – more than Mother, I think. She goes along
because he enjoys it.
*   Have a good day!*

Love – much much love,
Rosemary

BROOKLYN TO WINONA

Tuesday [3/3/1970]

Dearest Rosemary my Francha,
*   The "Chum Chum" party was fun, but too long. I had*
one very light drink when I arrived and kept replenishing my
glass with Club Soda. Our hostess Ann and her roommate served
us all a delicious spaghetti supper. We played charades after the
meal.
*   Drinking anesthetizes me to the boredom of small-talk*
parties. It is much more difficult to endure an evening without
libation. During the course of the evening I made a couple of
remarks which made them all roar (there were ten people in all),

so my sense of humor did rise to the occasion. But after 11 p.m. I couldn't wait to make the move to leave. I was in bed at 1 a.m.

I kept thinking about today. My first assignment is a meeting at a school for retarded children. A new psychiatric center is opening up near Bedford-Stuyvesant and it looks as if the directors of the school (or a certain faction among them) want to fix the catchment area so as to exclude our Bed-Stuy children. Ann did a study on mental health facilities in Bed-Stuy for "Public Services" and the services for children are almost nil. John Doar, Ann and I will go to the meeting for Bed-Stuy.

Next I will visit two narcotics treatment centers. One is run by the City; the other by a Protestant group. It's interesting to talk to the religious oriented people. They see the power of God as the only source of cure. The City people place all their emphasis on "encounter" therapy or "methadone maintenance" (a substitute for heroin which does not inhibit normal functioning).

Darling, you will be in my heart all day, as you were with me last night. I wish I had you to come home to this night and every night.

Love always, Chas

P.S. Hear you tomorrow.

BROOKLYN TO WINONA
Thursday [3/5/1970]

Darling,

I got up at 7 this morning. I wanted to write you and to clip some things out of the papers before going to work. But I've been in the bathroom so many times that it's now 9:20. I'm going to be good and late for work, but I wanted to write you so that I can mail it on the way. I must have some kind of virus. I haven't been eating much these past two days. I don't feel like myself.

A forward-looking Paulist wrote in a recent newsletter: "I hope our Community will be the first to include married priests as full members (Session 24 of 1968 Chapter). Secondly, I hope the principle of priest-worker will be fully accepted by our Community. And finally, I believe the Paulists should be the first to include ecumenical parish communities in which Catholics and other Christians will share a sacramental life, a joint concern for those alienated from organized religion, and a combined service of the local community."

Dearest, that 1ˢᵗ birthday picture of you could be shuffled among our family pictures and I don't think anyone would deny that it was a picture of my brother George. He had beautiful blond curly hair as a baby and his hair wasn't cut until he was four or five. I love your little fists in that first-year shot – so determined! Yet smiling – and fat!

Sweetie – I'd ask Joe at Queens College both about English and SEEK. I'll have to get in touch with Jim R and forward more pertinent information from him at a later date.

Darling, I'd better get to work. I love you. What a great feeling it is to know you love me and that we are planning a life together! When you get time why not send me a box score on replies, yes and no, from the colleges.

Devotedly,
Chas

WINONA TO BROOKLYN

March 6, 1970

Dearest,

The new liturgy can begin legally March 22. We had a 1¼ hour introduction to the sweeping changes by the diocesan liturgist yesterday. It's nice to see that the wheels are slowly rolling in the direction the CSC went 2-3 years ago.

I also enclose the discussion questions for Gatsby. My class today was about 300% better than it has been up to the present. So I feel great about it, and wonder how I can keep it going now, for the rest of the semester.

Later:

Joan called Eileen the other day; Eileen is going to Des Moines to an English meeting around April 1-4. Has to give a talk. Joan is going to offer to drive down and pick her up if Eileen wishes to visit up here. So that would mean I should be here when she comes, April 4 and 5. So I guess I'll have to wait, to make my spring break plans, till I know hers.

Later:
I just let your addressed envelope sit on a prominent table for an hour. Good Lord. (I got interested in a TV program and forgot it.)
This weekend I bury myself in term papers and try to make the Monday a.m. deadline for midterm grades. I can't seem to catch up on my work. My galavanting begins to tell!
Darling, I'd galavant anywhere for you!

LOVE
FRANCHA

NEW YORK TO WINONA

Saturday
3-7-70

Darling,
I'm on the train for Pawling, N.Y. Steve and Jean Smith invited me out for the weekend. I've got The Sun also Rises *and your discussion notes, plus the Saturday N.Y.T.*
I've just come from Dr. Doltolo's office. I spent most of my time today discussing my religious beliefs. I didn't see the relevancy until the very end of the hour when he asked me if I didn't see a pattern in relationship between what I was saying today and what I had said before. I guess I'd better explain some more.
Dr. D saw a confusion in my mind. He saw that I was rejecting the institution, but wanted to be part of Catholicism. I wanted to be the kind of Catholic I want to be, and I was in the process of being it. Yet the institution and Catholicism must in some ways be identified. At the same time there is another institution I carry around within me: the home and its strong influences. In relationship to my parents, I've also had difficulty being the person I want to be. In fact, as Dr. D pointed out at the end of the hour – I submitted in the relationship with my parents. Now I'm trying to win that battle against the Church, which I've substituted for the home, or those forces which exert a shaping influence over me.
Darling, I realize all this is not fully lucid, because there is still some confusion in my own mind. I have decided to continue the abstinence from alcohol.

*Last evening I went to Duke's and met with eight
Paulists, old friends. I must say it was enjoyable to see old
friends, but I felt very uncomfortable among them, as if I had to
continually explain myself. I had half a drink before dinner and a
glass of wine with my meal. I didn't enjoy the drink at all – only
took it to be polite. Most of the conversation was small talk and I
was bored. But I didn't get home until 2 a.m. I'd just taken off
my coat when the phone rang. It was Ed and Eileen.*

*They asked about you. Eileen may have a job in Austin.
Ed said that he had told the Community he was going to study
full time in the summer and next year. He also plans to live by
himself next year, but has not announced this yet. Eileen said
that the Federal Department of Health, Education, and Welfare
people were coming to Austin around March 16 to recruit
English specialists to work in their programs. Eileen is going to
write you about it. I encouraged her to get all the facts. There
might be an opening in New York.*

*SEEK stands for Search for Evaluation, Education and
Knowledge. I haven't reached Jim R yet, but will this coming
week. I made a mistake when I spoke to you on Wednesday. I
thought that our "meeting" was <u>this</u> Saturday; it's next
Saturday.*

*Eileen said that teachers usually give "notice" the first
week of April. Perhaps this is why you haven't had more positive
response from the colleges you applied to.*

*Dearest, at this point I'm wondering when we are going
to be with each other again. You were so right in perceiving my
loneliness. I wasn't that aware of it until you told me how much
you saw it in my letters. I miss your presence, your love,
understanding. We will have to decide whether it will be during
the Easter break or later. I don't like to think of our being
separated all summer. I will have two weeks vacation, and some
of that time I will want to visit the folks.*

*I finished the narcotics evaluation. I hope our
corporations do something about it. Now I know that large areas
of Bedford Stuyvesant have no services at all. My next important
task is to do a market evaluation of Bedford Stuyvesant for a
proposed radio station serving the community. I have to find out*

things like home ownership, buying habits, businesses, factories.
I'm learning a great deal about my "turf."

I've been writing this for about an hour. Now the train
has stopped for a few minutes and it's easier.

I love you my darling, and miss you. This is a hard year
for me because I'm in a state of in-between – between one kind
of life and another. And at the same time trying to work through
some things that should have been part of much earlier growth.
But basically, I know I'm on the right track. It's just that I can't
see where it leads. Except I feel so much better when I think of
you being with me.

Love always,
Charlie

BROOKLYN TO WINONA

Monday March 9 [1970]

Dearest,

Before I head down to Duke's in the East Village, I
wanted to drop you a line. I include Jim R's address. He will be
able to help you in your application for SEEK at Brooklyn
College.

After our telephone conversation last night, I finished
The Sun Also Rises. *I read your questions over briefly. I haven't*
had a chance to think about them at any length. One thing that
kept going through my mind during the whole book was the
question of Hemingway's ability to develop the feminine
character. Remember the critic who asserted that Melville,
Hemingway, Steinbeck and others could not relate adequately to
women in their writings. I must say Hemingway was much easier
with the male character. I don't know much about Brett, except
that she had a kind of attractive masculine quality, and that she
brought out the worst in men. I didn't find any attraction for her
in myself. I liked Jake because he was good at his work; he knew
a lot about fishing and bull fighting; he didn't let Brett get him
down. But he didn't seem to be going anywhere. I felt sorry for
Cohn. I could identify with him. I've moped around like he did
and I detest it. Even though he could floor everyone with his
fists, he had the respect of no one. The end of the novel surprised
me. It ended as it had begun. I felt a dull pain as I closed the

*book. I'll take a closer look at your questions and see if I have
more reactions.*

*My health is completely restored now. I feel fine. It was
very thoughtful of you to call me. I was touched by your concern.*

*I do feel funny about our next meeting. I don't like the
delay. I have the feeling I am being self-centered about it. But
after all, I <u>do love</u> you Francha, my Rosemary.*

Affectionately,
Charlie

WINONA TO BROOKLYN

3-10-70

Dearest Chas —

*My thoughts are with you so much lately. I guess it's
because I love you....*

*I got grades in yesterday by giving a semi-blanket grade
to two classes. I finished only 18 of the 70 term papers. I figured
it was better to take more time and grade them carefully, and
also to be prepared for classes. For the most part, the students
seem to see my point. No complaints, at any rate.*

*Did you watch the eclipse Saturday? It must have been
almost total where you were — or was it cloudy? The skies were
sunny here, so lots of little kids were running around excitedly.
The best I did was look at a pin-hole shadow on another piece of
paper.*

*I wrote to Pam, urging her to come in April or May
when it becomes beautiful around here.*

*I overslept this morning – forgot to pull out the alarm
button – and I was supposed to lead office. The theme this
morning was on our call to the religious life, so I bet there was
some kind of subconscious motivation in my neglect to pull out
that button!*

*I am glad Dr. Doltolo and you are making headway. You
<u>do</u> express yourself well in your letters. I feel close to you.*

Love, my dear,
Rosemary

BROOKLYN TO WINONA

Thursday nite [3/12/1970]

Dearest,

 It's awfully late. I read the review of the new Fellini movie "Satyricon" while eating lunch. By 4:30 p.m. I had to go. I could only get tickets for the 9:45 p.m. showing, so I purchased the ticket and then holed up in the N.Y. Public Library where I finished a report on the population and business characteristics of Bed-Stuy.

 The movie is plotless and indescribable. Fellini's imagination runs riot in color. The film portrays life in Rome before the Christian era. I left the movie with the impression that <u>we</u> are living in the <u>post</u> Christian era. There doesn't seem much that removes us from the violence and debauchery of those times. What a beautiful/ugly film!

 Darling, I love you. Now I must sleep. I'll finish this in the morning.

[3/13/1970]

 I awoke at 8:15 a.m. – and you know my rule – I leave the apartment at 8:30 a.m. – so I didn't have a chance to finish writing you until now. <u>We</u> will have to see "Satyricon" together. And another thing we will have to see is Robert Marasco's "Childs Play" – it's about the conflict within a school. It's supposed to be the best serious theater in New York.

 Yesterday I called both Brooklyn College and New York City Community College. I talked to Professor Quinn's secretary. She was aware of your application without having to look it up. I thought this encouraging. However, she said that the week of March 27 to April 3 was poor for interviewing. Brooklyn College is on vacation that week (as is the whole City University system, including New York City Community). Miss whatshername said that Professor Quinn would be in touch with you if they wanted an interview (you were right). Professor Becker at NY City Community College was much easier to talk to. He repeated the pessimistic note about the week of March 27 to April 3, and also said that April 21, Passover, would be a bad time. Professor Becker is in the department of commercial arts and skills. He didn't remember your application, but seemed interested when I said you had finished your course work and

*were in the process of writing your dissertation. He said he
would like an interview. That he is in the process now of
narrowing down the candidates for teaching next year. (He also
remarked that I was a "good advocate." I didn't realize I was
pushing that much – he said it with a chuckle.) So there we are,
darling. We'll be discussing it again this Sunday nite. I think we
ought to time your visit with interviews. It looks like sometime
after the Easter week but before the end of May, would be best.*

    *Had a good session with Dr. Doltolo again. We talked
about my father. We also discussed my vocation. I brought <u>you</u>
up purposely, but Dr. D stuck to authority and vocation.*

    *I said that sometimes I felt in a world of unreality. If my
struggle was to be myself vis-a-vis parental authority (to which I
had unwittingly submitted), how real is my decision about
leaving the priesthood? Is there not a danger that my decision
for laicization is simply a prolongation of the battle against
parental authority? Doltolo recognized this as a danger, but he
in turn raised the question: How valid was your original
decision to be a priest? He sees it tied in with parental authority
and escape and "doing right," after the broken engagement.*
[Charlie's fiancée after law school had worried that he was so
conflicted about a priestly vocation that he couldn't make a valid
decision about marriage; so she broke off the engagement.] *I
shouldn't say Dr. D "sees it," rather he raises the question. That
is, if the first decision wasn't real, maybe this decision is real,
not an escape, etc.*

    *Dr. D further specified my problems with authority.
Apparently people in authority, like John Doar, teachers,
superiors, etc., are threats to me. It has become clear to me now,
that I cannot bring myself to disagree with authority. The basic
authority figure for us all is our father. My Dad is good. He is
thoughtful, kind, responsible, funny – an amazing guy. I hold him
in awe. He never <u>said</u> I shouldn't disagree with him. But his
whole bearing, everything about him, indicated: "You just don't
confront me." I didn't. And I hated myself when he disapproved
of me. Whenever I deal with authority, I put the best construction
on authoritative decisions, e.g., John Doar <u>wouldn't think</u> of
doing anything to the detriment of the people of Bed-Stuy. I had
to defend John last week in a meeting with some of the girls in*

the office who thought he was encouraging housing for the middle class rather than the poor. When John summons me to his office, my heart starts pounding – what have I done? Has he finally caught up with me? Dr. D thinks I carry upstairs with me the guilt for the Flatbush Ave. tour [of bar-hopping]. *Of course, John is not concerned with my personal life. But I carry guilt, fear of punishment around with me. Sweetie, this is where we're at. I understand a lot better, but I still have to deal with these guilt feelings, and overcome them. I will be a much more effective person when I do, I think.*

Your "coming to join you soon" really touched me. I've affixed it to the door of my apartment. I want you to come soon, darling. Your letters aren't long, but they are signs of your love and heralds of your coming. Keep 'em coming. They are especially appreciated because I can feel the pressure you must be under. God does exist, darling. Our love is the surest sign. Bless you –

Love always,
Charlie

WINONA TO BROOKLYN

3-13 [1970]

Dearest C,

I enclose the liturgy that left me in tears, feeling I was an "unbeliever" and therefore an outsider. (I follow a year or two after Eileen — she felt this way once, too.)

On the other side are quotes of travel costs. I'm tempted to take a less expensive mode (unless I have to be there for an interview fast). Okay?

My love,
Francha

[Other side:]
PLANE *(round trip)*
Winona- Chicago by train plus taxi, about 25.00
Chicago-NYC excursion 86.00 = $111.00
RAILROAD (round trip — clergy rate)
Winona – NYC 46.00
(24-hour trip one way) plus eating
(arrive NYC around 9 a.m.)

BUS (round trip – clergy)
Winona – NYC 54.00
Plus eating
(arrive NYC around 8:00 p.m.)
BUS (clergy)
Winona—NYC—Des Moines—Winona
About 68.00 plus eating

WINONA TO BROOKLYN

Enclosed is a chart listing institutions for possible job applications, with a record of applications sent and responses received.

3-15-70

Here is the list, darling.

I spent 4 hours yesterday compiling results, typing 5 more letters, and poring over an old (Nov.) "vacancies" list to find other possibilities. I put these on the list (after looking them up in an atlas) for your opinion. They are close enough for weekends together, anyway – at least those I could find on the map. I'll mention this tonight on the phone.

This weekend some (three) classmates are visiting at CST, so once again I'm not getting as much done as I "should." But it's <u>good</u>.

I believe in God again! LOVE, Francha

3-15-70
Later on Sunday

Dah-ling —

The black bar on the envelopes lately covers up <u>my</u> name: using up more already-been-used envelopes.... ok?

I watched <u>David Copperfield</u> tonight: Well done, new "edition." The sentimental parts still make me teary – good ol' Dickens.

I'm writing again cuz I'm lonesome again, not because I have anything to say except I LOVE YOU –

Rosie

BROOKLYN TO WINONA

Monday [3/16 (?)/1970]

Dearest Rosemary,

I never thought about the bus or train. We can swing that easily.

I've got The Great Gatsby *and have read the first 22 pages. I didn't realize Fitzgerald was as "formal" a writer. His life was so hectic and impulsive. Wasn't Zelda his Brett?*

Some reflections on The Sun Also Rises. *If Hemingway writes of a sick civilization which doesn't grow up, I wonder if the horror of the war in Vietnam, the abandonment of the ghettos, the slow suicide of narcotics addiction aren't symptomatic of a society which has not grown through, or solved, its own identity crisis. We cannot even declare war and accept responsibility for it! The sun has not yet risen!*

Two further comments. I saw no change in Jake. Lady Brett is neither abnormal, self-deluded, nor a victim of circumstances. She appears to me to be consummate selfishness. I guess, because she wants Jake's total love while soliciting the attentions of Michael, Robert and Romero.

Why is it important that Robert Cohn be Jewish? I detected anti-Semitism in Hemingway.

I like #9: the novel is not a portrait of a "generation" at all, rather it is an examination of the subject which preoccupied Hemingway throughout his life: the definition of manhood. This ties in with the observation that H writes with greater depth when probing the male character.

I could not see how Jake could pander for his siren (#11). This was abhorrent to me. I could only see it as Jake's way of saying to Brett, "You don't have any real control over me."

COME JOIN ME SOON.

All my love,
Chas

WINONA TO BROOKLYN

[March 17 1970]

Hi!

> *"Hope lives in doubt*
> *Faith is trying to do without faith."*
> *--Robert Lowell, American poet*

I saw a cute comic strip today – "Sally Bananas." The little girl is plucking "petals" off a "flower," saying: "He loves me. He loves me not. He loves me. With a shamrock you can't lose!"

Sweetie, in a few minutes I'm going to "A Sacred Concert" — Sister Lalonde's baby. For someone who is not supposed to direct, she does get around.

She <u>was</u> going to Boston over spring break, but her father is getting worse (dying of cancer) and her mother (who is <u>very</u> nervous) wants her at hand. And Lalonde needs to get away <u>bad</u>.

Today I believe in God more – even in Jesus more, a little. What a strange mind I have. I suppose the spring weather helped.

Today we voted on the curriculum proposals – and it all went in, to go into effect this coming September. Wow. It's new, and theoretically it's great. (It would be exciting to stick around.) I was undecided as to how to vote (or <u>whether</u> to vote), since I would not be here to suffer the consequences and growing pains; I ended by abstaining on the crucial question of <u>WHEN</u>; but I voted on the rest (which weren't close), figuring I knew the situation better than some who hadn't heard any of the debates or who don't even teach, and who were voting. The final package vote passed 2 to 1 (82 yes, 43 no).

Off I go concerting. Cheers.

My love, dear.
Rosemary

BROOKLYN TO WINONA

In this letter Charlie referred to Deane, a first cousin and semi-closeted gay man. Here he has married a princess (by virtue of her having married and divorced a prince) and has (I suspect half-jokingly) established himself to be a titled aristocrat, a Baron von Ruekfrang, as a wedding present to his new bride. This new marriage lasted only briefly.

Good Friday morning [3/27/1970]
Dearest Francha my Rosemary,
The mails once again go through. Two letters came from you yesterday, including the "score sheet." I'll have to study it carefully and then we can plan our job strategy.

In this letter, I'll enclose some stuff I've been saving, including the Mass sheet, a description of SEEK, some assorted N.Y.Times clippings, and a stalk of wheat from Anne and Harry B's Paschal Supper. The news accounts of Deane's wedding are unreal. Deane has never been married before, and the oil in Oregon is a figment of his delightful imagination. My feeling is that the whole thing has been tongue-in-cheek. DR has disliked Grosse Pointe intently for years. Now he is out-grossing Grosse Pointe; out-snobbing the snobs.

I called brother Joe yesterday and we had a great talk. He says he thinks I took the only step I could take, the Church being what it is today. (I wrote him on his birthday -- March 19 -- explaining my life and my decisions.) Now Joe is very anxious to meet you. I was pleased because, of all the family, I felt Joe would be the least understanding. Joe now has two plants, one for design outside the city, and one for production inside the city. He has about thirty men working for him, plus an apprentice program for black men who want to learn the trade.

I saw something very beautiful the other day as I walked by Long Island University. A student in a wheel chair who could not use his legs was being pushed by a blind girl. They were obviously devoted to one another. I could tell by the way they were dressed (alike) and the way they were talking. He was her eyes and she was his legs.

*My life is so incomplete without you, darling. Now I'm
beginning to feel "whole" again as the mail resumes, and as we
talk and laugh on the phone. But it won't be fully complete until
we can share all of the days and nights. Happy Easter and all my
love.*

Charlie

BROOKLYN TO WINONA

Holy Saturday [3/28/1970]

Darling,

*I've been looking over "Job Hunting" and after the
Spring break I'm going to start making some calls for you. We'll
have to decide upon a time for your visit. I'm also enclosing the
teacher opportunities section of the* N.Y.Times. *I've Xed a few of
them. I'm enthusiastic and feel certain you will find something in
the NYC area. I hate to think of you miles away from me. Think
of the travel and telephone expense! (I'm appealing to a sensitive
spot – the economic argument!)*

*What did you think of Bishop Buswell's advice to Bob B?
Joanie told me that he told Bob M and Mary B to get married
without applying for laicization.* [Bishop Charles Buswell was a
very liberal prelate.] *This appealed to Bob because he was
resisting Mary's arguments for going through the channels. BM
doesn't want to give up the priesthood. In some ways I do; in
some ways I don't. I couldn't be an official representative of the
Church at this point. When the open Church is a reality I would
feel more comfortable, and then, if both a bishop and the people
invited me. One of the conditions would be a job like I have now.
I could not be a full time cleric, i.e., full-time sacrament
dispenser. The sacraments celebrate life, and I would have to be
living, i.e., loving you and working with you for others.*

*These are my Holy Saturday thoughts, darling. I love
you and miss you. But I know you're happy this weekend with
your family. I'll be happy when we don't have to hide anything
any more from anybody. When I can trudge joyfully through the
Harmony countryside with your Dad and brothers.*

*Love,
Charlie*

WINONA TO BROOKLYN

CST March 31, 1970
10 a.m.

Dearest C,

 March is going out like a lamb today. Lovely. Hard to be inside.

 I just spent almost an hour reading mail and clippings and descriptions of SEEK, etc. Thanks for all the info. Among other things, I got a brief note from Professor Quinn of Brooklyn College saying: "I regret to inform you that the committee on appointments can offer no encouragement about an appointment for next year in this department...." So that's that.

 I hope Professor Becker of NYC Community College really is interested. I'll try to finish sending letters to everyone on the checklist I sent you. Today and tomorrow will be for that purpose primarily, and we'll see what happens.

 A note from Eileen says that she has nothing definite yet either (close to Austin, that is – too bad we all are so fussy!). She hopes something may develop from her paper at the convention in Des Moines. She is coming here to visit this Saturday, and staying till Tuesday a.m. Ain't that nice? She says the visit has been in her dreams in one way or another for several days...!

 I'll head for Des Moines via bus Thursday a.m. Eight hours later ☺ I'll be there. Joanie will bring us back via Volks Sat. night.

 How about tentatively setting up the last weekend in April for interviews? (To be terribly optimistic....) That will be after Passover. That would be Friday, April 24, or Monday, April 27. I think I could make up classes for a Thursday (for travel) and Friday or a Monday and Tuesday (for travel). It would also give those people I'll write to today and tomorrow time to answer me.

five application letters later (4 p.m.)
 It takes a long time, especially when one types the way I do.

 For your record, I sent letters to:

  1. Jim R, SEEK
  2. Joe D, SEEK
  3. Queens College, CUNY

4. New York U.

5. Staten Island Community Col., CUNY

6. York College, CUNY

By the way, what is your favorite Rouault painting? Was it <u>The Old King</u>? I think you said <u>The Lord</u>, but I was thinking of Guardini's book <u>The Lord</u>, and Rouault's painting on the cover of that book is <u>Christ Mocked by Soldiers</u>, and I don't think that is what you said.

I checked the employment pages you sent me, and I checked only one that you had checked! That was for the English-reading teacher for high school dropouts in Harlem. Sounds like one just drops in to apply, résumé in hand, no letter necessary. We could try that when I come to NY. Others you checked were for Junior High (shudder) or for a Ph.D. Not I, sir.

Back to one more letter before I go to supper. Godspeed!

Love   love   love   love

Rosemary

WINONA TO BROOKLYN

March 31 '70

Dearest –

It's 9 p.m. I've really been writing to you all day, but I sent the earlier thoughts. I miss you. When I miss you most, I start re-reading your last letter, which is what I'm doing now. Your Holy Saturday thoughts.

One thing that strikes me on second reading is your idea of priesthood. Bob M's course of action appeals to you, doesn't it? What do you mean by "open church"? In what ways <u>don't</u> you want to give up your priesthood, dear? Be absolutely sure of what you give up when you get me.

I was touched by the mental picture of you trudging through the Harmony countryside with my Dad and brothers. Hunting? It's hard for me to picture you a hunter. You won't even kill cockroaches! I wonder what you would talk about with my father. He told me yesterday that he thinks Lyndon Johnson is great, and he believes Eugene McCarthy was hitting soft spots mostly for his own advantage. I have never heard my father give his political opinion before, so I only mildly disagreed with the latter statement and let Lyndon go by unscathed.

Silent majority. That's the Grebin stock.
I got a huge kick out of Deane's antics – speaking of
stock! A baron, no less! Who was the brave Father George,
marrying 2 – it says – double divorcés? (Are you a baron, too?)
Enough for now....

April 1, 1970

Sweetie,

I just finished more letters. Check these off:
1. *East Stroudsburg State College*
2. *St. Joseph's (Philadelphia)*
3. *Villanova U.*
4. *Williamsport Area Com. College*
5. *Providence College*
6. *Orange County Com. College*
7. *Cooperative College Registry (placement*
   service – free)

If I hurry, I'll get them in the mailbox before the next
pickup.

I told a dear 60-year-old nun yesterday about my leave
of absence. She said she felt I should not go — that I had a
vocation. She said she has seen, all year, love and sorrow in my
face. Then she began to cry and walked away. I was touched.
Darling, I must run. I'm calling you tonight anyway!

Love,
Rosie

April Fool !

BROOKLYN TO WINONA

March 31 [1970]

Dearest,

It was great to be back in touch with you by phone. The
sound of your voice does things to me.

Once again I'm enclosing some things to read. The most
important for us at the moment is "teacher openings" which are
pretty thin, unfortunately.

Toby and Dan have come to town. After we spoke, I had
a call from Susan, Toby's friend. After school this evening, I'm

*going over to see the happy couple. I haven't heard from Toby
since I declined an invitation to visit them for a weekend.*

*I've had a hard time getting a copy of <u>Invisible Man</u>. My
library didn't have it; two book stores were unable to find it in
stock. Finally, after telephoning around I am told I can get a
copy at Brooklyn Heights Library. I finished <u>Gatsby</u>, but I don't
have time to go into it now. I felt very sad on finishing it. No one
in the book proved strong enough or honorable enough – yet in a
sense "they had everything." What a wreckage of human lives;
what hypocritical compromises they were satisfied to live with.
As Fitzgerald reflects America of the 'twenties, no wonder the
tragedies of the 'sixties; no wonder we can live through the
wreckage, compromises and hypocrisy of a war in Vietnam and
the racial ghettos of our cities. (I've summed up my thoughts
more than I expected I could.)*

I love you, my beautiful blooming Rosemary.

Devotedly,
Chas

WINONA TO BROOKLYN

April 1, 1970

*So I don't forget — my last letters of job-hunting for a
while (I hope):*

1. *Educational Career Service (according to NY Times,
   a free placement service)*
2. *Saint Francis College, Brooklyn*
3. *The New School for Social Research*

(Later) Dear,

*I always meant to comment on your comments on <u>The
Sun Also Rises</u>. Do you remember your comments? Generally I
agree with your ideas. Exceptions:*

*I do see a change in Jake — from the pleading man at
the beginning of the novel who asks Brett if there isn't some way
they can still make a go of it, to the older, sadder, wiser Jake
who says, "Isn't it pretty to think so?" as a comment about
Brett's <u>self-delusion</u>. I agree that Brett is consummate
selfishness, but I maintain that she rationalizes it to herself by
the self-delusion that she is a little noble at times – e.g., when
she gives up Romero and feels "less a bitch" for a while. Does*

*she give up Romero or does he see he can never make her into
the lady he wants?*

*I think it's important that Cohn be Jewish just in the
sense that he belongs to a minority group and had to fight to be
the All-American boy-man, a star boxer. He tries too hard and
we don't like him for it. (Hemingway modeled Cohn on someone
he actually knew and didn't like too well — a few hard feelings
came of it when the book came out!)*

*Jake did pander for Brett when he put her and Romero
together. She did have control over him. He was disgusted with
himself for betraying the aficionados and consequently losing the
friendship of Montoya. He finally shakes himself free of this
control, I believe, when he sends the telegram to her and signs it
"Love, Jake," and has his little moment of truth. When he can
finally say cynically, "Isn't it pretty to think so?" he is a free
man. That is when he was at last saying to Brett, "You don't
have any real control over me."*

*I can send you pages of notes on The Great Gatsby if
you want them. Or shall we wait to talk when I come in late
April? (When, I said, not if! What optimism!)*

Will close now, for second time today.

Love, Francha

BROOKLYN TO WINONA

April 2, 1970

Darling,

*I had my first evening as a politico. Peter Eikenberry
has a storefront campaign office. The primary isn't until June
23. Things were very quiet. I answered three or four phone calls
and stuffed about 500 envelopes.*

*I'm enclosing the photos.
Most you will enjoy. I just love the
expression in "WELCOME ROSIE."
The early morning shots leave
something to be desired.*

*This is vacation week so I couldn't call New York City
Community College. When I telephoned College for Human
Services, the gal in charge of personnel was away. I am to call*

*back again on Monday. I'll also try NYCCC at that time (and
speak to Professor Becker).*

*I did reach the New York City Board of Education and
asked them to send you materials on their adult education
programs. The State Board of Education was also very helpful.
You should send a résumé to the Personnel Director in Albany.
You ask for info about the "Specialist-in-Education" program,
which requires only a Master's Degree. I would also suggest
that you indicate you prefer living in the New York City area.*

*Another résumé should be sent to the Personnel Director
to the State University of New York in Albany. Their Urban
Center is affiliated with N.Y.C. Community College. Again, you
should indicate that you are interested in locating in the N.Y.C.
area.*

*I just feel sure we are going to find something that will
be a challenge and a joy for you.*

*Why don't you send me a copy of your résumé and I will
Xerox about 25 copies, returning them to you. This way you can
write a brief personal note and enclose the Xeroxed vitae. It will
save you a great deal of typing. I could kick myself for not
suggesting this sooner. You shouldn't be wasting it on such a
simply mechanical task.*

*Yesterday I visited a public school in Long Island. They
have been experimenting in using TV as a teaching aid. The
class we observed is called TV reading (not remedial reading).
The kids choose, research, produce and direct their own TV
productions. In the process they learn basic research and how to
communicate: read, speak, write. Something they refused to
learn by attacking directly, they learn indirectly. The teachers
marvel (1) how the basic attitudes of the kids change, as learning
becomes fun! and (2) how reading scores and communication
skills show marked improvement.*

*The future use of Brooklyn Prep is clearer now. There is
a proposal for (1) a pre-prep; (2) a 4-year academic H.S.; and
(3) an M-A-T teacher-training program. Now to find funds! Ugh!*

*Darling, I love you and miss you. There is a WELCOME
ROSIE branded in my heart.*

*Devotedly,
Charlie*

BROOKLYN TO WINONA

Sunday [April 5, 1970]

My dearest,

I've tallied your job-hunt report. You wrote sixteen letters in two days. That must have been a terrific ordeal. But I am confident that a good opportunity will present itself. I had lunch with Jody today and told her about what you were doing. I urge you to write one more letter, to Seton Hall University. The application should be addressed to the Dean of the School of Arts and Sciences. Jody said that you should use her name in the letter. Seton Hall is co-ed and medium-sized within commuting distance of NYC. Jody works there at the Institute of Judeo-Christian Studies. We are going to have to pack a helluva lot into those few days you are here.

One of the things we will have to do is see "Z" – which I understand means, "He is risen" in Greek. Don't ask me why. Jody says we'll have to see it. I also want to get tickets for "A Child's Play."

Today was a beautiful sunny-blue day. The kids were riding their bikes and some were roller-skating – one of the surest signs of spring. We have had day after day of rain and snow, and the wind is too strong for umbrellas. It has been a long hard winter. I miss Austin, where I could play tennis all-year-round.

Had a good talk with John Doar on Friday. He brought up the subject of my salary. He asked me if I had enough to live on, almost as if he felt guilty about my wages. I said I was doing all right, and that in time I would speak to him about a revision. I said I wanted to stay with the Corporation (giving no specific date). He replied with a half smile: "You've got to." This exchange made me feel good. But I had to assert myself to go into his office. What an important year this is for me! What an opportunity for growth. Dr. Doltolo told me yesterday that my passivity may be a defense against a deep, unconscious anger rooted back in my childhood. Being a "nice guy" is a great quality, and I shouldn't lose it necessarily, but I must assert myself so that I can discover the "me" beneath the façade. The defense against anger (passivity) that worked well for me as a child (it helped keep the anger down and won parental approval)

*now holds me back from being a more effective person. I have to
make the effort to be assertive and I shy away from this because
I am afraid of the person I may discover in the assertiveness.*

*About the priesthood. Bob M's course of action doesn't
so much appeal to me. I find it curious. I am especially interested
in the advice of the Bishop. I cannot go back to the priesthood,
full time with the sacraments and the sanctuary. By open church
I meant (1) a church that accepts a married clergy; (2) a church
that does not require rigid doctrinal conformity, but is primarily
a community in process of discovery – whatever direction that
search may lead to. I have a dream, darling – that some day,
long after we are married, an appeal may come from Rome for
"ex-priests" to resume their duties. I could respond to this call
provided it didn't interfere with (1) my family; (2) my work; (3)
my "seeking" Catholic conscience. Meanwhile I am happy to
remain in the pews.*

*Today was especially good at St Thomas in Harlem. A
liturgy committee chose the readings, wrote the canon, selected
some of the music. The theme was joy – in the little things and
big things. Little things: Being tucked into bed, a smile, a warm
sunny day, vanilla ice cream.... Big things: friendship, marriage,
a clear conscience. It was a beautiful experience and reminded
me of some of the best things we did at the Student Center. At the
end of Mass, one of the members of the congregation said there
is also a joy in giving, and everyone was handed a flower!
(Maybe it was better than anything we ever did at the Student
Center – and it came from the pews!)*

Some items of shorter note –

*You are right. I wouldn't enjoy hunting, but I do enjoy
walking and talking. Remember our walk down the road at
Bastrop State Park in Texas! What a great feeling it was to be
with you outdoors. Didn't we have blankets around us, like
Indians? Remember our brief walk through the Botanical
Gardens here? This is the kind of walking, darling. But what
would your Dad and I talk about? The land? Certainly not
Lyndon. Perhaps I'd make a joke about the Austin businessman
(can't think of his name) whose campaign signs – black with
white lettering – amused the nation: "Bring Lyndon Home."*

*I am not a baron and neither is Deane. I really think
Deane is thumbing his nose at Grosse Pointe and Palm Beach
society; getting his long-earned revenge. He is showing us all
how stupid so many of our conventions are. I am not sure he is
conscious of this (maybe I'm Dr. Doltolo-izing too much).
Father George is, I am told, an Orthodox priest. I was kidding
with my brother Bob, and said, really, Father George might have
been someone Deane met in a bar and put up to the job. Deane
is capable of such a hoax. He is really down to earth in person,
but only to those closest to him. He is so terribly vulnerable and
has created a fantastic defense around himself. I can't believe he
and his wife will share the same room. But I'll bet they are
scheming together.*

*I think my favorite painting
by Rouault is <u>Christ Mocked</u>. His
head is slightly bowed. By a few
heavy lives Rouault can say so much
– there is so much dignity and
suffering in that rendering of Jesus.*

*I am waiting for your call
this evening, and even though I am
going to be talking with you in a
little while, I can't seem to stop
writing. Next Saturday I pick up my
new suit. I realize, as I sit here facing the curtains, that my new
suit resembles the color of the curtains! Isn't that funny. And I
had a crazy dream the other night. I was trying to call the folks
long distance and I couldn't get them. I awoke with the number I
was dialing fresh in my memory – 55987 – your zip code!*

*Your comments on Hemingway are clarifying. I still
wonder about the relationship between Jake and Brett. Is "Isn't
it pretty to think so?" a wistful desire of Jake to be under her
control, i.e., a childlike impulse, a longing for childhood; yet he
realizes he couldn't live with himself in this kind of relationship,
so he has to break with her. The only kind of relationship that
Brett can have with Jake is one of control over him? Is this the
tragedy? Even though Jake is free, he can't have what he wants
most of all?*

You know what, sweetie – our phone bill was only $35 last month!

I think I'll sign off now. I'm getting a little tired.

Reading your last three letters – all the love and beauty in them – makes me realize what a fortunate man I am to have your love and to be able to give you mine. COME JOIN ME SOON!

Affectionately,
Chas

P.S. "I thank you God for most this amazing day!" e.e.

P.S. Darling, the darn phone is out of order again, so I won't be hearing from you tonight. Love, but disappointed, Chas

WINONA TO BROOKLYN

CST
April 7, 1970

Dearest C,

As soon as I get a free minute I shall write to those new addresses you sent me. Just as I catch up he sends me more!

I met the Nassau and Catonsville men listed at the Des Moines Convention. The Nassau guy said about 2 Sundays ago the NY Times ran a huge ad for the CUNY system for teachers. Is it too late for you to find that ad?

Eileen and I had a great visit and good time at the convention. Then Sat. night we stayed with Joanie in Decorah. (Ed is now the only one of us who has not been at Joanie's!) Sunday Joanie drove us to Rochester. Today I put Eileen on the bus for Minneapolis and airport after she had a great visit with her sisters in Minnesota. She still loves us, and we still love her.

I tried to call you Sunday night and your phone is messed up again. Sigh. Last night I didn't get a chance to try. I'll try late tonight and here's hoping. I miss your voice very much. Sure hope the electronic equipment comes to our aid.

I am especially eager to hear if Ed has reached you and told you that the Law School is interested in you for running the Office of Equal Opportunity office in Austin. Would you be tempted? I can't stop thinking how tantalized you will be.

I'm running now to hear visiting poet Dan Gerber....

Love,
Francha

4/8/70

I just typed out Give a Damn [adapted from the song by
A Rocket to the Moon]. *Do you know the song? At any rate, it
reminded me of you and your efforts and aspirations.*

> *If you'd take the train with me*
> *Uptown, thru the misery*
> *Of ghetto streets...*
> *it might begin to teach you*
> *How to give a damn*
> *about your fellow man....*

I'd better get this in the mail.

*Oh – I got your long Sunday letter this a.m. Your letters
are so thoughtful and well-said. I love them. I love you.*

BROOKLYN TO WINONA

Wednesday a.m. [April 8, 1970]

Darling,

*It's a beautiful sunny spring morning in Brooklyn. The
intense yellow brightness penetrates the tiny weave-openings of
the curtains giving them a deeper, richer color. The birds are
chirping. It's too early for traffic sounds. I'm still "up" from
having heard the sound of your voice last night. All systems are
"come join me"! Come soon!*

*I thought you might like to file the Hemingway article for
the next time you teach* The Sun Also Rises.

*Dolores wrote a rambling Easter letter describing her
white feelings teaching Mexican kids, the joy of planting sweet
peas with her daughter, and her worries about her teenagers
who went to a rock festival in Lubbock, a Texas town with an
"Easy Rider" resistance to the young. She looks forward to your
coming to Austin. Dolores is very discreet. She never mentions
you and me in the same line. She continues to urge me to visit
though. Very thoughtful.*

*I mailed in my income tax returns yesterday and if my
computations are correct, I will have enough refund from
federal, state* and *city taxes to finance your trip to NYC the last
weekend of April. I have enough in the bank to take care of
everything, but I would much rather have the refund money so
that we can save the other for this summer. I'm going to have to*

ask for a raise soon. We need the money for our future. In order to ask for it I want to have accomplished something for the Bedford-Stuyvesant people. Yet I realize the self-imposed standard is not realistic; it takes so long to accomplish things here. I also detect a little pride. We can talk about it when you're here. It's great to have your visit to look forward to. Love, love, love dear.

Charlie

WINONA TO BROOKLYN

April 10, 1970

Darling,

It's Friday night, and I have a few minutes, before I tumble into bed, to collect my thoughts and send them on to you. Earlier the sisters at St. Anne's Hospice a few blocks away invited us over for fun and games — and a few of us went. We did a few round dances, polkas, and schottisches (sp?) and were done in. It's fun to be silly once in a while, although I have to admit I missed the mixed company of other "silly" fun times. You in particular, dear. It reminded me of the silly charades we played at Holy Cross HS — when you called us ladies BROADS!

Darling, I got a positive response from Orange County Community College in Middletown, NY. I am to send in the application form and they will arrange for an interview by telephone. What do you say to that?

Rejections: 1) Williamsport Area Com. College 4/7
2) Villanova U. 4/7
3) St. Francis College (Brooklyn)
(no date)
4) Trenton State College 4/2
5) Newark Col. of Engineering 4/1

NYU says (4/6): "As soon as we know what vacancies exist for next year we will consider your application...."
So that's the state of the union at this minute.

Did you celebrate properly the defeat of Carswell and mediocrity? [The U.S. Senate had just rejected this Nixon nominee for the U.S. Supreme Court.]

Thank you for all the goodies you enclose – from Eddie
Bonnemère to Papa Hemingway!

I love you –
Francha

BROOKLYN TO WINONA

Saturday [April 11, 1970]

Darling,

I'm going to write very quickly now – more tomorrow.
I've been on the run all day. Here are some of the things
I've done – Saturday laundry and cleaners, bought a beautiful
mirror at St Vincent de Paul for my bureau ($2.00), breakfast of
bacon and eggs and Sara Lee coffee cake (love the stuff), Dr
Doltolo – he is beginning to help me to see the kinds of conflicts
that have been going on within me that have been taking up a
great deal of my energies – e.g., the conflict between the real self
and the image I have of myself, the conflict between the man and
the child within me, the conflict between the desire I have to
assert myself and the desire I have not to assert (in order to be
loved). I can't think of others at the moment. Then I picked up
my new suit which I will wear to church tomorrow for the first
time (an old family custom), I bought you a present which I will
give you when you arrive, I went to a health fair in Bedford
Stuyvesant and learned a lot more about the health delivery
system here, I got my shoes shined for Sunday, and in a few
moments I'm on my way to the the parents of Joe [who had
recently left the Paulists]. *I'm enclosing some more about the*
"head-hunter." I'll check with CUNY on Monday. I can't
understand how I missed that ad! Got Mary B and Bob M's
wedding invite. What kind of invitation will we send?

Charlie and Francha love each other; Francha and
Charlie love you.
God is love.
Charlie and Francha and all of us have love.
Let's celebrate our love, especially the love of Francha
and Charlie
which they will mutually promise to share together,
under the same roof, for as long as they live.

Just off the top, darling. We can do better if we put our heads and hearts together.

Chas

What is the melody to "Give a Damn"? I like it!

WINONA TO BROOKLYN

April 11, 1970

Dear —

     Latest "no openings": Fordham U. – 4/7; Beaver College – 4/8; Providence College – 4/8.

     Joe says that he gave my credentials to Queens' SEEK director; jobs are scarce with SEEK as everywhere, but they still will be in touch with me later....?

     I just finished my application form to Orange. Co. Community College. 4/11

     Later: also sent application form to Cooperative College Registry – 4/11

Letters of inquiry to: *SEEK – 4/11*
                           NY State Dept. of Ed. – 4/11
                           State U. of NY – 4/11
                           Seton Hall U. – 4/11

     Counting those listed above, I now have 20 letters unanswered. 21 have been answered.

     Wow! No wonder I can't keep up with papers to correct. Which is what I must do now....

R
4/13/70

Sweetie,

     Just came from a MARVILLOSA concert—Stanley Plummer, violinist. Wow.

     Staten Is. Com. College, CUNY, sent an application form but little hope. I may as well send it in, although I'm getting mighty sick of the whole business.

     I enclose a note from an elderly sister in our house. The first hint of blaming others for me leaving. I consider the source (she's approaching senility perhaps, though very sincere) and I'll thank her & reassure her, and that will be that.

CST 4/13/70

While I'm in the "letter-writing business" I'll
write one to you! These thoughts will have to be written
for tears would fall speaking them — just as they did
when I recently heard of your plan to leave us.

You are a beautiful young sister, a good faithful
religious and an excellent teacher. You have <u>so much</u> to
give to God, through our Community, and your vocation
is a personal call to this service.

Sister, please think this over before acting
finally. I'm sure your faithfulness in prayer will merit
sufficient grace to strengthen you in this matter if you
place <u>all</u> your trust in God.

It seems to me that you have been unduly
influenced. Sister, please do not consider this as
meddling — I do not mean it so.

You have your own life to live and your own
soul to save. God be with you, Sister, whatever you
decide. My prayers are with you.

Sincerely,
SMB

Many others are expressing regrets in person – 2 today,
for example. But NOBODY has been ugly.

You would laugh to see me now – straight hair hanging
in my face, sitting awkwardly on my bed in my PJs, writing on
top of my briefcase. I hope you can read this.

Snow today!!! Land o'Goshen! A couple of inches, I'd
guess.

And a nice note from Eileen today, thanking me for the
good visit and saying that all is well, and Ed was warm to come
home to.

Makes me lonesome, dear, for you. I love you.

Rosie

BROOKLYN TO WINONA

Sunday evening [April 12, 1970]

Dearest,

Here I am on Sunday evening, once again waiting for
your call. I just got up to check – the phone <u>is</u> working! Hurrah!

I am relaxed. I just finished a chicken pie. The radio is on. I'm listening to a Villa Lobos (sp?) composition. The music is a little distracting because the composer is original. He's one of my favorites – a Brazilian who can communicate the experience of that country which mixes the savage [i.e., indigenous] *with the old world.*

I've had a good day. I traveled to Harlem for Mass. This morning they had a play as part of the fore-Mass. I'm enclosing the script. I wore my new suit. The Harlem parish is the only parish I feel at home in. I wish it weren't so far away.

After Mass I took the D train to 59th St. I had an appointment with Fr. Jim L [at the Paulist "mother church" on 59th Street], *a good Paulist friend, who is doing a dissertation on the priesthood. I am one of his interviewees. This was the first time I was to visit my old haunt since requesting the leave of absence and laicization. I was apprehensive. I got to 59th St early, so I walked down Central Park South to the Plaza Hotel – the only way I can give you a feel for the hotel is to say it's the kind of hotel Gatsby would have felt comfortable in. I went to the bar and had one expensive drink ($1.80 for a martini). While sitting at the bar I read the last few pages of the Autobiography of Malcolm X. I amused myself at the contrast between my reading matter and my plush surroundings.*

I had a good visit with Jim L. His questions helped me to articulate my present position. I quickly lost my uneasiness. JL urged me to visit more often, and I will. Jim's theory is that the men who are role-changing are persons who can live with ambivalence, are very open, non-authoritative persons.

When I left 59th St I decided I didn't want to talk any more. I'd been with Jim in intensive conversation for an hour and a half. I took the subway to my park, Prospect Park, and it was delightful. It was cold enough to wear an overcoat, but the sun was out, bright and warm. The park was full of people – typical Brooklynites – just like a subway car population, multiplied hundreds of times – blacks in all forms of colorful dress, Puerto Rican families jabbering in their clacking Spanish, well-dressed Jewish ladies and men, hippies, fat people, skinny people, pimply faces, brown complexions, charcoal black faces, tans and pale whites. A galaxy of humanity. I dodged bicycle

riders, paused to watch young lovers for a moment or two,
sauntered by family groups, and listened to parents disciplining
their children. As I paused on a promenade, below me there
were about thirty young people in what looked like Scot
uniforms, marching in military fashion. It was fun. I didn't know
what I'd see next. The skating rink was closed so I walked by the
zoo. The white polar bears were clumsily begging for food. Most
of the crowd was absorbed by the seals. The merry-go-round
was delightful, all ages riding. One boy was smiling and waving
at everyone; another was in misery, crying the whole time. I
picked a few little shoots which are promises of spring. These I
enclose. Then I walked back to my apartment, and here I am
anxiously awaiting your voice, my love. I imagined that you were
with me on that walk this afternoon, enjoying the same things
and pointing out to me things I'd never have noticed. My love
always.

Devotedly,
Chas

BROOKLYN TO WINONA

Thursday p.m. [April 16, 1970]

Darling,

> *Enclosed is the blank check. It expresses my trust in you;*
my desire to see you and to be with you, the unlimited way in
which I want to give to you and be for you.

> *Tomorrow I meet with my public services staff to review*
our goals and timetables for the next two years. Most of my work
thus far is in terms of promise, the future. I can't point to a
single de facto accomplishment, yet each day I learn a little
more, or make another contact, and hopefully this will culminate
in something positive for the community. There are many irons
in the fire. I am hopeful. There is a chemistry for
accomplishment and I continue to experiment with ingredients.

> *The radio just announced that Apollo 13 is on course*
and will splash down close to target. I am happy for the families
of these brave men. My thoughts of course return to Bedford-
Stuyvesant and the threat to daily life that puts fear into
thousands of people whose concerns do not make the papers
except in terms of high infant mortality rates, increased narcotic

deaths, and more muggings. Until the nation can focus on the concrete crust of our cities the way it rivets attention on the moon crust – we are off course.

With this bit of homily, I will close with all my love, dear.

PAY TO THE ORDER OF FRANCHA MY ROSEMARY ALL MY LOVE FOREVER.

Chas

BROOKLYN TO WINONA
Thursday [April 16, 1970]

Dearest,

I wrote you this morning – my blank check. Jean Smith called me at work and invited me out for the weekend. I accepted, cancelled my appointment with Dr. Doltolo and called Jody to say I'd miss seeing her this Sunday (next Sunday too). In some ways I didn't want to go; I can't relax completely with Steve and Jean. But the country is beautiful now and the prospect of playing tennis lures me. Also curiosity – why do they want me? So I won't be at the apartment if you call on Saturday, but I will be there Sunday p.m., looking forward to hearing your voice and putting the final touches on our plans for the coming week.

Had a good meeting of the public services staff today. There is a possibility of latching onto some government money for a narcotics facility. There is also the possibility of a model sanitation project taking place in Bedford-Stuyvesant.

This carries all my love, Rosemary my Francha.

Devotedly,
Charlie

BROOKLYN TO WINONA
Thursday evening [April 16, 1970]

Dearest,

This is my third letter today! I hope my handwriting is disguised enough. It's 11 p.m.

I'm going to write Mary B tonight. We'll have to select a gift that we can give together. I'm telling Mary that I can't make the wedding, but I'm sending my better half!

*Tonight was uneventful at the storefront political base. I
just sat in the office and made small talk. There was really
nothing to do. I'm coming to the conclusion that I'm not
politically oriented. It seems strange that I will be spending the
weekend with Robert Kennedy's campaign manager, and the
man behind Arthur Goldberg's nomination for governor of NY.*

My love, love,
Charlie

WINONA TO BROOKLYN

Enclosed are two hand-copied "concrete poems": Pedro
Xisto's "Epithalalium" and e.e. cummings' "loneliness."

CST 4/16/70

Dearest,
*A sister, who is very fond of me, gave me a passage to
read last night from Louis Evely's A RELIGION FOR OUR
TIME. I quote from it for you, in order to get your impression
and opinion:*

….To separate yourself from the Church would be to
separate yourself from Christ, to rend the communion of
charity which he wants among all his members. And
what will you represent then? Will you preach in your
own name? Will you preach a doctrine of love and union
which you have already denied?...

And this came out in 1968, at least in the English edition.
*I must run off to a committee meeting—my first all year!
– on preparation of the culture and entertainment we will bring
to the college next year. But I want you to know that, in the midst
of term papers and frantic preparations to meet the next hour or
day, you are in my heart and often in my musings.*
*I was especially touched in your last letter with your
composition for our wedding invitation. It makes it seem so near,
dear.*
More later…

Love always,
Rosemary

I traveled to New York in late April in order to interview at two institutions for a teaching assignment: Orange County Community College in Middletown, NY; and New York City Community College in Brooklyn. I brought a gift for Charlie: a copy of Rouault's painting, *The Old King.* And we found time for exploring corners of New York, like walking on the beach at Coney Island.

BROOKLYN TO WINONA

Tuesday [April 28, 1970]

Dearest,

There are so many evidences of your presence that your absence is that much more

difficult to bear. There are the graham crackers in the cabinet; the extra dishes in the sink; your big white bath towel; the green wash cloth and towel; the strong royal profile, eyes fixed on your curtains – clutching yellow flowers.

As I reflect on the weekend I hesitate to single out events, but you can file the following in the easy-to-please category: the way you took my arm when we walked; the conversation about teaching, over chicken-pie suppers on Sunday evening.

I called Nancy tonight. The reason we couldn't reach her was typical of NYC – their phone was out of order. She repeated how much they had enjoyed Sunday. Me too. That's another for the file. I told you how much you added to my being with Nancy and Warren.

I'm enclosing another notice about fall teaching opportunities. And don't forget to send a résumé to OPEN

*ADMISSIONS, CUNY, 535 EAST 80th ST, NYC 10021. This is the
response to the N.Y. Times ad, and should touch all CUNY
possibilities. I'll be anxious to hear tomorrow if there are any
more positive responses.*

*Had a good chat with John Doar today. When I walked
in the office, he looked up at me and said, "How are things
going?" I replied (instead of my usual "Fine"), "I'm struggling.
I wouldn't want to be working any place else at the moment." He
responded with a half-smile. "It's tough, isn't it!" Then I
peppered three questions at him and he fired back quick but
helpful answers. I felt I communicated much better, but I had to
prepare for that brief meeting. Before going in, I asked myself,
"What do I want?"*

*As I repeat that question now, the answer is clear! "You,
and to be with you."*

My love, darling—
Chas

WINONA TO BROOKLYN

28 April, 1970
St. Teresa's

Dear C,

*Got home safely and comfortably. The 5 o'clock United
got into Chicago at 6 o'clock Central time. I grabbed a cart and
wheeled colorfully (got lots of stares!) through the length of the
terminal, arrived at Mississippi Valley's terminal at about 6:30,
learned that, sure enough, they had changed their schedule as of
April 26, but that their 6 o'clock flight to Winona was late and I
could still catch it. So ten minutes later I was on board once
again (couldn't even go to the bathroom) and got into Winona at
8:30. I was met by two young sisters who then treated me to a
Dairy Queen (a big one for a dime, non-New York prices!) and
then came to my room for a festive chat and presented me with
some bright purple gorgeous fabric with which they are going to
make me a going-away dress!!! Ain't that sweet? They stayed in
my room till eleven (with a couple of others coming in and out)
and by that time I was really tired – remember, we got up at 6:30
NY time—so I just rolled into bed, not even unpacking my
toothbrush. Today I arose at 7:30 to unpack and get ready to*

confront my eager students. All afternoon I have been here in my office getting organized, reading mail, writing a couple letters.

*I got an application form from Catonsville Community College and a letter asking me to specify which days I can come to interview in early May. They sound interested. My friend the Dean must have said something very nice. But Middletown is closer, yes? I'll probably send in the application but also write "Please consider me" to Orange Co.

*Materials and brochures arrived from NY State Ed. Dep't about Specialists in Education.

*"No openings" from St. Joseph's College, Philadelphia.

*"No foreseen needs" from Seton Hall, but something unforeseen may show up.

*Brochures, etc., from Albany central office of SUNY, encouraging me to write to individual colleges.

As you can see, my mailbox was packed. I should have asked Lalonde to check it, but did not think of it.

Believe it or not, Lalonde's <u>mother</u> was operated upon in my absence. Hemorrhaging and they did not know what they would find, but it was certainly unexpected. I guess she came home within two days and is fine again — will be able to resume nursing duties for her dying husband later this week. Lalonde left yesterday for two days at home, so I missed her. What <u>more</u> can happen in that family?????

I hope the old king is keeping you sufficient company these days. Whenever you need to be cheered up, just imagine the face of the thief as he looks in your window and changes his mind about coming in....

You know I love you.

Rosie

By now I had made my summer plans – to go to Austin to continue work on my dissertation.

BROOKLYN TO WINONA

Saturday [May 2 (?), 1970]

Dearest,

The old king is looking out the window and I don't know why he scowls; it's a warm bright day. I've spent the morning puttering – sewing and cleaning and cooking. I haven't read the paper yet, but I did read your cheerful letter. I miss you. I can't help but think of how we enjoyed Coney Island last Saturday. I wish we could take the Circle Line today!

Yesterday I received a long involved letter from Bob T [a U of Texas professor]. *He is studying religion in London. Family life is wonderful but he is disenchanted with the Church of England which decided not to demonstrate against the visiting South African cricket players.*

Pat W [a member of the U of Texas CSC community] *called from Texas last night. She was cheerful and said that Bernie seemed to be pulling out of the drug scene. That strange group he lived with has broken up. They worry about me because I don't write. She said Joseph W* [a UT professor] *wants me to return! I told her I was on a leave of absence and had applied for laicization. I didn't mention our plans. I think it's better if you do that. I have no idea how prevalent the rumors are, but the less you have to explain, the easier it will be on you this summer. I leave public relations up to you, because you will be on the scene, dear.*

Izzie [a first cousin of Charlie's] *telephoned this morning from California. She thought I was ill in Louisiana. I apologized for my silence and said we had tried to call her last Sunday. She sends her love. I told her about our plans. She was delighted!*

My cold has a bark much worse than its bite, but I sound so stuffed up that I've cancelled appointments rather than expose persons to my germs. I've been at the office every day, trying to keep my distance and do my work.

I think your strategy on the schools is good. As I said on the phone, the other night, if you feel Middletown, then I think you should make your pitch. I must say that as the whole N.Y. experience hits me now, I react the way you do. Middletown makes sense; so does the State University program on Atlantic Avenue. I think SEEK would too. Catonsville is too far! I think

*you are going to be awfully good at the challenge and will enjoy
it – even if some aspects of NY life (subways at rush hour) are
hard to take.*

*This room is so quiet and lonely without you. Yet, there
are so many reminders of your presence. Hurry back, darling.
I'll be hearing from you tomorrow evening.*

*Sorry to hear there is so much for Lalonde and her
parents to bear.*

This carries all my love, Rosemary my Francha.

*The bright purple will look great as we sashay down
Underhill!*

*Your devoted
Chas*

BROOKLYN TO WINONA

*Monday morning
Just before going to work*
[May 4, 1970]

Dearest,

*I'm enclosing the interesting review of Max Brand's life
because of his doppelganger image* [an aspect of my
dissertation-in-progress]. *There must be something of this in all
of us – the person we really are and the person we want to be or
imagine ourselves to be. Would Faust have been a happier or
better adjusted person if he had read this and understood himself
as Dempsey understands him? Or was it terribly important for
Faust-Brand to spend those lonely morning hours at his poetry?
The Anthony Lewis piece puts Cambodia and campus unrest in
perspective for me.*

*I love you.
Charlie*

WINONA TO BROOKLYN

*May 4, 1970
CST*

Dear Chas,

*Another letter from you today—your Sat. one! What mail
service!*

My best news today is that I heard from Pam – a short letter but a very welcome one. She assures me that she is not dead; asks about you; says she just can't get to MN before May 16 (my "graduation" date) and damn; says she has been at her "motherhouse" a lot helping with Christian weekends or something; the deaconesses are out to get her, help! and (casually) she almost got married but saved herself in the nick of time, realizing that it just wouldn't work, but she still sees him, an ex-seminarian and Catholic.

My God, what a girl!

Tomorrow and Wednesday I teach my last classes of the year. Thursday I begin tests (which I haven't made out yet, naturally). Friday is Pledge Day – the Teresans (many with tongue in cheek at the required convocation) pledge themselves to the ideals on our college seal, namely purity, loyalty, and truth. Today was May crowning, initiated by a few junior girls and attended mostly by sisters. I went out of a feeling of loyalty rather than devotion — in much the spirit that I went to see their prom. I wish it were a devotion but it just isn't.

Today was a lovely May day—and still I'm grouchy! I think part of it is the realization that only 2 weeks of convent life remain, and that is bound to be a somewhat painful severance.

Can you take me for better or worse?

Love,
Rosemary

WINONA TO BROOKLYN

I enclosed the lyrics of Paul Simon's "Bridge over Troubled Waters."

May 7, 1970

Hi,

Did I tell you that Rollo May [author of Man's Search for Meaning] has been ill and his doctor will not let him keep his speaking engagements? I was very disappointed, thinking quite selfishly about it all. I understand he is practicing clinically again, however.

I enclose what your description of your photograph of
the Brooklyn Bridge [see this book's cover] *reminded me of. And*
how I feel in relation with you.

I think a bunch of us will go to St. Paul to see <u>*Fiddler on*</u>
<u>*the Roof*</u> *next week. My cousin gave the singing group at her*
wedding some money for such an outing, and, although I have
seen it – remember? (That was before September 21 [our
"anniversary"]*, do you remember that?) – the other young sisters*
are delighted with the prospect, and there isn't much choice in
the limited time we have left.

It's Ascension Thursday (did you go to Mass?) and I am
reminded of my homily in Texas a year ago. "The good old
days...." [While I was a staff member at the CSC, the priests
invited me to give the Ascension Thursday homily – a first for
me and a rarity for a woman to preach in the Catholic Church. I
took for my text the following words, from a greeting card.]

>*He came singing love*
>*He died singing love*
>*He rose singing love*
>*If His song is to continue,*
> *we must do the singing.*

Two finals have been given now, and await correcting. I
just typed out the third, and must still make up the fourth. The
pressure is letting up, and the days are lovely. All continues to
go fairly well, considering everything.

The peace and rally signs have been matched on campus
with "Tell it to Hanoi" and the like – products of "Young
Americans for Freedom." Incredible, but they too have a right to
speak out. One little sign has only a picture, a white dove
stabbed and bleeding (dead?) by the red sickle of Soviet Russia.

Must go to lunch. I love you.

Rosie

BROOKLYN TO WINONA
Thursday – no – really Friday [May 7/8, 1970

Darling,

Your "mood" letter didn't arrive today. I'm really tired.
I've been on the run all day. After a routine morning of research
and telephone calls, I tried to see John Doar. He was too busy to

*take time in the office, so I rode the subway with him and
brought up the most pressing matters. When I returned to the
office, I met with a Presbyterian minister interested in economic
development in Asia. I toured him through Bed-Stuy. We visited
IBM where 400 are employed. It was RFK's influence that
pressed [IBM's CEO] Thomas J. Watson to bring his business to
Brooklyn. The operation is "beautiful." I was thrilled at the
order, the spirit of the workers, the ingenuity of converting an
old warehouse into a computer manufacturing plant. Then we
visited a shoe store that has been helped by one of our economic
development (no interest) loans. I saw more attractive shoes in
this store than any we saw together. Believe it or not, the shoes
are imported from Italy – real leather and great variety in color.
Send me your shoe size, dearest, and I will venture a purchase
for you. Our next stop was the Sheffield Community Center
where my office will soon be (July), in the middle of Bed-Stuy.*

*When the tour was over, I returned to the office to finish
a memo on the present lack of veteran participation in the G.I.
Bill, and then headed to 110 Livingston Street for a meeting of
the Board of Education. The community people were in full force
telling the Board "how it is." In order to get more community
people (Blacks and Puerto Ricans) as principals and
supervisors, they want to do away with the Board of Examiners,
which they say gives an "idiot test," and make performance "the
test."*

*I didn't wait for the meeting to end, but kept my
commitment to report at Peter Eikenberry's Democratic
headquarters. This evening I typed an anti-war campaign flyer
on a stencil. I had to do it three times to get it right. Before
heading home I picked up my Brooklyn Bridge photograph. Then
I stopped back at the Board of Education for another hour of
community rhetoric, before catching the 41 bus which took me
almost to Grand Army Plaza.*

*Now it's 12:35 a.m. darling. My eyes are burning. I
skipped supper tonight, but am not hungry. I'm just tired; I miss
you. I love you. I look forward to Sunday evening. I hope there is
some good news by then from Orange County.*

My love always,
Chas

Fri a.m.

*P.S. Did you get a wedding invitation from your faithful St
Vincent de Paul workers Hal and Sue?*

   *May is the anniversary of Georgia's baptism. I must
write her.*

   *George H is in Mt. Sinai Hospital. He had a serious
breakdown.*

   Saturday I play my first tennis of the year with George L.
   Love you dear. Chas

WINONA TO BROOKLYN

May 8, 1970

Darling,

   *I see by my trusty calendar that you are about to
celebrate (?) your tenth anniversary as priest. How does that
make you feel, my dear? This year is my tenth since first vows,
too.*

   *Today is "Pledge Day" at CST – the girls gather in
required convocation to honor the seniors. The seniors receive
the pin with the college seal, and later today all are invited to
pledge themselves to the ideals on the college seal, "Purity,
Loyalty, and Truth." It used to be a sacred ceremony as late as
my graduation, 1963.Today it's PLT Day, butt of many unkind
jokes. Well, Truth is still respected, it seems!*

   Milton Friedman [the conservative economist] *comes to
Winona tonight to shake us up a bit.*

   Enclosed is an anniversary present! Can you find me?
[A photo.]

Love,
Rosemary

WINONA TO BROOKLYN

May 11, 1970

Dearest,

   *HAPPY ANNIVERSARY. I hope you got my card today.
You probably got 2 letters. I got 2 from you today.*

   *Georgia wrote, too, sending a new address in De Ridder,
Louisiana. 90 acres. They like it. She seems happy.*

I loved little Edith's letter! [Charlie's eleven-year-old goddaughter.]

Sorry about George H. He seemed well enough – what I saw of him – at Toby's wedding. You have been wondering about him, though, haven't you? Any progress for him?

Yes, I got invited to Hal and Sue's wedding. I wrote a note to Sue that I would miss it; I will arrive in Texas a little too late.

Milton Friedman is a close-minded economist who counsels Nixon. But he's an engaging speaker. He's against do-good gov't plans — used welfare and prohibition as examples of why do-gooders won't work. Basically he says he's against all coercion, including the draft and prohibition of marijuana, as long as no one hurts somebody else. He said some things I agreed with and lots of things I didn't, but he was stimulating, anyway.

How do you like my last purple letter? End with a bang. [I enclosed the dittoed letter, which included a cartoon saying, "Think, but groove a little." I signed off for the school year but did not mention that I was signing off forever.]

I'm having trouble locating the Bianchi article [discussing lay affiliation]. *I'll keep trying.*

For better or worse....

Rosie

P.S. I found the article this a.m. (Tues.) and am duplicating it. Will send it on shortly.

LOVE

BROOKLYN TO WINONA

Tuesday [May 12, 1970]

Darling,

I came home very late last night from a soul-searching, identity-seeking evening [during a gathering of Paulist brothers] *at Duke's . Not many problems were solved, but I feel more sure than ever that most of us want some sort of relationship with the Community. I didn't put forth my ideas on affiliation, but am encouraged to put something down on paper. Joe has been laicized.*

Anyway, when I came home, I read your beautiful letter, and the Paul Simon poem about the bridge, and fell asleep, untroubled, with you very present to me. That touching expression of your love made you very real. Whatever wrinkles (like troubled waters) surfaced on my forehead (after that soul-searching evening) were smoothed. You were the bridge over troubled waters, and because you were bridge I could reach you, though miles apart.

I feel we must do something to bridge the communication gap these next few weeks. Can't I write you at St. Teresa's, using "Educational Affiliate, 268 Ashland Place, Brooklyn" as my return address? Won't you have to communicate with English departments? I will be so happy when we can be open. The strictures of tradition and society bear heavy upon us, forcing us to conceal something that is good and beautiful and true – our love – which will, like the sturdy and majestic Brooklyn Bridge, twin towers inseparably joined, survive the storm.

All my love, my darling
Chas
off to work

P.S. We had another bomb scare yesterday.

BROOKLYN TO WINONA
Friday [May 15, 1970]

Darling,

Your "mood" letter came!

Do you know what I was immediately reminded of? Remember once, after I gave a sermon at daily Mass (before September 21), I thought I had been too positive? You smiled and said, "You're never positive enough!" This isn't an exact quote, but it is a recollected impression.

This is how I felt when I read your letter. After our telephone conversation, and your warning, I didn't know quite what to expect. Yet after reading the "indictment" all I could do was smile – and say, as I finished the letter, "YES" – "I do take you for better or for worse." Sweetie – can you take me? ...

Why don't you come to N.Y. rather than Austin for the summer? Much less strain. Remember, you're mine for better or for worse. And I'm yours –

Devotedly,
Charlie

Graduation at CST passed. I said my final farewells, as a sister, to my Franciscan sisters, and I accepted a teaching job at Orange County Community College in Middletown, NY. I then spent a few days back on the Harmony farm with my parents.

HARMONY TO BROOKLYN

May 20, 1970
11 p.m.

Dearest Charlie,

It has been 2 days now at home. Usually there are sisters-in-law, babies, and aunts around enough to keep me happy. When Mom and I are alone she gets on my nerves. I wish I could be more objective.

I miss you so much, but I just can't call here. The telephone is central and right in front of the stairs, and privacy does not exist here. I guess that wears on me most.

Mother already hopes to visit me in (if not drive me out to) New York with Daddy. That may be the time for you to meet them — who knows?

I had a nice talk with the Harmony pastor, this afternoon. You would like him. He is open, well-read, a peacenik. He'd like, for instance, to go to Washington for the May 26 clergy rally for peace. (Are you going?) I finally managed to get it out that I wanted to marry a priest, and he encouraged me in my mature (?) decisions and promised to help, whenever I feel the time is right to tell my parents. I feel good about our talk.

We have been working hard at sewing. We got a lot done but have a lot to go. I'm shortening skirts and hoping I won't have to wear those awful midis. If they are the only acceptable garb next fall, I'll have to start all over again!

Friday evening Lalonde and three others are coming to our farm for dinner. Saturday night we go to Stewartville for a

*picnic at my godparents' home. Sunday I am driving 3
classmates to visit an ex-classmate in New Ulm, MN (about a 4-
hour drive), who just got married a few days ago (she told me
when I called her Monday night – talk about bad
communications!!). Sometime next week we'll go see Joanie –
only ½ hour away – and finalize plans to go to Texas.*

*I will even have a hard time mailing this secretly! Our
mailbox is a mile away and usually someone drops the mail in
the box for the rest of us. So I may carry this around a while.
SIGH....*

*Some day, dear – soon – all will be open and nothing
will need to be hidden. I long for that day because I love you,
Charles dear.*

Rosemary

BROOKLYN TO AUSTIN
Wednesday morning, May 20 [1970]

Dearest,

*Even though I can't mail this now, I thought I'd begin a
letter to you.*

*Last evening I had my first guests since we invited
Warren and Nancy – No, I guess since my Martin Luther King
birthday party. And incidentally, yesterday was Malcolm X's
birthday. Lily and Chuck arrived half an hour early. Fortunately,
I had cleaned the apartment on Saturday. Lily smoked and
Chuck smoked and drank a Fresca. I had a gin and tonic and ate
most of a can of peanuts. Lily was finicky about cockroaches so
there was no eating. Chuck made a thorough search and only
found one. Despite roach phobia, we had good conversation for
an hour and a half and then went to the opening of an African
sculpture exhibit at the Brooklyn Museum. They were both like
children, running excitedly from one art object to another. Lily is
an artist and Chuck collects African sculptures. The show is
superb. The artists, all unknown, in their masks and carvings of
men and women and animals, catch the mystery of the
relationship between the world of nature and the spirit world. I
shall return. There was too much to see at once.*

Love, dear.

Thursday morning May 21

Happy anniversary, dear!
Is it 20 months? It's a stunning day! Perfect to celebrate
our love. Last evening I had dinner with the young man who
lives across the hall in 6B. He teaches in J.H.S. 271 in the Ocean
Hill-Brownsville section of Brooklyn (where everything erupted
in '68). He's a Catholic (ex, he says) and spent three years in the
Peace Corps in India. We talked for hours – dinner in Brooklyn
Heights and then walked to the promenade where there is a
magnificent view of the tip of Manhattan. The Staten Island
Ferry was lighted up, creeping into its Manhattan berth. When
you next visit, this will be one of the first places we go. You were
in my heart, darling. Wherever I go I keep thinking of your
reaction. You would have been excited at the beauty last evening.
(Did you know that Lindsay wants to raise the S.I. Ferry fare to
25 cents?)
I have your birthday in mind and know what I want to
get you, but don't know which store to go to, or how much I'll
pay. I'm going to send it to Texas. It's a surprise!
This morning I'm going to have a talk with John Doar.
He's hard to see – so busy. Love you, dear – and can almost say,
love what I'm doing.

Chas

Saturday May 23

Darling,
Today was a good day. I saw Dr. Doltolo at 10. Most of
our conversation revolves around self-affirmation, and the
emotions that must be challenged to make that affirmation. I'm
beginning to understand more about what holds me back, and I
shrink from the continuing struggle. He asked me today what I
thought my visits to him had done for me. I replied that he simply
re-affirmed objectively, what I had suspected subjectively. Then
he said, "You really knew or suspected all along?" I said yes,
but that I needed verification. I added that I knew the real
struggle (answer) had to come from me.
This evening I've just returned from an AA meeting near
the apartment. I haven't taken the pledge, but I attended because
I'm studying the alcohol problem in Bed-Stuy. I really feared

going to that meeting because it was in Bed-Stuy. And after what happened last Saturday night (the rock incident) [he must have mentioned this incident on the phone] *I was wary about wandering alone. I didn't wear my watch or carry my wallet. I did have $6 just in case – money I would be happy to part with to avoid an incident. I also carried my Blue Cross card for identification. The meeting was in St. Gregory's (RC) school. It was 99% black and black was beautiful. To hear these people speak so openly of themselves – as Edmond might say – "touchingly human." They were very friendly towards me. My early evening fears seem so unwarranted.*

When I returned from Dr. D's office I met George L, and we had a good tennis game. He sends his love. We will have to go out with him the next time you come to N.Y. When will that be, darling? I don't want to wait until August 31. My income tax refund came today ($135.70), and Monday I will have over $700 in the bank.

My dinner is on the stove, darling. I wish you were here and that you had cooked it. I haven't heard from you in a week (as of tomorrow nite) but I understand. I'm just so happy you will be only 66 miles away next year.

Still haven't had my meeting with John Doar. He's been too busy. But tomorrow (Sunday) afternoon we have a tentative date.

All my love –
Charlie

P.S. I bought your present and it's on the way. I got it in Brooklyn!

Sunday May 24

Darling,

Mass at St. Thomas was beautiful today. I not only "served" but distributed communion. It felt "funny" putting on the alb and stole. I enjoyed my role, because <u>*that Mass*</u> *helps me to express my love and hope and struggle in the ghetto. I was called upon by the community to act and I did so with ease. Now I return to my ghetto and my struggle. I can't return to a rectory. I will not be segregated from the people nor can I be stopped from loving or expressing my love for you. I cannot give myself*

*to an institutional framework that keeps me from being myself,
from giving as I need and want to give.* [Theologian] *Ivan Illich
distinguishes between the Church as "it" and the Church as
"her." He loves "her" but not "it." I can be part of "her," but
not "it." Dig?*

*This afternoon I had a good long session with John Doar
– about an hour and a half. He is ready to beef up Public
Services with two assistants! He knows that I know the problem
of the politics of action in our corporate structure – that no
matter how many memos I write (or we will soon be writing), we
can only do what Restoration (the community corporation) wants
to do. Restoration's corporate structure is being modified and I
know my new counterpart in Restoration, Charlie I. And I feel
sure I will be able to work with him. So I am very hopeful today.*

*The only thing is, both the people who work for me will
be making more than I do. I decided not to bring this up yet.
After all, I'm living well enough. I still have the "thing" about
not making too much money. I hate to get "fat" in poverty work.
But as I think of our future, I know I must at some point demand
more to provide for our future. But I'd feel better about making
that demand if a narcotics half-way house that I had planned for
were in operation!*

*These are my thoughts today, darling. I haven't heard
from you and I miss your words and your voice.*

*Love,
Charlie*

Wednesday May 27, your birthday!
Happy Birthday, darling!

*Even if it was only for a few minutes, hearing from you
both by phone and by mail turned me on. I wish I could mail my
letters to you. But on Friday, as you leave with Joanie, I'll
gather all my jottings together and send them to you in Texas.*

*Darling, I had an experience last evening that shook me
up. I don't know how well I'll be able to write about it. About ten
days ago when I took my clothes to the cleaners I noticed that a
new Phoenix Center was opening up on Washington Ave., about
two blocks from here (on the way to St Teresa's Church). This
Center is a storefront intake center for narcotic addicts. I*

decided to follow up on its operation for two reasons. (1) I am interested in learning as much as I can about the problem and its treatment; (2) the facility is in my neighborhood. The director of the center, whom I contacted by phone, invited me to what sounded like an open-house last evening.

It was pouring rain. I was soaked and to add to my discomfort, my shoes were soggy. I'd left my rubbers in church last Sunday. I called Phoenix up and asked if they were going ahead with the meeting. The answer was, yes: so I trudged over in the rain. When I got to the center, I discovered a group of people, mostly white, sitting in a large circle. I was invited in and discovered that I was in the middle of an encounter group.

On the one hand I wanted to leave. I felt I was seeing a psychiatrist and that was enough; besides I don't like encounters (remember?). On the other hand, here were a group of people I'd never seen before – what an opportunity! The very reason that repelled me from encounters, attracted me. That is, I wanted to find out why I was so closed.

Well, it didn't take long. The leader, a Black man named Barry, turned to me and said, "Are you bored?" and then it began. "Are you drunk?" "You seemed so out of it you seemed to be drunk." Then they zeroed in on me, darling. They asked me how old I was, what I stood for, if I had ever done anybody any good, if I'd ever done anything for anybody, if I was a man. I seemed to close up all the more, but I would not leave. All I could have done was get up and slug the red-mustachioed man who was screaming at me, but I know that kind of action was destructive, even though I felt like it. They were on me for what seemed like an hour. I couldn't believe what was happening. But in some sense I was glad, because I felt – though nothing may happen tonight – this is an earthy experience through which I can grow. Barry terminated the attack with some healing remarks, I can't remember now, but he indicated he wanted me back. The group meets again in two weeks. As I left the meeting, Barry patted me on the cheek (like a Bishop at confirmation) and said, "Charlie, I want you to stop drinking. You don't need a chemical to be a man." Actually, all I had had before coming to the group was two drinks with dinner. But I had told the group I thought I drank too much.

*It was after midnight when I got back safely to my little
apartment. I wanted so much to pour myself a good stiff drink.
But darling, I didn't. I went to bed and slept soundly. Even
though it's your birthday, dear, I feel that in a sense I was
reborn a little last night.*

[Charlie here copied a short poem by Lawrence
Ferlinghetti, which begins: "I am waiting/ For a rebirth/ Of
wonder."] *I gave $ to the Vietnam Moratorium Committee and
the above poem came to me on their "thank you" card.*

*Let's just keep wondering thru life together, dear!
Happy Birthday, sweetie.*

*Love,
Charlie*

Friday morning May 29 [1970]

Dearest,

*You're on your way to Texas with Joanie today and I
think it's about time to send this "diary to dearie" on its way.*

*Today is a holiday for us, darling. I'm going to work this
morning until noon. Then I've been invited on a picnic by some
of the people at the office. Late in the afternoon, I'll be calling
cousin Cleve at the Waldorf. He and his wife E.M. and daughter
MiMi are in town for her graduation from Briarcliff. Tonight I'll
go to dinner with them and we are going to see "Promises
Promises."*

*We had to evacuate the building twice on your birthday
– bomb scares both times. We have had four bomb scares in all
and one not so serious fire in the hotel. But that's five
evacuations and everyone is edgy. I have no idea who was doing
the harassing. This July we move into our new building in Bed-
Stuy on Fulton Street. I think we should make the move very
quietly.*

*I will have two assistants by July 15. They both are
highly qualified people, and within six months we should know
whether or not we can really <u>do</u> anything in Bed-Stuy. It will be
a real test for me darling, because I will have to solve the
"politics of action" – how to move the bureaucracy and the
community – which I call solving the technology of bureaucracy.
It's easier to land men on the moon than to put up a building in*

*Bed-Stuy – that requires the cooperation of the office
bureaucracy (ours), the city, the state, the feds and community
groups.*

*I may move my vacation (my visit home) back a few
weeks, to June, because I want to be on the job when my co-
workers report. Then I also want to be with you to help you get
settled, so I can shift my August vacation back a week if
necessary. These shifts we can talk about.*

*I'm happy that Texas means our writing and telephoning
can resume, but I do want to see you and be with you, and this
we will have to plan – maybe a weekend in Dallas. Darling, I
miss you and love you. Have a safe trip.*

Devotedly,
Charlie

My letters from Austin began. I was house-sitting with
Barbara W at 904 Terrace Mountain Drive, Austin TX. This
letter is written on the back of a newsletter from Students for a
Democratic Society (SDS).

AUSTIN TO BROOKLYN

Thurs. June 4 [1970]

Dear Charlie,

*Barb arrived this morning in the midst of my cleaning
out the fridge (moldy oysters, moldy caviar – ye gods, how our
tastes differ!). On the way in to school I told Barb about US and
she was just delighted! How often, she said, she had wanted to
tell me what a good couple we would make, but she thought that
was not an appropriate comment. Best news she ever had. The 2
people (excepting Nick) she's closest to, she said. (!)*

*I miss you. It's hard to be on our old stamping ground,
among mutual friends, without often thinking of you.*

*I spent the afternoon in the library, and am now waiting
for Barb to pick me up to go grocery shopping. I must get used to
being dependent on someone else for transportation. I'm used to
simply walking home when I'm ready. We might just park at the
end of the shuttle-bus line and end traffic and parking
headaches. A lot of students seem to use them. (See SDS plan on
back for socializing transportation and child care.)*

I was distracted in my research on [dissertation subject]
*John Knowles today by an English teaching suggestion: teach
Robert Ardrey's* African Genesis, *followed by Wm. Golding's*
Lord of the Flies. *Have you read either? I can remember going
to see* Lord of the Flies *(film) in the Union with you in the early
days of our courtship, but it was a damaged or worn out film.
Are you interested in reading* A. Genesis *with me? It's in
paperback (Dell) and I think I'll get it and read it. Maybe this is
the book I need to make 3 composition courses interesting in
Middletown, New York.*

*Barb is 40 minutes late.... Say, I never sent my shoe size
to you (9½ very narrow), because it's so hard to fit my foot that
it would be risky for you to buy me a pair of shoes. Also
expensive to mail! I'll let you take me there personally, however*
☺.

*45 minutes! The familiar UT tower bell gong just
sounded. Well, this is one way to get a letter off to you – right?*
So you want to get together in Dallas?!!

Love, Rosemary

BROOKLYN TO AUSTIN

June 5, 1970

Darling,

*It's been a week since I sent my "epistle." How are the
Christians in Austin? As St Paul* [Philippians 1:8] *would say, "I
long for you."*

*I saw Dr. Doltolo yesterday and he seemed quite
interested in my encounter experience. He wants to use it in our
discussions. That experience illustrated one of the big problems
– my fear of my own anger. My reaction to the attack was one of
two extremes, either to stand up and slug my oppressor or to
close up and defend myself against the blows, take the abuse. I
took the habitual stance, defensive – for which I hate myself and
build up more anger! I have to find the middle ground – being
assertive without losing my cool. It sounds easy, doesn't it, dear?
But emotionally, it's terribly difficult for me.*

*Last night John Doar and his wife Anne had a party and
I was one of the guests. I thoroughly enjoyed myself. He comes
from a small town (4,000) in Wisconsin. His brother, who was*

also a guest, still practices law there. A cousin of theirs, also among the 30 invited, directed "Butch Cassidy and the Sun Dance Kid." The handsome director always seemed to have a circle of ladies around him. Burke Marshall, famous civil rights attorney, was there with his wife. He is now general counsel for IBM.

Eva [Charlie's secretary] has just walked in the office and it's time to put the show on the road. TGIF. Tonight I go to John Doar's for a party. I wish you were going to be with me. Last night, I kept thinking how much you would enjoy the Doars and how they would be attracted to you. I love you, darling.

Your own,
Charlie

BROOKLYN TO AUSTIN
Monday June 8 [1970]

Dearest,

If I sounded scolding last night on the phone, please accept my behavior as (a) a sign of how much I miss you and need you, (b) an indication that I am getting better at expressing my feelings, (c) perhaps anger at myself for having let a week go by without writing – I wasn't that busy.

It is funny how I hate to show the scolding side of me. But it is there – for better or for worse.

I was also upset when you told me about that young Paulist's remark about my being mixed up. (1) I wish he had expressed himself to me *rather than to you; (2) everyone who takes a leave of absence is assumed to be mixed up; (3) I still have a lot of thinking-through to do.*

So much for my Monday morning analyses. I did sleep well.

When I come back from vacation, I'll begin investigating quarters [in Middletown, NY] *for you. I don't see how you can expect to find something in the last week of August.*

If you get a car, perhaps I can fly to, say Houston, and we can drive north together – assuming your apartment is set. I should be able to help you with the purchase of the vehicle.

*It looks like you picked a charming section of New York
to live and work in. We will have a great time next year
exploring the territory. I love you darling.*

Devotedly,
Charlie

*P.S.   Remember me to Barb.
How is Lalonde's family?
How do you feel, having been away for a month? You
said you felt in arriving in Texas you were coming home.
What about Belinda?*

AUSTIN TO BROOKLYN

June 8, 1970

Dearest Charlie,

*No need to send this letter yet, since you will be in
Detroit, but I'm sticking things in the envelope. (1) Lay
affiliation – sorry about the appearance of the proposal. My
typing is bad enough on a typewriter I'm used to! But there's no
excuse for putting a carbon in backwards....* ☹ [See Appendix
for a copy of the proposal.] *(2) Society for a Free Ministry
propaganda is from my old friend Marion in Atlanta (now in
Athens, GA), who married a priest who refused to be laicized.
Their baby, I think I told you, was baptized by Eugene Bianchi.*

*Darling, I miss you <u>very much</u>. I could hardly bear being
cut off from you after our phone conversation last night.*

Till later—

Rosemary

June 9

Tomorrow you leave for home [that is, Grosse Pointe].
Bon courage!

*I'd like to locate a writer-critic WALTER CLEMONS
who I think lives in New York City. At least he did in 1965. Does
your phone directory have 16 of them?*

Rosie

Friday, June 11 [1970]

Sweetie,

I was <u>so</u> delighted that you wanted to talk to <u>me</u> Tuesday night after your very hard day. Despite the sad news [that his brother Bob was ill] *you told me, I felt GOOD. The next day I received your very interesting letter analyzing why you scolded me on the phone Sunday. I think I needed the scolding.*

Work is progressing satisfactorily enough here. <u>A Separate Peace</u> [a dissertation subject] *is coming out of my ears. I will soon have it memorized.* ☺

Larry and Margie stayed at my house Wednesday night. We talked into the night about you and me (Margie suspected it <u>before</u> Sept. 21, 1968!) and how great it is; about God and if he exists (mathematically, Larry says, there is no need for a Prime Mover since there is no need for a <u>beginning</u>. Interesting, yes?). They are still happy with each other and still hoping Margie will get pregnant soon.

Earlier Wednesday, at Nick's birthday dinner, I told him, too, about us. It was funny. I'll try to reproduce the conversation:

<u>Rosemary:</u> Did you know that Father Harry M is getting married? He got instant laicization.

<u>Nick and Barb</u>: I remember him. No kidding!

(A significant glance between Barb and me: I asked silently, shall I tell him now? She nodded.)

<u>R</u>: He's not the only one being laicized.

<u>N</u> (looking oddly at me): I know.

<u>R and B</u>: You do!

<u>N</u> (to B): You know, too?

<u>BW</u>: Francha told me a couple of days ago.

<u>Rosie</u>: Who told you, N?

<u>N</u>: Edmond. Who told you? (At this point I realized he didn't know about <u>us</u> yet!)

The long and short of it is that Nick is extremely pleased. "A great birthday gift, that news!" he said. Whew! He admires you so very much, and almost is relieved that you, too, want to get married. It's so human, you know!

Last night I went over to Mary C's and Elaine's for a spaghetti dinner. With (as usual) lots of other people. Joanie

*lives there this summer too, you know. It's constant open house,
never a dull moment, and Joan likes it that way.*

*I really enjoyed the article on the "Perilous Route 17"
to* [my job in Middletown and] *the Catskills! Won't we have fun?*

*Well, sweetie, I'm waiting for a call from Detroit. My
thoughts are constantly with you.*

Eileen bought a Peugeot (foreign car).

Love, Francha

BROOKLYN TO AUSTIN
Tuesday [June 9, 1970]

Dearest,

*I called Orange County Community College yesterday
about finding an apartment for you. I didn't get in touch with the
chair of the English Department, but did talk to the charmer,
your Dean. He urged me to read the <u>Middletown Times Herald
Record</u>, which I will subscribe to when I return from Detroit. He
also said he would send a note to the secretary to the President. I
will follow up on this for you. Your Dean seemed pleased that I
was helping out.*

Last night I met with [Paulists and former Paulists] *Joe,
John B, Jerry S and Jerry T. The two Jerrys are active priests.
Duke was "sitting in" with some squatters in the Village and
couldn't make the meeting. The squatters are protesting the
dearth of housing facilities and are seeking to prevent the
takeover of an apartment building by N.Y. Eye and Ear Hospital.
I learned last evening that Harry M is married and that Tom S*
[new President of the Paulists] *telephoned long distance to Rome
to get the dispensation. I feel that I know Tom well enough to ask
him to do the same for us. I think we should consider this
possibility. Called the Brooklyn Chancery now – it takes about
11 months. I was there Feb. 10.*

*My folks just called to say that my brother Bob collapsed
at work and is in inten-sive care at St John's Hospital in Detroit.
Bob has been calling faithfully every week. Mother & Dad think
he has been under pressure because of the failure in the
economy (tho he's top salesman at Lochmoor-Chrysler) and
because he's trying to raise 3 teens. Both Bob and Sue work, but
she has had her illnesses too, and hasn't been able to pitch in as*

*much as she used to. This also puts more pressure on Bob.
Mother & Dad won't be able to meet me at the airport. Bob's
illness puts a cloud on my visit, but I look forward to seeing him.*

*I realize all of this is old news now after our
conversation of last evening. It was beautiful just talking to you.*

*Brad just called and he is going to pick me up at the
airport. A wonderful friend.*

*I promised myself I'd leave the apartment at 9 a.m., so
darling I've got to scoot. While you are munching on caviar, I
am finishing up a can of peaches for breakfast.*

I love you my sweet,

Devotedly, Charlie

GROSSE POINTE TO AUSTIN

June 16 [1970]

Dearest,

*It's 7:30 a.m., my last full day home. In a few minutes
I'll be leaving for the tennis courts. I have an 8 a.m. game (and
one again at 4:30 p.m.). How I wish I were driving over to pick
you up. I loved those early morning games* [during our Texas
courtship]. *I'm enclosing a red leaf out of love – and as a symbol
of my longing to be with you. It won't be long, darling.*

*You have been in my thoughts and desires so much
during this visit. I feel that Mother and Dad accept me and my
decisions. I haven't been the subject of their concerns these few
days as much as Bob, and our common concern for him has
drawn us closer together. Bob had a serious test yesterday. They
injected a colored liquid into the veins of his brain. Today we
should hear from the doctors the prognosis. Bob is cheerful, but
he only admits to feeling "fair." He has intermittent headaches.
We are all praying.*

*My trees, the Rose of Sharons that I planted last fall, are
sturdy and green. They don't bloom until September – our
anniversary.*

*I've seen more of Brad than anyone else. He has been
over here for dinner on three evenings. Last night we talked
about what it would be like to live in Marquette, Michigan, in the
Northern Peninsula. There is a college campus there; it's*

beautiful northern country and business is beginning to boom
(though the town is small).
     I'll be telephoning you tomorrow evening. This carries
all my love.

Devotedly,
Charlie

AUSTIN TO BROOKLYN

June 17, 1970

Darling,
     Two days ago the Franciscans of Rochester MN elected
the most liberal candidate on the five-woman slate as their
president! Sister Gretchen Berg, who has been in charge of our
"Pastoral Program." The last two years, full time. She has a
Ph.D. in English and is solidly based on prayer, theology,
Scripture.
     Now can you beat that?
     It wasn't easy. It took four ballots and I imagine some
hard feelings. The second highest was my second choice, so I'm
hoping she was put on the council yesterday.
     I got this news from Sister Lalonde Monday night. She
has been feeling pretty well. Her father has been almost dying
almost daily. Very hard. It was great to talk with her. I also got
another MN call later with the same good news, and also that
Pat S and two other dear Franciscans are coming through
Austin on June 27. Yippee! (If plans work out.)
     More good news! I wrote to Marion telling her about
you and me, and telling her I would love to visit them in Athens,
GA. She called last night, overjoyed that I may come. She invites
you, too, with open arms. She and Don will have much to share
with us. So-------- we can plan to stop there on the way to NY or
we can meet half-way at some point sooner. Athens must be
about half-way! What do you say, Mr. Palms?
     And tonight you will call. I am happy.

Love, Francha

     The chair of the English Department at Orange County
Community College, my new employer as of September 1970,
called to ask if I would like to teach an additional freshman level

class offered in the evening once a week, for a little extra money. I said yes.

BROOKLYN TO AUSTIN
Thursday evening [June 18, 1970]

Darling,

What a boost your surprise call gave me ☺. We seem to be able to make decisions easily. My greatest concern on Orange County was whether it would mean extensive additional preparation. I think it's better to grow into the job and accept more responsibility gradually, but the extra evening class sounds reasonable. On Athens, I think being a little Spartan was wise [that is, to save money on our trip from Austin to New York by staying overnight with Marion and Don].

I called Walter Clemons and he was friendly. He said he was in the process of moving and had a couple of things on the fire this summer, so that he could not respond in any very detailed way, but he urges you to write. He suggested you reach him at the New York Times Book Review. I introduced myself to him and said I had a friend in Texas who was using A Separate Peace in a study of "the double." In all the excitement of my successful detective work I forgot to give him your name. I also said I thought you had finished the chapter on the Knowles book. So take it from there, kid!

I thought you might be interested in my latest memo on the alcohol problem. It gives you a good idea of what I'm trying to do and how serious things are. Tomorrow I begin research on sickle cell disease. Ever heard of it?

This carries all my love, darling.

Charlie

HOW ABOUT THE WEEKEND OF JULY 17-19 [for a visit to Brooklyn]*?*

P.S. Did you know that Thomas Aquinas held with Larry that you could not rationally prove that the world needed a beginning? Thomas accepted the beginning of the world as a revealed truth. Scripture scholars today insist that the Bible is not a book of cosmic science.

AUSTIN TO BROOKLYN

June 20, 1970

Dearest Charlie,

I miss you.

I just figured out that, even if the income tax takes ½ of my salary, and even if I pay as high as $150 monthly for rent, I still should be able to save $200 monthly.

Nevertheless, I will add $720 to that savings in the fall semester and work myself a little more [by teaching the extra night course]. *I may need to keep busy in order not to be lonely.*

Then I can either (1) buy a car, or (2) pay back the Franciscans what they started me out with (although they don't expect it). [My college president in Winona had given me $500, no strings attached, to get me through to my first paycheck.]

It's Saturday morning – a late start at the library today, to make up for doodling away yesterday afternoon. I went swimming with Barb and Nick at Campbell's Hole (above Zilker Park).

Do you get an extra day off for the 4th of July? I was thinking that, if you want to come to Texas that weekend, there's no reason why you shouldn't. When I'm busy, you could be visiting your thousands of friends here. It may be worth the extra day. (Couldn't you fly here late Thursday without taking a vacation-day away?)

I must get to work. Sweetie, I miss you.

Love, Rosemary

How is Bob?

We had decided that I would visit New York in July, rather than Charlie visit Austin.

BROOKLYN TO AUSTIN

Monday morning June 22 [1970]

Darling –

Do you realize that June 21 was our anniversary – 21 months? I forgot to mention it in our conversation last night.

I am enclosing the attractive invitation that Harry and Aurelia sent. I enjoyed their party, did a little dancing. This week

*I am going to play tennis with Harry and invite both Harry &
Aurelia out to dinner afterward.*

*In visiting the African sculpture exhibit yesterday, my
curiosity was aroused by the fact that a significant number of
works had the "double" motif. For example, there would be a
figure with two heads, or, one head and two masks. I don't know
the cultural or spiritual significance. I'm sorry the exhibit is
leaving the museum. Did you know that Picasso and the modern
art movement have been strongly influenced by African art? It's
much the same as our music has been influenced by jazz.*

*Darling, I'm off to work. I wanted to send you my fragile
treasures from the Botanical Gardens (which incidentally were
inspired by a Belgian whose name begins with P – Parmentier).*

My love always. Can't wait for July 10!

Devotedly,
Charlie

BROOKLYN TO AUSTIN

The morning after: June 24 [1970]

Dearest,

*Our candidate Pete Eikenberry lost by 1,000 votes
yesterday (21,000 votes cast), and his brave attempt to unseat a
27-year (72-year-old) veteran of Congress failed. The
"machine" was able to resist the movement. I could see the party
hacks in operation at my polling place, a neighborhood
community center near massive housing projects that contain
hundreds of Blacks and Puerto Ricans. They hung around the
entrance; they manned the tables; they kept waving hello and
greeting voters. Pete's youthful idealists were unable to work a
system built on party favors over the years. Old John Rooney
even came out against Vietnam involvement towards the end of
the campaign, which left Pete without one of his stiffest weapons
against his wily opponent – who ridiculed his youthful adversary
with crude remarks.*

*I feel let down. And for some unfathomed reason I want
to bear guilt for the loss. I didn't work hard enough – is the self-
reproach I feel. Yet I think Pete's campaign man-agers could
have done better. They always made me feel I was sort of a fifth
wheel when I turned up at headquarters. But again, the old guilt*

answers: well, you could've thought out a helpful way to advance the campaign instead of waiting around to be put to work....

Thus far readeth the political analysis of Palms. My poll watching was without too much incident. I won every point I took a stand on; but not with table pounding assertion. Rather, I found myself smilingly making suggestions that were yielded to. By the end of the day, the adversaries were cooperating generously. They could; they sensed themselves winning. I learned a little more about myself through the experience.

I've met some great people this past week. My faith in this country keeps being renewed in the goodness of people. The evening I went to Harry and Aurelia's party, I was worried about getting home (because the neighborhood was unfamiliar and appeared a little threatening to me – on my way to the party a friendly black woman urged me to leave the streets). The black couple who gave me a ride to the subway almost insisted (1) that they drive me all the way to Brooklyn (two-hour detour), or (2) that I spend the night with them in the Bronx. I resisted and compromised – I would call them so they would know I got home safely.

Then on Monday evening I had dinner with Pat W's sister Peggy and her husband Finley. It was a delightful evening. They made me feel part of the family – took my shoes off. And they insisted on walking with me three blocks, where I caught the subway at 11 p.m. Their two pre-school age children ran along too as escorts. I climbed the steps to the elevated train and looked over the railing as this couple walked arm in arm back to their modest apartment, the kids hanging on, laughing and running up to a mail box and back to their parents. – I couldn't help but think of us, darling. How I love to have you take my arm. And very soon you'll be here; and tonight we hear each other's voices.

My love always, Charlie

AUSTIN TO BROOKLYN

Enclosed is a second-hand birthday card: "Happy Birthday – why does everybody love you? I don't know... ...but

you must be doing something right." "Love from 'everybody'!
Rosemary"

This letter hints at a struggle I was facing, although I
spared Charlie the cause: I was experiencing an infatuation with
an eligible young man I had just met that summer. Thus my
haste in arranging to see Charlie sooner rather than later.

June 25, 1970

Dearest C,

*I sent off your birthday present today, and, while I'm not
sure of its appropriateness, I think it will at least surprise you.
The card is appropriate, tho.*

*The enclosed birthday card is to hold you until the other
comes! I sent it, second hand though it is, because I was
immediately reminded of you when I received it myself.*

*I am very tired today, and the result is a rather
unproductive stint at the library. I'm too far from home to go
steal a nap.*

*We got up at 6 this a.m. to take the car in for a routine
check. If you can get it there by 7, they'll try to fix it in one day.
Noble, eh?*

*I have a yen to go shopping. I get this idea in my head
and it's like an obsession; it won't go away.... until I go
shopping! So I think I'll take off shortly. It's 5 o'clock anyway.
Barb is going to stay in and study until an 8:30 movie, which I
just begged out of.*

*Darling, I feel a great need to see you. I feel remote from
you and I don't like the feeling. If it weren't for that, I would
probably argue for saving our money and waiting another month
for our reunion. You know miserly me!*

*I'm also amazed at myself for accepting an additional
class for money. Perhaps I'm the worst kind of crass materialist
– the penny-pinching kind without other priorities! God forbid!
Or maybe in this case I just dislike the idea of buying on credit
and I know I'll need a car....*

Meantime, dearest, Happy 45th Birthday.

Love,
Rosemary

BROOKLYN TO AUSTIN

June 27 [1970]

Dearest,

It looks like we have your apartment problem solved. Yesterday I received an excited call from the secretary of the Orange County president. The academic dean was chatting with the dean of students, about your plight, and the latter disclosed that he owned the perfect spot. It is a furnished studio apartment, $125 a month including heat, electricity, cooking gas and janitorial service. There is a large living room with wood-burning fireplace, a dressing room and bath and kitchen. A large picture window overlooks a courtyard. The location is in the city, so that it is near the shopping area, theater and stores. In addition, it is within ½ mile of the school. They wanted you to have first crack at it, so I thanked them and said we would be visiting on July 11. The only catch is, they want to rent it as of August 1. With all of these conveniences, I feel that it's worth the investment. Besides, it may bring you to New York sooner! I conditioned your acceptance upon a view of the premises. But it sounds like a superb deal! I can't wait to tell you about it by phone.

I'm home this weekend after all. The Smiths never called. Last night I had dinner with Duke. We supped at Tuesdays. The place has changed; it's getting too posh. Afterwards we walked over to visit the apartments where the squatters are living despite the expansion plans of N.Y. Eye and Ear Hospital. One of the apartments had a warning to police about breaking and entering. We also visited a "freedom park," a vacant lot that had been cleaned up and "taken over" by the residents for their children to play in. The owner had sealed up the lot with a wire fence topped by mean-looking barbed wire. But the people had defiantly ripped up the fence so their children could play. It was a rainy night. We walked through the Village and ended our evening at McSorley's Ale House. The place was packed with men – talking and drinking and singing as if to hold on to the last shred of their masculinity. You and I walked by the place on our tour of the Village. A man stands at the door to make sure no women are admitted. Recently a group of women have brought a suit to challenge the all-male restriction,

*arguing, rightly so, that it is a public facility, and therefore must
be open to women as well as men. I am confident they will win
their case, but I do not believe that many ladies will be knocking
the doors down for admission. It's dirty and vulgar. If a lady
does by chance force her way in now, an elaborate alarm system
is triggered, sounding whistles and bells and arousing the
patronage to the "danger." There were no alarms last evening,
and after walking Duke to E. 4th St, I headed for my subway to
Brooklyn.*

*Today, I'll write some things at the office and put on an
offensive against the roaches in my apartment. My neighbor,
who lives in 6B, has given me some deadly powder.*

*My love to you, darling. Just a few more days and we
will trip the light fantastic on the sidewalks of New York.*

*Devotedly,
Charlie*

AUSTIN TO BROOKLYN

June 29, 1970

Dearest Charlie,

*I'm reading a few of your last letters. I miss you so
much.*

*I was especially touched by your description of Peggy
and her family, and how you brought me into it! You are so
sensitive and beautiful, and I love you. Very humbly I love you.*

*A Dominican (Houston) sister called last night to ask
about my lay affiliation plan. The word surely gets around!*

*I am amused at the 2 of us debating on the phone on how
to save money on the plane ticket. We must have spent 5 dollars
deciding!*

*Dolores and her 3 youngest are coming July 5-July 17.
A Chicano workshop. Barb's birthday is Wednesday.*

*Did I tell you that the (Harmony) liberal priest, with
whom I carefully confided, has been transferred? D___! In
Norwegian Harmony he made a terrific impression on the
Protestants. Mother said that at the Farewell Party 4 ministers
and lots of kids not "our own" were there.*

*Georgia wrote and sounds well and happy. Says she
enjoyed a letter from you.*

I need your help on how the black is a double of the white (or vice versa? Jazz, e.g.?). I'm trying to get going on [the next dissertation chapter] *Ralph Ellison.*

I went to a lovely ballet production of Tchaikowsky's Romeo and Juliet, *produced by the Drama Dept. here. I wish you could have been with me. Tomorrow Bonnie has talked me into seeing John Wayne in* Chisum. *God forbid!*

I love you,
Rosemary

BROOKLYN TO AUSTIN

June 29 [1970]

Darling,

My offensive against the cockroaches has been a complete success. Not a one in either kitchen or bathroom when I returned this evening. I destroyed their sanctuaries (and supplies), but unlike the Cambodian fiasco, there was no counter-offensive. I hope the little rascals don't embarrass me upon your arrival.

One thing I haven't figured out is the heat. I'm perspiring right now and it's not very comfortable. I can't afford an air-conditioner. Maybe I'll get a fan. Otherwise, everything is ready!

Toby called and invited me for lunch tomorrow. She is as direct and self expressive as ever. I had to hold the phone close to my ear so my secretary couldn't hear Toby's "rich" language.

My love, darling. You caught my depression last evening. I was surprised, and a little relieved that you were depressed, too. I wasn't alone. It's hard to share when so many miles and so much time separate us. I look forward to the 10th.

My love always,
Charlie

AUSTIN TO BROOKLYN

July 2, 1970

Dearest C,

I have almost decided to bring my work to New York for a full week. Your eagerness on the telephone warmed my whole being. I miss you so much.

The Passion of Anna sounds fascinating and of course will no doubt merit mention in that elusive Chapter II on the double [in Flannery O'Connor's *Everything That Rises Must Converge.*] *Thank you for being so alert.*

Edmond is really rather depressed: by pressures of time; economics; and decisions regarding his return to Cairo and his Jesuit province or staying here where he says he feels much more free. He suggested last night that we travel in 2 cars together in August to New York, because he wants to visit his brother in Atlantic City. I told him you would probably be with me, but that did not deter him – may have, in fact, added to his enthusiasm! ☹

We had a nice outing for Barb's birthday: canoeing where you and I went a year ago – 4th of July! I am reminded of you constantly! Later we had a Mass at a girl's apartment with friends, Edmond presiding.

Love, Rosemary

AUSTIN TO BROOKLYN

July 3, 1970

Dearest—

I love you---.

Alsop's article [enclosed in this letter] *was perhaps also in the* NYTimes, *but I wanted to be sure you see it. He doesn't mention some factors you did. I guess he's rather anti-student. He had a vicious article on the new conscientious objector rating (on moral or intellectual bases) saying that now all a student needs to do to become a CO is sharpen up his intellect; and what this country needs most is some Walter Mittys who will volunteer for the dangerous jobs. (That was in last week's* Newsweek, *last page.)*

I see by a motherhouse communication that a sister of ours in San Antonio – and a friend of mine – will be there

*(teaching) only till July 12. I may have to delay my NY plans a
few days and go see her. But also, Bonnie's roomer moved out
and she offered the room to us at $120 for six weeks. If we take
that (and it's a generous price) I could just move my stuff over
before I go to NY, and then I would not have to be back by July
13. (In order to move out of this house July 14.) In other words, I
might come to see you from Wednesday to Wednesday instead of
Monday to Monday. Follow?*

Will write more later. Now to work!

*Later: I just ran across a small discussion concerning the
concept of race in Winthrop Jordan's <u>White Over Black</u>. "Race"
now anthropologically is defined in terms of a gene pool; but
what interested me was his mention of sickle cells in Africans as
a racial characteristic. Now I am really curious as to how <u>you</u>
are studying sickle cells in Bed-Stuy!! Do you have a lot of cases
of fatal anemia there?*

We will have a lot to talk about, I think--- yes?

Love
Rosemary

BROOKLYN TO AUSTIN

*It was beautiful reading your letters and talking with you
last night and dreaming about your coming on Monday. I'm not
sure that this will reach you in time, but I'll mail it at the post
office on my way to the office this morning.*

*How is the black a double of the white or vice versa? I
really think you should try to write this chapter in Bedford-
Stuyvesant. I think we should have dinner with Harry and
Aurelia – not to discuss these questions, but to get to know them.
I see three kinds of Black people now – the militants who are
trying to discover Black identity, purging it of everything white.
They disparagingly refer to Blacks who try to be white as
"oreos" – black on the outside and white on the inside. This is*

the second kind of Black person, one who tries to ape the white in everything – taste in food, clothing, lifestyle. Then there is the great mass of Black people who are simply themselves or who don't much care or worry about the problem. *The Autobiography of Malcolm X* is a fascinating account of his 3 conversions: (1) From a pimp and a junkie to a Muslim; (2) from a strict follower of Elijah Muhammed (sp?) to an orthodox Mohammedan; (3) from a white hater to openness and toleration. I guess I need to know more about the concept of the double to be of help to you. I know there are ever so many levels of the double in me: (1) The child and the man; (2) the id and the ego; (3) the masculine and the feminine; (4) the passive and the aggressive. It's a life-long tension.

Oh darling, I long for your coming. I love your response. See you soon.

BROOKLYN TO AUSTIN
Wednesday [July 8, 1970]

Darling,

I'll be speaking with you on the phone tonight so that much of what I say here may seem redundant. Yet I know I enjoy getting your letters, and you've told me how much you appreciate mine.

The President's secretary at OCCC will be happy to see us at 2 p.m. Saturday, July 18. In fact, she said it was more convenient for her than the 11th. School begins on Wednesday, September 9. I didn't think to ask her when you were expected to report in case there are any orientation programs for you. At any rate, you can discuss this with her when you see her. Jody's offer of a car is still open.

I wish you were here even though this week may not be as convenient as next. I almost telephoned you on Monday. I felt very depressed. It's hard to say why one has feelings of depression. I felt let down that you weren't coming, even tho I assured you *rationally* that it was better to wait a week. I felt a

kind of undertow of depression as I welcomed my new associates
Barbara and Jon. And I was confused all the more because I
reasoned that I should be overjoyed that I have assistance; that I
finally have the cooperation of Restoration. The only things I can
point to that caused that depression were: The increased
responsibility and what is expected of me; the fear for my own
job since, on paper, they have more experience and know-how
than I; I just don't understand it. I had to walk home for lunch
and back again to the office to dissipate the tension.

Tuesday was much better. I began to reflect on my
contribution to the new team. If it weren't for my ability to win
the confidence of Charlie I (of Restoration), we would still be
facing a blank wall. Maybe Barbara and Jon will be better "at
the job than I am." So what! All the better for the people of
Bedford-Stuyvesant. If I weren't their manager, they wouldn't be
giving their services.

Sweetie, I've got to run to work. I'm sending a couple of
more "lures" [that is, photos]. *Please save them for our album. I*
love you.

Charlie

BROOKLYN TO AUSTIN
Saturday [July 11, 1970]

Darling,

I've tried to call you a couple times, but to no avail. I
tried Thursday night and this morning. I'm just looking forward
to Thursday when we will be able to communicate at a moment's
notice.

I got a card from Mary C. She said she tried, but
couldn't reach me. Then – surprisingly – "I'm hoping to get in
touch with Fr Lundy over here." Is he in Ireland?

Cousin Izzie called me twice last week – just to say
hello! She always calls at about 2 or 3 in the morning, and is
very concerned about <u>us</u>. She always asks very specially for you.
She and Mark have no telephone, I guess because of Izzie's
addiction to the phone. So they call when they're out with
friends. They have a beach house for us for a honeymoon!

George L is looking forward to seeing you and so is
Jody. Both have offered cars for our trip to Middletown. How do

you like an address like "Middletown"? That name says a lot! I like "Harmony" much better, but I reject the geography of Harmony, at this time.

    This carries all my love, Darling! I need you and I look forward so to being with you.

Devotedly,
Charlie

    I spent a week, July 16-23, visiting Charlie in Brooklyn, firmly reassuring myself that he and I were going in the right direction. We secured an apartment in Middletown for me and generally had a wonderful time.

BROOKLYN TO AUSTIN

Saturday [July 25, 1970]

Darling,

    What a void in this little apartment. And so many reminders of your presence – the uke hanging on the wall, the position of the fan, the rice in the cabinet, no sound but the radio and the whirring of the fan. I feel incomplete without you. I am existing, not living. I spent the afternoon at the office going through my education files, overwhelmed by the magnitude of the problems and unable yet to think through proposals for their solution. I also did some more research on the anti-lead poisoning campaign which has already begun. Neighborhood Youth Corps kids are already canvassing the blocks of Bedford-Stuyvesant lining up kids for screening.

    Last evening I had dinner with [Paulists and former Paulists] *Duke, Tom S, Dave O, John B, Jerry S and George L. It was a friendly evening. No serious discussion. Dave promised to get in touch with me about my letter on lay affiliation. He said he could not foresee anything "formal" yet; he would like to see Harry M teach at St Paul's* [Paulist Seminary] *as a beginning; he expressed his regrets about "losing" so many of his "friends." I insist we are not lost. After they left, Duke and I had a talk. Duke said how much he enjoyed meeting you and liked you – that he wished we three could have gone to dinner together. I promised him a date in September. OK?*

Now I'm on my way back to the Doors. I'll call you
tomorrow nite. My love, my darling --

Longing for you,
Charlie

P.S. What a wonderful day we had last Saturday. I've been
thinking about it all day. Remember how hot I was on the court!

About July 24 I wrote a painfully difficult letter to my
parents, with copies to my siblings, telling them that Charlie was
in my life, and that I intended to ask for a dispensation from my
religious vows and then marry him. I so dreaded causing them
sorrow and disappointment, but I felt I could not delay the news
any longer.

The next letter is written from a new address. Barbara
and I finished our stint housesitting, rent-free, for a vacationing
professor in West Lake Hills, and moved to a house in south
Austin for the next six weeks, along with another housemate to
help with the rent.

902A JESSIE STREET, AUSTIN TO BROOKLYN

July 26 '70

Dearest Charlie,

After you called, Kathy did — because I had not written
to her for so long she was worried. So I talked to her about THE
LETTER for a while, which she will probably get tomorrow.
Then she called me back to suggest I ask our old pastor to pay
the family a call. So I just wrote him a letter.

I told Sam and Jean [Pam's friends] *this afternoon that I*
was going to marry you within the year, and they were delighted.

So you have been very much on my mind today and I just
want to tell you that!

Tomorrow afternoon I'm going to Boerne with Barb for
Polly's profession with the Benedictines. I'm doing it more out of
loyalty than desire. Tuesday a.m. I help Eileen pack. She's going
to take her stuff to Dallas [where she had secured a teaching job]
at the end of the week and come back as she needs (wants?) to
for conferences with her prof. (and Ed?). (Or will Ed be in
Ireland?)

I have been typing a while this evening but I'm a slow worker. Still haven't started writing the Ellison chapter. Dear me!

I miss you so much!

Love, Rosemary

BROOKLYN TO AUSTIN

Wednesday [July 29, 1970]

Darling,

Just a few lines before walking to work this morning. The heat has been terrific. This will be our third day in 90 degree heat, and you know how different 90 degrees in NYC is from 90 degrees in dry hot Texas. I wear a suit one day and it looks like it has to go to the cleaners. I feel as if I should change shirts twice a day. My little Rosemary (plant) seems to be thriving through it all.

We'll be talking together on the phone this evening. Last night I attended a meeting of the St. Thomas "community." [Pastor] Kevin K has put it on the line to us. He wants a one-year commitment from the members of his floating parish. I feel that you and I must talk this over because, though I hope we will be going to church together most of the Sundays of next year, where will this be? You've already spoken about the active Newman Club at OCCC. Maybe we'll have to go half and half – or at least work it out as the year progresses. I shy away from commitment to one parish. As I told them last night, I didn't commit myself to St Thomas last year, but it was where I could celebrate the mystery of the world and of God and I came again and again as if committed. Kevin also feels the community must get to know one another better and to "do" something of social purpose.

It's 8:30 darling. Time to go to work. I love you.

Charlie

An acquaintance had a car he wanted moved from Austin to New York. A plan was made for Charlie to fly to Austin, then drive back to New York with me.

AUSTIN TO BROOKLYN

July 31, 1970

Darling,

    I have been collecting things for you but have not actually got them off in the mail; now today your second letter arrived (only took 2 days!) since I wrote last, so I'll write now and mail it on the way to noon Mass.

    We have started taking the morning paper, and since I have Vic's car now and need not go to campus with Barb, I mosey around reading the paper over breakfast; then the mail comes; and now it's 10 o'clock! I could easily become lazy.

    Last night we went over to friends for dinner. There we met 2 new couples (to us) and Ed Lundy, and Barb threw a bomb at them by telling them she no longer stands for the pledge of allegiance. It's amazing how volatile the word "patriotism" is – and how many meanings it carries – a different one for everyone.

    I'm glad you're not making a commitment to St. Thomas. Just as you want to live in the area you work, I would like to worship (if at all possible) in the area I work and live.

    The excitement of having my mother call and tell me she supports me and loves me was hard to convey to you over a bad connection. I burst into sobs of relief and gratitude after I had talked to her. Can you share with me that intense emotion when I shout it faintly over 2000 miles? (Why didn't I offer to call you back? The connection is usually good from here to there. Let's do that after this.)

    Eileen leaves for Dallas Sunday with Ed, whom she will shortly put on a plane there for New York. I hope you get together there. I like his growing mustache!

Love, Rosemary

BROOKLYN TO AUSTIN

[July 31, 1970]

Darling,

    Had dinner last night with Martha and Larry G and Martha's lawyer brother. Martha used to work for us. It was a delightful evening. We had Irish "soul food" – corned beef and cabbage. We discussed religious life, the war, revolution, the Panthers, music and art. They promised to give me "The

*Bridge" for Christmas if I give them "Universal Soldier." I
promised to let them meet you early in September.*

I'm enclosing some encouraging news on Cesar Chavez.

*These days make NYC a trial even for a Gotham-lover
like me. I'm dripping continually and can feel the smog in my
lungs. It's kept me from smoking!*

*I miss you, my love. Great news about your folks. When
do we meet for the trip up?*

Devotedly,
Charlie

BROOKLYN TO AUSTIN

Sunday [August 2, 1970]

Darling,

*I worked most of the day yesterday and finished my study
of lead paint poisoning, the most serious childhood disease in
New York City. We estimate there are 30,000 children between
the ages of one and six who live in housing built before 1940 and
painted with lead-based paint, which was then considered
quality paint. You know the story of landlord neglect in New
York. The paint in these old dwellings is cracking and peeling
and kids eat it. If they ingest it over a three-month period, they
may become retarded or sustain serious brain damage. It's more
of a housing problem than a medical one. Our attack will be to
have children tested and at the same time to force landlords to
make repairs. It will be my first action project, darling, and I'm
anxious!*

*I was lonely last night. I didn't want to go to a movie,
but felt I needed a "reward" for my hard work yesterday, so I
went to a football game – all by myself. But I had some enjoyable
surprises. The game was played at Boy's High Field (Bed-Stuy's
only high school). The players were semi-pro's (looked like they
drank beer as part of their training), tough young black and
white guys who aren't good enough for the big time, but love the
rough and tumble of the sport. The tickets were all $2.00 and
went for the benefit of the local sickle-cell project. I met one of
the girls from my encounter group (who dreads the encounters
as much as I do) and the two people I work with and Harry
Salmon's sister, who surprisingly enough won the prize of the*

best-dressed person at the game. It was fun, but I just wish you had been by my side.

I am enclosing an interesting article that reminds me of Hershey and Dora [both from Laredo, both Mexican-Americans, but from different social classes]. *The dismissal of John Silber* [Dean of Liberal Arts at the U of Texas] *appeared in a small column in yesterday's paper. The country is polarizing, my darling. Meanwhile I am drawn more and more to you.*

Devotedly,
Chas

BROOKLYN TO AUSTIN

Tuesday [August 4, 1970]
Dearest,

I hasten to enclose the materials from your friendly OCCC president. As you can see, they still use [the Winona MN address] *P.O. Box 106. (You are earning $35 more than I am!) I know you will be happy to see your due date is September 9. Didn't I write you about this once before?*

Had a wonderful evening with George L and Valerie F. We had a Danish delight supper. Rosemary is one of the herbs used on the chicken – with thyme and something else that begins with a "b." I confirmed the herb use by sniffing my rosemary when I returned home. George was ecstatic, glowing and confident in a way I have never seen him before. As you might expect, he was extremely amorous, kissing Valerie's hand at every other mouthful. I sang for them, and as George pointed out, I played the songs differently – I knew it was different, but the evening inspired me to be creative. I felt good. Especially when I talked with you.

I went to bed early (10:30). I had one call at 11:30 and then little Penny called at 3 a.m. in tears. She was leaving the convent, blaming herself for "letting the same thing happen again." Remember, you predicted it. I told her to write about it and I would answer her. I felt very sorry for her and tried to cheer her up. She is going to teach in Brownsville and live in a home for wayward girls (same thing?).

Off to the office, darling. My love always,
Charlie

BROOKLYN TO AUSTIN

Sunday [August 9, 1970]

Darling,

We will be speaking together tonight, but I thought I ought to get some of this collection to you with my love.

*Notice of a meeting at OCCC on September 12. I'm amused about the impression I've made at OCCC. Your notices come c/o "me"! In the spirit of that "Peanuts" strip – I must have "yelled" at them!

*The interesting article about the meaning of the peace symbol. My tie clasp gets much attention. I'm very fond of it.

*I thought that "History and Human Survival" might interest you in view of your teaching responsibilities. Soon you will be facing "protean man." I'm slowly plowing through Harrington's book. All signs point to the fact that we are in the midst of a revolution. The old structures (both in Church and State) are still operative. But the crime, the recession, the narcotics, the unemployment, the high welfare rolls, the takeover of hospitals, the rioting in the schools – all indicate the need for fundamental changes. I don't think we really know how structures should be changed. And reactionary forces like unions and business groups, the vested interests, will not give up their security or take risks to encourage fundamental change.

*David Ignatow's poem "Bowery" reminded me of Jerry's work. What's the status of the publication? Do you still have any ms. copies? Wesleyan University Press might be interested???

Darling, I'm enclosing another photo of us in case you lost yours. I had two more made. One goes in the album.

I want to get this mailed now. I'd like to be able to talk to you about the job and my last meeting with Dr. Doltolo. We'll be with each other soon. I miss you. I've been very lonely. I did go to a party Friday night and danced myself silly until I was dripping wet. The party was a going-away blast for one of the gals in the office. Eva, my secretary, complimented me and said, "You've got it in you." It's all for you, darling.

Love,
Charlie

AUSTIN TO BROOKLYN

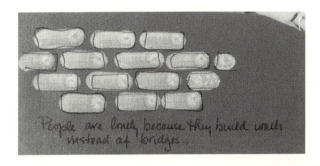

People are lonely because they build walls instead of bridges...

August 12, 1970

Darling,

I know you will like this stationery.

Why can't I get letters off to you as frequently as you write to me? I love your letters; I don't deserve your thoughtfulness. Somehow I get snowed under by <u>PEOPLE</u>. *People are so wonderful I can't get enough of them; consequently when I'm alone I read the paper or go to bed – that's all the time left in the day!*

I drove [visiting cousin] *Judy and* [her husband] *Hamdy to the San Antonio Airport Monday p.m.—after a lazy morning full of good conversation with them. So that was Monday. Yesterday I washed linens and, believe it or not, worked in the library all afternoon (except for four carrel-callers ☺). Last night I cooked an elaborate casserole which tasted pasty ☹, and then read 3 days' newspapers which had stacked up. This morning I'm trying to write some overdue letters. This p.m. I'll go back to dissertation work, and tonight I'm going to a 20th-century music concert (concerto-jazz-Shiva's Head Band rock) at the Music Recital Hall.*

Today is the Feast of St. Clare. Ten years ago today I first professed vows. Today I renew my admiration for the Franciscan ideals and renew my love for you, Charlie Palms, whom I love in your poorness of spirit, your dedication to the poor, in your joie de vivre, in your gentleness and sensitivity.

I shall call you late tonight. Be patient!

My love, dear,

Rosemary

AUSTIN TO BROOKLYN

August 13, 1970

Dearest Charlie,

I have just been reading the articles you sent me on:

*Ignatow's poems — I like them and I plan to put the "Bowery" one up with the subway ad for the Bowery Savings Bank I brought home for Barb;

* "Flyer about Peace Symbol" — [drawing of peace symbol] *Viva Nuclear Disarmament! Isn't it amazing how facts can be twisted to that extent? Satanism, black magic, anti-Christ!*

*Book review of "History and Human Survival" — "Protean man" is a remarkable concept. Ellison says somewhere that the P. initial in his character Rinehart's name stands for Proteus. I can use the Lifton concept in my current chapter. Thanx!

Charlie, if you don't feel this is the time to come to Austin, I will willingly meet you in Dallas. I don't mean to pressure you; I just want to reassure you that you may well be magnifying difficulties. My experience this summer has been friendly acceptance, and I should think that anyone as loved as you would experience at least the same dosage!

Curt called Tuesday when I wasn't home and wanted to be sure I wasn't leaving town before seeing him. And I haven't seen him all summer. Does he know about us? I'm sure he must by now. Curt and Joan have often formed a foursome with Ed and Eileen, and they have become good friends.

I love you even when I don't write! You know that, don't you!

Love, Rosie

BROOKLYN TO AUSTIN

Monday [August 17, 1970]

Dearest,

I have two of your letters to respond to. I especially loved "People are lonely because they build walls instead of bridges...." You know my bias for bridges. To build a bridge is my goal in life. This may come as a surprise to you, but I accuse myself of building attractive walls rather than bridges.

I hope I can always live up to the conclusion of that letter in which you see in me the Franciscan Spirit. You can help me to <u>be</u>. That letter gave me a terrific boost and I worked all Saturday afternoon.

I was tired when you called last night, and went to bed annoyed that you hadn't called, and awoke annoyed, and then it took me a long time to get back to sleep. I kept nodding at my desk this afternoon. I've just been very tired lately. I need a vacation, and I look forward to being with you! But let's keep my coming secret, relatively quiet. How about seeing Curt and Joan! I don't know yet what to do about Walter. I'll have to see him. I know he'd be crushed if I didn't. Remember, I told him about us from the beginning. (See the walls!)

I enjoyed reading the music program. It's the kind of recital I would love to have been with you at. (Syntax! ☺ !) I'm enclosing the program from the Sunday service next door. Note the subtle Negroid features on the Christus.

Here is what I'm etching at art school. It expresses my love for you darling, with apologies to Picasso.

Devotedly,

Charlie

AUSTIN TO BROOKLYN

August 20, 1970

Dear Charlie,

Your letter came today describing your annoyance with me for not having called you earlier, and your lack of sleep. Darling, I'm sorry to have annoyed you, but I know that, when you think about it, you would not want me to stay home on Wednesdays and Sundays just to be sure I call you before it gets too late. Or leave a movie early because it turns out to be "sneak" night. I chose to see "Oliver" on Wednesday, last night, so that Nick could go along. He works some nights. (As it turns out, he didn't go anyway.) Nevertheless, I felt blue after reading your letter, as if I had let you down. And my letter-writing habits don't help much, either, do they?

Curt called this morning to say he was leaving town tomorrow and wants to see me. I told him he was going to miss you (top secret, of course) and he regrets that.

Pam drove down from Dallas to see me and Roz [her close friend], *since we'll both be gone when she comes to school. She looks great, seems happy to be back, and says she has a date with you and me on October 11 for an all-night jazz stand with Eddie Bonnemere and Louis Armstrong. !! Did you say anything about that to me?*

I'm in the library now, trying to shepherd my thoughts on to the paper on the Ellison chapter. It will be a mad dash to finish the chapter, but I still have hopes to do it.

Barb decided to live with some shut-in for board and room next year, so bowed out of her agreement to live with Dora. So Dora found an efficiency for/by herself.

My love, dear,
Rosemary

P.S. – Thoughts from James Baldwin's <u>The Fire Next Time</u>*:*

"Love takes off the masks that we fear we cannot live without and know we cannot live within." *(Walls = masks. Moral: build bridges.)*

"People who cannot suffer can never grow up, can never discover who they are."

BROOKLYN TO AUSTIN

Thursday [August 20, 1970]

Dearest,

After my ranting and raving about the dearth of correspondence last evening, I realize that I have been lethargic about writing this week.

In a few minutes I leave for the Harvard Club and a squash game with Harry B. Then I will meet Jon W and his wife and her cousin from England for dinner at "Tuesdays." After dinner we plan to go to a special coffee shop in the East 90's that Jon recommends where they have excellent folk music. I guess I should really be writing this after my evening. It's interesting how both of us always seem to be invited out with "people."

I'm excited about going to Hyannis [to the Kennedy Compound on Cape Cod] *for the weekend, but fear I will not be in shape for the strenuous exercise. I know I will be on the tennis court for hours and hours and I will be expected to win. I haven't played tennis since Middletown.*

Today the temperature got back up to 90 degrees. I've been dripping. And to add to the discomfort the apartment has had no hot water since Sunday nite. They are making major repairs to the boiler.

George L was like the cat that swallowed the mouse. I've never seen him so happy. I'm amused at how he invites his other gal friends (like Diane and Joan W) to share in his joy. He's just a totally open person, and cannot bear not to be loved by everyone. And all of us do!

Another beauty of Bedford-Stuyvesant has become evident these past two weeks. There are "Rose of Sharon" trees in nearly every block. Some have white blossoms, others lavender and pink. They are so beautiful and they remind me of you, of us, and the two trees I planted at home that you will see within the year.

Love,
Charlie

BROOKLYN TO AUSTIN

August 21, 1970

Dearest,

It's just after midnight, our 23rd anniversary! I'm sending you a little check for $25 -- $21 plus a few dollars to "grow on." How about going to one of the enclosed plays for our 24th anniversary? Isn't it great to look forward to next year! A year in which we will see each other so much more, and a year within which we will be married! (Let me know by phone before the 28th so I can get the tickets.)

I'm also enclosing an article on sailplanes. Note there is an airport in Middletown! This is something I've always longed to do. Will you join me? I love sailing and skiing. Sailplaning seems to be a delight of the same species. I would love to be aloft

*with only the sound & feel of the wind. It must be like looking
down from a high bridge in the sunlight!*

*I worked late tonight in preparation for my departure.
There is always so much <u>more</u> to do. Deadlines help to get things
done.*

*I have procrastinated two days on my "raise"
memorandum. Your advice of taking it in stages helped. I'll
submit it tomorrow as I leave for Hyannisport!*

*I noticed yesterday the first signs of fall. The leaves on
some of the trees are beginning to turn brown, ever so slightly on
the edges. The color in the sky was different, a darker smoky
blue, and it seemed to get dark an hour or so earlier.
Middletown and its environs will be a riot of color in a few
weeks!*

*I really can't get myself to make out a list of people to
see in Austin. It's so hard to draw lines. Certainly Mary C et al*
[mutual friends]; *Myrtle and Birdie and Marian* [staff at St.
Austin rectory]; *Walter, Ed P, Bert R* [Paulists]; *some of the
gang at Aquinas* [the graduate student group at the Catholic
Student Center]; *faculty members; Hershey, Bernie, José* [other
students at the CSC].... *My head is swimming.... Curt & Joan,
Charlie C* [pastors at Protestant student centers]! *Wow! Joseph
W* [faculty member]!

*I DO NOT WANT TO SEE ANY TEXAS REGENT,
TEXAS RANGERS OR POLICEMEN.*

Most of all, darling, I want to see you.

Devotedly,
Chas

AUSTIN TO BROOKLYN

Sat. p.m. 2:30
8/22/70

*I'm on a study break, dear, sitting by the biology pond I
can see through my carrel window. I have been working
intensely and yet sporadically for 3 hours, hoping to finish the
Ellison chapter before I pack everything up once again. The
lilies in the pond are perfectly beautiful — blue, pink-violet, pale
yellow, peach. I can see one tiny frog on each of the 5 clusters of
lily pads nearest me; tiny minnows swarm below them; a fat six-*

inch goldfish glides around as if he owns the place. It's a nice break, and I'm thinking of you and missing you.

Our separation is almost ended, dear – at last and I hope forever!

I got up to leave, just when a photographer asked me if I would sit there a little longer and he took a couple of shots catching shadows and reflections on the pond. (Flattering – don't you know? He said he may want to use them for something and will write for my permission in that case.)

Thinking of you in Hyannis Port and hoping you are having a good time.

Back to work.

Love, Rosie

AUSTIN TO BROOKLYN

August 24, 1970

Dear Charlie,

This letterhead of Colegio Jacinto Treviño constitutes the current address of Hershey. He asked me to give it to you. Jacinto Treviño, he tells me, killed more Texas Rangers than other Mexicans! That may be his only claim to fame(?).

I enclose yesterday's song sheet from the Catholic Student Center liturgy. We sang "Oh Happy Day" but you may be interested in the next song [Paul Simon's "Bridge Over Troubled Water"].

Five days till you arrive! Whom can I tell? Elaine says when you two talked on the telephone you promised her a long chat....I haven't heard from Georgia! Off to the library—

Love, Rosemary

[over] *I also saw Bob and Barb B at Mass yesterday – just visiting. He has a position with "Chicano Studies" at the U of Texas at El Paso. Bob is pleased (and surprised) about "you and me." XX R*

[written on envelope] *Chas—your big packet – check, sailplanes, plays — just arrived. Thanx. I opt for "No Place to Be Somebody." Also a letter from Georgia, who is* <u>*very*</u> *eager to see us* [during our drive back to New York]. *Will have "something to eat" for us, and we are welcome to spend the night if we wish.* ☺

Chapter 9 – Waiting for Word from the Vatican

The year of separation, and thus the year of intense letter-writing and intensely difficult self-examination and decision-making, was over.

Charlie and I spent three or four days driving Vic's automobile from Austin to Yonkers, New York. On the way we paid a call in Louisiana to our dear friend Georgia and her new husband Ron, and spent a night in New Orleans. We also stopped to visit my former convent classmate and dear friend Marion, with her husband Don and their baby, Katie, who lived in Athens, Georgia.

After arriving safely in Middletown, New York, I put Charlie on a bus back to New York City. Then I had a few days to settle into my new apartment and prepare for new teaching responsibilities at Orange County Community College. Once the academic year started, we settled into a pattern of alternating weekends together in either Middletown or Brooklyn.

The first big purchase we made together was a little car, which we bought and financed through Charlie's brother Bob, our car dealer in the family. Soon we were exploring the beautiful Catskill environs around the Middletown area. And soon I was learning to drive in the big city, finding my way from Middletown to Brooklyn.

It was in general a busy and happy year. We were waiting for news from the Vatican regarding our dispensations from our religious vows, so that we could set a date for our wedding. While we waited, we undertook the next step with our families.

I took Charlie to meet my parents, who lived on a little "retirement farm" near Harmony, Minnesota. I remember that, from my point of view, the visit went smoothly. While I'm sure my parents and brothers must have had a difficult time accepting our decision, the "Minnesota nice" culture came through for us: everyone was polite and avoided any hint of conflicts. Charlie remembered that he had had a visit-long case of nerves. He later reported to his parents that he had longed for a drink, but in my parents' house there was not even a beer to be found.

A couple of months later Charlie took me to Grosse Pointe, Michigan, to meet his parents, and it was my turn to be nervous. "Papa" Charlie and Marion were absolutely gracious and kind. To welcome me, Papa Charlie had ordered the sheet music for "Rosie, You Are My Posie," and performed it for me at the piano. But what set us all at ease at once was Papa Charlie's innocent gaffe as he met us at the door and faultily remembered Charlie's report on his Harmony visit. "Welcome, Rosie!" he said, "and you're from Temperance, Minnesota?"

In a lovely coincidence, word reached us both on exactly the same February day that the Vatican had granted our dispensations. Since we wanted children and were conscious of our delayed start, we settled on an early wedding date – a Saturday during my spring break from teaching. My mother took care of local arrangements with the little Catholic church in Harmony, including the reception afterward in the parish hall.

Charlie and I printed and mailed invitations. (See Appendices.) We decided on our own liturgy, building on the traditional Mass but incorporating our own theme of building bridges instead of walls. The first reading would be Robert Frost's poem that begins: "Something there is that doesn't love a wall." We wrote our own creed, one that we could say in complete honesty. We composed our own vows. The music included Paul Simon's "Bridge over Troubled Water" and Billy Taylor's "I Wish I Knew How It Would Feel to Be Free" (with the line, "I wish I could break all the chains holding me").

Among the guests were many Franciscan sisters, coming from the College of St. Teresa and other Minnesota locations; they would constitute most of the choir and guitar players. Two carloads of dear friends represented a Texas contingent. A Michigan contingent included Charlie's brother George as his best man, with George's wife Mickey loyally accompanying him. Charlie's cousins Cleve T and Charlie C were a supportive and loving presence.

My sister, Kathy, was my matron of honor, and her two older children along with brother Gary's older children were adorable ring-bearers and flower girls.

My brother Mike was assigned to tape-record the whole event.

The best-laid plans....

First, a heavy snowstorm. But Minnesotans knew how to handle that: my brothers Gary and John, for example, wouldn't let the arriving Texans drive down my parents' steep and winding driveway. They met them at the top of the hill and sternly ordered the drivers to "move over" so that they could pilot them safely to the warm farmhouse awaiting them.

The most potentially devastating event, we learned on the day of the wedding, was that the bishop of the Winona diocese was sending his personal envoy to be sure that this wedding would not occasion a local scandal. The envoy made his presence felt first by bringing official papers to the sacristy, where the groom was waiting for the ceremony to start. The papers demanded Charlie's signature: that he understood that he was, in Latin, being "reduced to the lay state," and that he was to desist from associating with anyone who had known him as a priest. Charlie, who after all was a lawyer, knew that any documents signed "under duress" would be invalid, and signed.

Learning of the presence of this envoy caused me acute anxiety, which naturally colored my experience of my own wedding. I worried that this priest, hearing our readings, our creed, our vows, would stop the whole proceeding. My brother Gary, for the first reading, recited Robert Frost's poem, "Mending Wall" while I held my breath. That poem wasn't anything like the usual Hebrew Bible reading or an epistle from the New Testament. Desperate, Charlie and I decided in the moment to scrap our planned wording of our vows and revert to the usual standard form, and we stumbled through our nervous faulty recall of those familiar words.

This spy in our midst stopped nothing. Was this because, as I learned years and years later, he had been standing in the choir loft when one of my sister friends recognized him? She divined his purpose in being there, and roundly scolded him for playing such a nefarious role.

Other smaller events came to light. The first was that brother Mike's tape recorder malfunctioned, so I will never know what celebrant Ed Lundy said about Dairy Queens in his homily. (He claimed not to remember either.)

A favorite memory, retold and embroidered many times, concerned my mother, who worried that guests would get tipsy at the reception. She asked my brother John to keep an eye on the punch. John decided that the punch didn't need to be spiked. One bottle of gin was supposed to be diluted in enough punch for one hundred guests. John took that one bottle and locked it in the trunk of his car. Guest George L, when asked to help find the gin, solved the matter by driving to the liquor store and bringing back two more bottles.

My mother had asked us not to tell my Grandma Rose that Charlie had been a priest. I had told our guests of Mother's request. Well, George, who had known Charlie since seminary days, stood up to make a toast. He carried on for five long minutes, telling stories of their many adventures together while I held my breath. Happily, he managed not to mention the forbidden topic. (As I think back, I suspect Grandma had figured it out anyway.)

What would a wedding be without a few stories like these? So many happy surprises contributed to making our wedding day, in sum, a supremely joyous day. A dear friend, Meg, designed a huge banner depicting the Brooklyn Bridge, which was hung from the altar. A special wedding present was a movie camera, used to record many of the bustling activities

before and after the ceremony. A convent classmate created a beautiful wedding candle. Above all, Charlie and I felt very much loved – by the numerous Franciscans there, by the Texans making the journey (including Pam, who crafted our exquisite wedding rings), by parents and siblings and aunts and uncles and cousins and sweet little nieces and nephews. We were an extraordinarily happy couple.

On to the honeymoon – but that's another story.

Yes: Beauty enough.

Afterword -- On Beauty

When old age shall this generation waste,
Thou shalt remain, in midst of other woe
Than ours, a friend to man, to whom thou sayst,
"Beauty is truth, truth beauty," – that is all
Ye know on earth, and all ye need to know.
                    --John Keats, last lines of
                    "Ode on a Grecian Urn"

Memoirs can be suspect for a variety of reasons. Why do people write memoirs? In my case:

- It's true that I want to live on after my death. It would be nice if this memoir could keep the memory of Charlie and me around for a generation or two.
- It's true that I want to control how I am remembered. Thus I may be tempted to emphasize my good qualities and de-emphasize my darker side.
- It's true that what I do remember is dimming as the years pass. It has been nearly 50 years, after all, since the central events recorded here.
- It's true that sensational events tend to be the most compelling. Charlie and I lived rather ordinary lives in the end. My son urged me to ratchet up the love scenes and the crises. My daughter asked me, suspiciously, if I had edited out the most intimate details in the letters. The fact is, I didn't edit out and I didn't ratchet up.

The letters kept me honest. The letters prompted and corrected my memory. They are what they are, frozen in time like the figures on Keats' Grecian urn. The little editing I did was intended to keep the focus on *our* story, Charlie's and mine. For example, I tried to eliminate needless repetitions, the rare misspellings, and names of persons not essential to our story.

"Beauty is truth, truth beauty." What is beautiful? What is true? To these eternal questions I venture a subjective response. For me, the bonds between humans are what create the most significant beauty. These ties that bind help us to live in the moment. They support us as we take risks, step into the unknown, seize the day. These bonds show us what is beautiful because they encourage us to get in touch with and express what moves us as human beings. Relationships confront us with our pretenses and lead us to find what is true.

My poet friend Jerry sought these bonds in his search for beauty. His poems tell of this search. I quote him once more:

I have crossed the streets of nervous light
I have slipped through the fields of wet grass
I have silently passed the darkened houses
But nowhere, O Moon, rising full in the East,
Do I find beauty enough
For my lame soul.

Others could see the truth, that *he* was beautiful. His beauty was in his humanness, in his search for beauty, and in his poems. It was the beauty of Jerry's soul that brought his friends together around him. We all sought to strengthen bonds of friendship with him, in order to feed his hunger for beauty. Sadly, his soul was too lame to go onward, and our efforts were not *enough*.

Those bonds among Jerry's friends, however, led directly to my deepening friendship with Charlie. I believe that our romance blossomed with the catalyst of Jerry. Thus the title of this memoir and its dedication, in part, to Jerry's memory.

Building bonds, building bridges. For Charlie and me, the Brooklyn Bridge, as crystallized in the photograph on the cover of this book, became a central metaphor in our own relationship. Charlie worked and lived in the urban decay of central Brooklyn in the early 1970s; yet he kept his spirits up by finding beauty everywhere, as he recounts in his letters: in the watery eyes of a homeless man, in the colorful leaves and art cards that he folded into his letters to me, in the diversity of the throngs of New Yorkers – and in the Brooklyn Bridge. This bridge was his Grecian urn. It was, in its constant beauty, a beacon of hope, a reason to celebrate the triumph of human endurance and ingenuity, a motivation to reach out to others to forge bonds, to tear down walls, to build bridges. He asked me to join him in this, his life's work. And together, in our triumphs and in our struggles, we found beauty enough.

Appendix 1 – Father Palms' Farewell Mass in Texas

FATHER PALMS' FAREWELL MASS

July 31, 1969

OPENING HYMN: They'll Know we are Christians, pp. 69-70

INTROIT: (Little Prince)
So the little prince tamed the fox. And when the hour of his departure drew near ---- "Ah," said the fox, "I shall cry." "It is your own fault," said the little prince. "I never wished you any sort of harm; but you wanted me to tame you..." "Yes, that is so," said the fox. "But now you are going to cry!" said the little prince. "Yes, that is so," said the fox. "Then it had done you no good at all!" "It has done me good," said the fox, "because of the color of the wheat fields." And then he added: "Go and look again at the roses. You will understand now that yours is unique in all the world. Then come back to say goodbye to me, and I will make you a present of a secret." The little prince went away, to look again at the roses. "You are not at all like my rose," he said. "As yet you are nothing. No one has tamed you, and you have tamed no one. You are like my fox when I first knew him. He was only a fox like a hundred thousand other foxes. But I have made him my friend, and now he is unique in all the world."

GRADUAL: (Hammarskjold's, Markings)
With all the powers of your body concentrated in the hand on the tiller, All the powers of your mind concentrated on the goal beyond the horizon, You laugh as the salt spray catches your face in the second of rest Before a new wave --- Sharing the happy freedom of the moment with those who share your responsibility. So -- in the self-forgetfulness of concentrated attention -- the door opens for you into a pure living intimacy, A shared, timeless happiness, Conveyed by a smile, A wave of the hand. Alleluia, alleluia. One runs the risk of weeping a little if one lets himself be tamed. Alleluia.

Offertory: (Little Prince)
And he went back to meet the fox. "Goodbye," he said. "Goodbye," said the fox. "And now here is my secret, a very simple secret: It is only with the heart that one can see rightly; what is essential is invisible to the eye." "What is essential is invisible to the eye," the little prince repeated, so that he would be sure to remember. "It is the time you have spent for your rose that makes your rose so important. Men have forgotten this truth," said the fox. "But you must not forget it. You become responsible, forever, for what you have tamed. You are responsible for your rose...." "I am responsible for my rose," the little prince repeated, so that he would be sure to remember.

FATHER PALMS' FAREWELL MASS ----------------------------- Page 2

OFFERTORY HYMN: TAKE MY ALL,   Page 3

COMMUNION HYMN: LAST THING ON MY MIND

It's a lesson too late for the learnin'
Made of sand, made of sand
In the twinkle of an eye my soul is turning
In your hand, in your hand.

Chorus: Are you going away with no word of farewell
         Will there be not a trace left behind
         Well, I could have loved you better
         Didn't mean to be unkind
         Y'know that was the last thing on my mind.

You've got reasons a-plenty for goin'
This I know, this I know
For the weeds have been steadily growin'
Please don't go, please don't go.
CHORUS

As I lie in my bed every mornin'
Dawn's anew, dawn's anew
Every song in my breast dies a'bornin'
Without you, without you
CHORUS

COMMUNION PRAYER: (Hammarskjold's _Markings_)
Thou who art over us,   Thou who art over us,   Thou who art ---
Also within us,   May all see Thee -- in me also,
May I prepare the way for Thee,   May I thank Thee for all that
shall fall to my lot.   May I also not forget the needs of
others,   Keep me in Thy love   As thou wouldest that all
should be kept in mine.   May everything in this my being be
directed to Thy glory   And may I never despair.
For I am under Thy hand,   And in Thee is all power and goodness.

RECESSIONAL: SPIRIT OF GOD,   Page 7

Appendix 2 – Sister Rosemary's Job Search

P.O. Box 106

February 5, 1970

Chairman, Department of English
Kingsborough Community College   [illegible]
Lafayette and Clermont Avenues
Brooklyn, New York

Dear Chairman:

I am very much interested in teaching English at a college in an
urban area, particularly in a tuition-free or low-tuition community
college. Your school has attracted my interest. Do you have openings
on your English faculty for the academic year 1970-71?

At present I am a Catholic Franciscan sister, teaching in a private
girls' college, the College of Saint Teresa, which enrolls about a
thousand full-time students. Here I teach a composition and readings
course to freshmen and American Literature to majors and minors in
English. I very much enjoy teaching on the college level, but at the
end of this school year I plan to leave the sisterhood, and consequently
I am job-hunting.

My *curriculum vitae* is enclosed, but I would like to elaborate on one
item on it. During 1968-69, while I was working on my doctoral dissertation, I worked part time as a staff assistant at the Catholic
Student Center on the campus of the University of Texas. I enjoyed
direct contact with students on various levels and in various settings:
office hours for counseling or just listening to the students; work
with the liturgy programs; social action activities concerned with
tutoring, housing problems, welfare, etc.; committee work with other
campus ministers in various projects; discussion groups; and contact
with the faculty at the university.

The following persons are some of those with whom I have worked quite
closely in the employments mentioned in the *vitae*, and whose letters
of recommendation, with other information in my dossier, are available
upon request: Sister Margaret Byron, Dean of the College of Saint
Teresa; the Reverend Edward Lundy and the Reverend Charles Palms,
Associate Directors at the Catholic Student Center, the University of
Texas; Sister M. Sheila Foley, my principal when I taught in high
school; and Doctor Joseph J. Jones, Director of my Ph.D. dissertation.
Please send your request for the dossier to: The Placement Service,
College of Saint Teresa, Winona, Minnesota, 55987.

On February 20 I shall be in the New York area and would be available
for an interview. Otherwise, perhaps an interview could be arranged
during our college's spring break, March 30 through April 3.

I would be happy to answer further questions. Hoping to hear from
you, I am

       Sincerely yours,

       Rosemary Grebin

Enclosure

C U R R I C U L U M   V I T A E

Rosemary Helen Grebin

b. Preston, Minnesota, May 27, 1940.   Daughter of Francis
   and Eloise Gossman Grebin.

Harmony (Minnesota) High School	1957	
B.A., College of Saint Teresa	1963	English
M.A., University of Texas at Austin	1967	English
Ph.D. (pending completion of dissertation), University of Texas at Austin	1971?	American Literature

Experience:
Instructor in Cathedral Grade School, Winona, Minnesota,
grade six, 1960-61; Instructor in Saint Adrian High
School, Adrian, Minnesota, grades nine through twelve,
1963-65; Graduate student in Communication Arts, Notre
Dame University, Summer, 1965; Student Assistant in
Department of English, University of Texas at Austin,
1966-67; Assistant to Chaplains of the Catholic Student
Center, University of Texas at Austin, 1968-69; In-
structor in Department of English, College of Saint
Teresa, Winona, Minnesota, 1969-70; Member of Public
Occasions Committee, College of Saint Teresa, 1969-70.

Memberships:
Modern Language Association.

Dissertation-in-progress:
The Double Motif in American Literature--Flannery
O'Connor's The Violent Bear It Away, John Knowles'
A Separate Peace, and Ralph Ellison's Invisible Man.

Present Address and Telephone:

P. O. Box 106
College of Saint Teresa
Winona, Minnesota 55987

(507)454-2930

February 9, 1970

Placement Center
College of St. Teresa
Winona, Minnesota 55987

To whom it may concern:

I am writing this letter to recommend Sister Rosemary Grebin
whom I have known since September 1966. I was associate director
of The Catholic Student Center, University of Texas at Austin from
1966 to 1969. In this position I was responsible for teaching
credit courses in religion and for planning discussions and programs
for the 3,000 Catholic students at the University of Texas. Sister
Rosemary was a graduate student in English. She was a frequent visitor
at the Center and participated in our programs. She fit in so well
that when we were looking for a young woman to help us at the Center
for the academic year 1968-69, we asked Sister Rosemary if she were
willing to accept this responsibility.

She accepted and during the year counseled students daily, helped
lead discussion groups, was responsible for our coffee hour on Sundays,
led the St. Vincent dePaul Society (a student-faculty group dedicated
to the poor of Austin), and participated in our weekly staff meetings
helping us to charter the direction of our services to students. She
did all this while continuing to work towards her doctorate in English.

I cannot vouch for her teaching ability. I have never observed
her in the classroom. I can only say that Sister Rosemary was excellent
as an organizer and prompt and responsible in carrying out her duties.
She also showed originality in her thinking and offered a number of
important suggestions which helped us in our relationships with students.
Most of all, she had the confidence of the students. From my own
teaching experience, I know that teaching (communication) is almost
impossible unless the teacher can relate to the students. In this
respect, she was superb.

If I can be of any further help, please do not hesitate to call
upon me.

Sincerely,

(Rev.) Charles Palms
195 Underhill Ave.
Brooklyn, New York 11238

Appendix 3 – A Proposal concerning Lay Affiliation

The lay and religious forms of living out the commitment of baptism are not antagonistic, but rather they are complementary. Neither is freer than the other; both are limited. Each one needs the other. Keeping this in mind, I propose some type of lay affiliation program specifically designed for former members of our congregation who retain a desire to be loosely affiliated but who choose a different style of life, married or single. In the past, the Church's official stance regarding a dispensation from final vows precluded any continuing affiliation: the wording of the dispensation virtually forbade it. The Church has now adopted a stance much more understanding and accepting, even making it possible to return to the congregation at any time after official dispensation. It seems the climate is right at this time to consider ways and means to make possible continuing affiliation with former members.

Thomas E. Clarke, S.J., has made some very pertinent observations and suggestions concerning "The Crisis of Permanent Consecration" and possible alternatives (see *Sisters Today* XLI, August-September, 1969, pp. 1-15). He writes in part:

> The life of the counsels, as a distinct Christian life-form, does call for a permanent engagement. But there are several things which this permanent engagement does not exclude: First, it does not exclude that we have some groups or communities in the Church, including celibate groups, in which permanency of commitment is not part of the structure, in which the decision to remain celibate for the sake of apostolic work in a particular group will have the nature of a career decision fully open to be changed. Secondly, it does not exclude that, within a community whose basic or core membership is committed on the basis of a life-time dedication, there should also be associate members who never make such a life-time commitment. In the conditions of life today, there would seem to be a good deal to be said for such

communities, which have historical antecedents in such kinds of membership as that of oblates and donnés.

A further question here would be whether such associate membership could be extended to married people. The various efforts made by heterogeneous communities (celibates and married) in the past are not entirely encouraging, but it may be that we are in a period of the life of the Church and the world where this difficult dream may be capable of realization. As I understand the Focolare movement, it represent such a heterogeneous grouping of dedicated Christians. I would understand such a conception as being in continuity with the association that religious and seculars had in the past through Third Orders, sodalities and similar groups. (p. 4)

"Similar groups" might include a new lay affiliation program inaugurated by the LaCrosse (Wisconsin) Franciscans and the current experiment of the California IHMs [Immaculate Heart of Mary Sisters].

Preliminary "feelers" concerning some type of lay affiliation have been sent to those women presently on leave of absence from our congregation (sent by myself) and to those who have signed dispensations within the past two years (sent by Sister Margaret Mary Modde). From these groups alone there are perhaps fifteen who showed interest in some type of affiliation, even though the concept remains rather vague.

Our reasons for desiring affiliation are probably varied. My own feeling is that I have a deep love for the Franciscan ideals and for many of my Franciscan sisters. I leave without bitterness and with a sense of gratitude for what my personhood has gained from my life as a religious. I leave with a sense of responsibility to those who have educated me and to those who have spent a lifetime in service and now deserve a cared-for retirement. Therefore I want to keep in touch in order to continue sharing friendships and sharing responsibilities.

The actual form this affiliation would take should be flexible and largely unstructured. In broad terms, as I see it, the auxiliary member could offer professional, financial, and/or moral support to the Rochester Franciscans, to the services this congregation performs, and to the ideals it strives for. The Rochester Franciscans as the nucleus group could in turn arrange an organ for communication and provide for occasional gatherings, perhaps similar to alumnae homecoming weekends, for the exchange of ideas, worship, and recreation.

For specific examples, let us say that it was agreed to send each issue of the *Tidings* to the lay affiliates, with an added page or two containing news about the affiliates or items that would be of special interest to them. If circumstances were such that a lay affiliate were free for the summer (for example) to donate services in a certain area, she would know that her services would be appreciated and even encouraged. She might be invited to a special "ex-nun retreat" at the motherhouse or to a liturgical weekend in a local parish. Some issues might come up at a Chapter about which she might profitably be consulted. There are almost endless possibilities and advantages to both the congregation and the lay affiliate with such an arrangement and cross-fertilization of ideas.

The exact nature of lay affiliation should perhaps never be defined. Part of its beauty is in its evolutionary nature. I propose that we let its form evolve as seems best from year to year. As a practical beginning, I propose that we write to all former members of our congregation and invite them to receive the *Tidings* or similar organ of communication, and then during the next year invite them to a homecoming weekend, to pastoral action weekends, and like events. The interested former members who respond to such invitations may well become the lay affiliates of the future. Let us rely on the Spirit and see how the wind blows.

I would be happy to hear reactions to these ideas. I earnestly hope for some action that will lead to a lay affiliate with the Rochester Franciscans, and I will gladly do my share of the groundwork. I ask this in the name of long friendships and with an eye on the needs of tomorrow's Church.

Respectfully submitted,
Rosemary Grebin, O.S.F.
June 2, 1970

Appendix 4 – Wedding Invitation

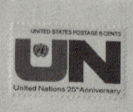

Charles Palms and Rosemary Grebin
joyously invite you
to celebrate with them
their union of marriage
in a Nuptial Mass
at two o'clock on Saturday
April 3, 1971
in the Church of the Nativity
Harmony, Minnesota
and at a reception in the parish hall
immediately following Mass.

If you can come, please write
Mr. and Mrs. Francis Grebin
Harmony, Minnesota 55939

Appendix 5 – From the Family Photo Album

Celebrating the Brooklyn Bridge Centennial, 1983
Michael, Charlie, Rosemary, Amy
Photo by Jeff Foxx

Charlie and Rosemary in December 2003

Acknowledgments

So many to thank:

The bridge photograph reproduced on the cover was purchased by Charles Palms in New York in 1970. Photographer unknown. The bridge photo in Appendix 5 is by Jeffrey J. Foxx.

The reproduction on the dedication page of Gerald D. McCarty is a detail from an oil portrait by his friend Marilyn Todd, circa 1967.

The image on the dedication page of Charles Palms is a detail from a photo taken by Steve Chappell during the March 2003 protest in New York City against the imminent U.S. invasion of Iraq.

My children have been staunch supporters. My daughter, Amy, an artist and a loyal sounding board, designed the front and back covers. My son, Michael, offered valuable critiques and networking opportunities.

I thank my longtime employer, Pratt Institute, and especially my chair in 2012, Ira Livingston. Ira advocated that I be awarded a sabbatical semester for the purpose of getting a start on this memoir. He encouraged me without pressuring me.

My grandnephew Eric McKay, a millennial techie, generously came to my rescue while I was preparing this manuscript.

I am grateful to my dear friend Liza Williams, who has listened to me and encouraged me for years. Her suggestions and professional copyediting have made this a better book. The inevitable errors are my own.

For most of the persons mentioned in these letters I have chosen not to use full names, keeping the focus on the story that the letters tell – the story of the two correspondents, Charlie and me. There are many family members and friends who played key roles in our lives during those long-ago years, to whom I owe special thanks and sometimes do use their partial or full names. Many have stayed in my life these many decades later, often encouraging me until finally this memoir was done.

Thank you, thank you, thank you all.

Rosemary

90321735R00183

Made in the USA
Columbia, SC
02 March 2018